Terrible Sanity

Other Books by Sam Pickering

Terrible Sanity

Sam Pickering

Lake Dallas, Texas

FIRST EDITION

Requests for permission to reprint material from this work should be sent to:

> Permissions
> Madville Publishing
> P.O. Box 358
> Lake Dallas, TX 75065

Acknowledgements:

The author and publisher gratefully acknowledge *River Teeth* and *The Chattahoochee Review* in which selections from these essays first appeared.

Author Photograph: Vicki Pickering
Cover Design: Kimberly Davis
Cover image: Detail from a twelve-pane panel by Pieter Bruegel the Elder—Scan aus: Rose Marie und Rainer Hagen—Pieter Bruegel d. Ä. um 1525—1569. Bauern, Narren und Dämonen, Köln: Benedikt Taschen Verlag GmbH 1999 S. 34 ISBN 3-8228-6590-7, Public Domain, https://commons.wikimedia.org/w/index.php?curid=6887712

ISBN: 978-1-948692-52-6 paperback, 978-1-948692-53-3 ebook
Library of Congress Control Number: 2020941271

Dedication

For Vicki whose remarks have enlivened my living for over forty years. She is eleven years younger than me, and her take on life is slightly different than mine. Two days ago, after returning home at the end of a long walk in the woods, she exclaimed, "God, am I tired! I just want to sit down and put my feet up. I feel like I am seventy-eight." "I know exactly how that feels," I said. "Oh, no," she said, "I didn't mean." "I know what you meant," I interrupted. "It feels like a bowl of chocolate ice cream." "And maybe a slice of coconut cake, too?" Vicki said. "Darn straight," I answered.

Table of Contents

Virus Days: A Preface of Sorts

The letters began as the life I had long known vanished. In early February things started to seem akimbo, bothersome but not frighteningly so, a bit like the Bombay Kipling's father Lockwood described in the nineteenth century. "No masonry is square, no railings are straight, no roads are level, no dishes taste quite like they should, but a strange and curious imperfection and falling short attends everything, so that one lives in a dream when things are just coming about but never quite happening." Age makes sane people fatalists. Vicki calls me a curmudgeon, but a curmudgeon is simply an old guy who tells the truth. He is someone who can't stomach the Wonder Bread soaked in messianic pap that society spoons down the gullets of the young and the naïve.

Actually, becoming a pessimist is a good prescription for increasing a person's zest for life. Unlike the optimist who mopes through days being continually disappointed, rarely is a pessimist depressed when the best-laid plans of the well-meaning mildew and turn dark. In fact, fatalism kindles high spirits. "The virus is quicker than dementia and not as hard on families and savings accounts," my friend Josh told Vicki then slapped his knee and laughed. Perhaps I shouldn't have said *kindles*. Vicki has yet to measure me for an oak kimono. In any case since funeral homes are closed, she'll have to jettison the sartorial box and settle for a fire bath, surely a high-octane immersion now that the price of gas is low. In truth, I don't know what plans Vicki has cooked up for me once I conk out, but if I see her storing kindling in the woodshed, I'll break quarantine and head for an Arcadian place beyond the evil eye of television. Every night on every channel, lollipops announce "good news." I realize that tolerance and lies bind society together. Nevertheless, although I discount the announcers' remarks, the phrase brings to mind the old gospel song "Good News. Chariot's Comin'." Although a white robe and a starry crown wait for me in Beulah Land, I prefer to ignore the entreaty and hope that the chariot makes a wrong turn and leaves me behind. Even the bonus of a personalized harp doesn't seduce me. I'm not musical. I am tone deaf. I've never played an instrument and couldn't learn even if that famous chorus of angels long heard on high tried to teach me.

The virus has not only affected how I act but also how I think. For decades I taught Thoreau and preached the virtues of simplicity. Now that my life is simple, I yearn for complexity. Many things I wrote in healthy decades past and which seemed to ring with sonorous rightness now appear silly. Boredom "with its blissful calm," I once declared, "is an aspiration devoutly to be labored for but impossible to achieve." Coping with momentary isolation isn't difficult. What's tough is adjusting to the realization that all I have to look forward to is isolation. In past years when winter became oppressive in Connecticut, Vicki and I decamped and took a warming cruise through the Caribbean. During the summer when society seemed too much with us "getting and spending," we went to Nova Scotia and rusticated on a farm her parents bought seventy-five years ago. Cruise ships are now mothballed, and the

Canadian border is padlocked, not depriving us of actuality because we hadn't planned to visit Canada this summer or book a cruise next winter, but denying possibility and impoverishing imagination. Aging constricts life, but I anticipated the natural loss of abilities and had adapted well to the diminished me. However, I resented the unexpected narrowing caused by the virus.

Of course, Vicki's and my isolation was not that of people confined to apartment buildings or tract housing. The quarantine was partial and only separated us from other people. We still received mail and robocalls. I adjusted to the university's shutting and curtailing my jogging rounds on the indoor track. Instead, I cycled to the soccer field and ran four miles around the artificial turf. The field was almost abandoned. Some days "the Chinese tire-tosser" appeared. He was a body-builder and spent hours lifting and pushing tractor tires. We smiled and waved but did not speak. My friends Tim and David showed up around 10:30, and we walked together for old time's sake. Conversation was difficult because we kept two lanes apart and David is deaf.

The few eateries that remained open limited purchases to take-out, not something that affected Vicki and me because in the best of culinary times we rarely dined outside the house. We continued eating dinner in the television room and watching movies on Netflix. Some nights we bought Indian, Chinese, or Lebanese take-out in hopes of seasoning the films, but we had done this long before the virus appeared and the purchases did not change the pattern of our evenings. Every afternoon we wrapped ourselves in coats and scarves and donning ear muffs and gloves walked downtown. Vicki bought coffee at Dog Lane

Café, and we drank it slowly, sitting on a bench in the town square. We did not speak to anyone. We told each other that we were such a regular sight that our figures should be bronzed and anchored to the bench. We stayed for an hour. We ignored cold and drizzling rain and studied the absence of people. Foreign students marooned by the virus crossed the square masked and walking slower than when the university was open. Joggers hurried around corners; all were alone and female. Every twenty minutes the man operating Insomnia Cookies came outside and cleaned the door to the shop after which he smoked a cigarette and called people on his cellphone. Workers from the branch of the university health center located in a row building behind us bought Mooyah Burgers, and teenage boys clacked by on skateboards, jumping from walkways to the tops of walls.

Dog walkers were the most ubiquitous breed of pedestrian. They were also the most alert, careful to prevent their animals from straying off sidewalks and ready to scoop up droppings. We often brought our dogs with us. Vicki leashed them to the bench and occasionally fed them kibble. They took their lead from us. They never barked and sitting motionless also looked bronzed. After finishing our coffee, we ambled to the university and freed the dogs letting them scamper about searching for groundhogs. The campus resembled an empty suburban park. Some evenings after daffodils began blooming, Vicki strolled around the corner to nearby dormitories and picked a bouquet for the kitchen table. Dogs, not words, harnessed people together. For years we've spent Saturday and Sunday afternoons walking dogs though the woods above the Fenton River. With the exception of mountain bikers, we didn't meet other people. Only rarely had we leashed the dogs, this only after Vicki noticed an abundance of coyote scat or someone spread alarmist news about the presence of a mountain lion. Now after the appearance of the virus, our bosky paths became thoroughfares. Tethered to their owners, packs of dogs pulled families: mothers, fathers, and cabooses of children. In contrast to the dogs which "verbally" acknowledged our canine threesome, people turned aside and looking irritated passed by silently.

Our walks were not as quiet and somber as tombs, however. The beaver pond was lively with amorous frogs: shrill spring peepers, wood frogs clacking, toads trilling, and green frogs thrumming. Later after the ardor of the other frogs cooled gray tree frogs began whistling. Early in the morning outside our house cardinals piped cheerfully through the trees, and blue birds perched on low limbs and chirruped tenderly and uncertainly. Would that I were the servant in the Grimm's tale who sliced a bit off the magical "White Snake" and as a result understood the language of animals. Still, if a person listened carefully, he could guess what young animals talked about in the spring. Moreover, he'd know not simply what friends, his bifurcated animal compatriots, said when they telephoned but also what they thought about saying. Aged friends don't wait for cronies to finish sentences. They complete predicates themselves, punctuating the thoughts with genial recollections. In fact, when my friends were young and gadded about in the garden with the angels, they didn't waste their salad days munching apples. They lived with gusto and ate all the snakes. The seedtimes of their lives were bright and gay, and as a result their later years did not wither, cankered by inanition, regret, and guilt but instead blossomed with feeling and kindly stories.

I have been bookish since childhood, and in part I escaped the quarantine by sauntering beyond Connecticut in the company of books. Because the university and town libraries were shuttered, I was limited to rereading volumes I owned. As the virus curtailed my travels, so age restricted my reading. The first book I pulled off the shelf was Oliver Goldsmith's *The Vicar of Wakefield*. I last read *The Vicar* in 1969, fifty-one years ago. Not my taste in novels but my vision had changed, however. The print was too small for my eyes, and words swarmed off the page like fire ants defending a colony. I lay Goldsmith down and picked up Henry Mackenzie's *The Man of Feeling*. After reading the book fifty-three years ago, I slotted it on a shelf, never thinking I'd look at it again. But since it was printed in a clear black font and the spaces between lines were generously eye-soothing, I spent an afternoon reading it. In *In Nature's Realm*, Charles Conrad Abbott urged ramblers to turn their eyes and steps toward home. The worlds surrounding their dooryards, he wrote, were inexhaustible. In comparison to such domestic studies, "the labors of Hercules were as child's play." My bookshelves were not stalls in the Augean Stables, but they had been neglected and were dusty. When I swept through them, I discovered volumes that I forgot I owned. Printed in big readable type were the works of Frederick Marryat and Bulwer-Lytton. Immediately I started reading two, alternating signatures of Bulwer's *Pelham; or the Adventures of a Gentleman* with those of Marryat's *Japhet in Search of a Father*.

No longer, though, was I capable of sitting with a novel in my hands for hours. Consequently, between chapters I stirred through the house, opening closets and drawers searching for surprising unknowns. "Pester patrolling," Vicki called it, not thinking the phrase complimentary. To avoid irritating Vicki, I stopped exploring the house and sandwiched relaxing nibbles of prose between signatures of novels. Over the years I'd written volumes of reviews, and I rummaged through them hoping to exhume the equivalent of snacks: a hunk of dark chocolate, a bag of Cheese Curls, and maybe a dollop of Original Seriousness. Amid the reviews I met old acquaintances. None were scintillating conversationalists, but their page presences were livelier than the silences of people from whom I maintained anti-social distance. I admired the catholic taste of William Buckland, the first professor of geology at Oxford, who bragged that he'd eaten his way through the animal creation. Initially he said the worst thing he ever ate was mole, but he revised his opinion after sampling a dish of bluebottle flies. The virus has led to comestibles vanishing from Price Chopper, not enough, however, for me to purchase fly paper in hopes of harvesting an aerial meal. The last request of a Mr. Boys was dated but light-heartedly affectionate. Supposedly, Boys left his body to a teaching hospital with the proviso that after the instructive slicing and dicing ended, his remnants would be reduced to salts and presented to his lady friends in order to invigorate their "drooping spirits."

Bulwer himself strolled into a paragraph, not only masking his mouth and nose, but his whole body, appearing at Little Holland House in Kensington in the nineteenth century leading a train of a dozen French poodles with his hair and theirs coiffed to match, a sight that surely made adults "laugh and play." Of course, virus and death were serious, and not exhuming examples of the didactic would have been irresponsible. In his introduction to *The Journal of a Voyage to Lisbon*, Henry Fielding demonstrated the instructive use of real events. "It is very hard, my Lord," pleaded a convicted felon before Judge Burnet, "to hang a poor man for stealing a horse." "You are not to be hanged, sir," the judge explained, "for stealing a horse, but you are to be hanged that horses may not be stolen."

Some of the more interesting folk whose company I enjoyed never breathed but had long been alive. A hag with a blue face and iron fingernails, Black Annis lived in a cave. When children wandered near the entrance, she pounced on them, ripped them into antipasti, and ate them. Unlike Annis, Aiken Drum didn't devour people. Instead he wore his meals. His hat was made of cream cheese, and his coat from roast beef, the buttons of which were penny loaves. When I was small, Uncle Remus was my closest chum. I suspect he sampled the White Snake because he understood the talk of animals. Once, he related, when Brer Tarrypin was visiting Miss Meadows and the gals, Brer Fox came up in conversation. When the terrapin asked the gals to guess how the fox had greeted him recently, the ladies "hilt der fans up 'fo' der faces," and Miss Meadows said, "Law, Brer Tarrypin ... you don't mean ter say he cust?

Despite keeping people at sentence distance, every day Vicki and I heard poor grammar. The disappearance of er-comparatives gave Vicki headaches. On public radio this week, an announcer said "more safe" rather than "safer," an illiteracy, the only antidote for which was a snort of wine. Last Saturday a committee appointed by the governor to control the spread and treatment of the virus appeared on television to answer inquiries from journalists. "That's a great question," a woman said responding to a columnist. "This is a great panel, and we are committed to accomplishing great things for the citizens of this great state." "Great God," I exclaimed. "Greats of Wrath," Vicki added and turned off the television. Vicki and I are not verbal couturiers. We are old-school grammarians. If words are the dress of thought, I often appear in silk stockings and knee breeches and Vicki in a mantua and matching petticoat. In digging through my reviews, I noticed many forgotten expressions, some ancient, others almost contemporary but rarely used. Because a few states and an assortment of countries closed their borders, no longer could tramps filch rides in side-door pullmans, that is, boxcars. Because of virus economics, many truckers were hauling potholes or empty trailers. If Mr. Buckland had called moles mouldywarps, they'd now be items on menus in French eateries, along with pootys or snails. I doubt that millers would appear even in these down-in-the-apron days of take-out, millers being rats dusty with flour found in and served below deck in the Horatio Hornblower years of British warships. A word to gourmands: if at the end of a formal dinner, life itself or a favorite hostess offers you a candy bowl heaped with sirreverence, turn it down. Even if the serving dish is sterling silver and the treat is sugar-coated, turn it down. But if a person does succumb to a hostess's aspartame entreaties and later suffers from gastroenteritis, he should consult Humphrie Lloyd's *The Treasury of Health*. "The doung of a Camell dried and dronke," Lloyd suggested, or "a Dogges toord that only eateth bones doth binde the belly mightily."

What did my miscellaneous readings amount

to? I wasn't sure. But my uncertainly was reassuring rather than nettlesome. "There is a danger in clarity," Alfred North Whitehead said, "the danger of overlooking the truth." And I did come across medicinal matters that valetudinarians might find salubrious. In *The Art of Cookery Made Plain and Easy*, Mrs. Hannah Glasse included a recipe for concocting a remedy against the plague. The plague Mrs. Glasse envisioned was bubonic rather than corona. For that matter she was probably not herself but instead was John Hill, a prominent eighteenth-century botanist and quacksalver. "Take of rue, sage, mint, rosemary, wormwood, lavender, a handful of each;" Hill instructed, "infuse them together in a gallon of white wine vinegar, put the whole into a stone-pot closely covered up, upon warm wood-ashes, for four days; after which draw off (or strain through fine flannel) the liquid, and put it into bottles well corked; and into every bottle put a quarter ounce of camphor. With this preparation wash your mouth, and rub your loins and your temples every day; snuff a little up your nostrils when you go into the air, and carry about you a bit of spunge dipped in the same, in order to smell upon all occasions, especially when you are near any place or person that is infected."

Hill's remedy and some of the cures now touted for coronavirus are similar albeit the latter are simpler: among a pharmacy of others, drinking cow urine or elderberry tea infused with lemon grass, guzzling bleach, rubbing one's back with lemon and lavender oil, and, most devoutly, praying because the virus cannot survive being rinsed in the Blood of the Lamb. No cure-all worth its ingredients appears without testimonials to its efficacy. "They write," Hill stated, "that four malefactors (who has robbed the infected houses, and murdered the people during the course of the plague) owned, when they came to the gallows, that they had preserved themselves from the contagion by using the above medicine only; and that they went the whole time from house to house without any fear of the distemper." The coronavirus has caused anxiety, and as a result many people suffer from insomnia. In his *A Thousand Notable Things of Sundrie Sorts* Thomas Lupton noted that "the soles of the feet anointed with the fat of a Dormouse doth procure sleep."

On the radio recently I heard a discussion of Time Travel. The subject is a weary perennial, and conversation about it always occurs during the somnolent digestive period after breakfast before the listener gathers his energies and abandons the kitchen. Hosts of the show are inevitably post-adolescents who haven't lived enough to package experience into thoughtful sentences. As a result, they haul empty bookcases. For them the subject resembles a video game in which past and present, beginnings and ends shift so rapidly they become hazy. In truth, all people are Time Travelers, riding memory into the past and imagination into the future. Today among people of a certain age, the future is too clear to be alluring. In contrast the past appeals to them, and since the start of the epidemic I have received innumerable letters, emails, and telephone calls from old friends. If I could travel to the eighteenth century and peruse *The Art of Cookery*, I suspect that in the snake-oil section I'd find a potion responsible for my correspondence, a compound composed, among other ingredients, of a tincture of unease, the balsam of idle time, and the honeyed essence of sentiment. My correspondents reached their majorities in the 1950s in a drugless society, when the advent of woman's libido was a pipedream, and before Gunga Din became Gunga Dell, when the regimental bhisti fetched water for battle-worn sahibs, not solace for IT managers in New York and London thirsty for answers to computer problems.

Memory fictionalizes, but from the Now cacophonous with requiems of sickness and death, the past seems simpler. "When I look back into the past," Samuel Smiles wrote as an Everyman in 1893, "it all seems a dream." Focus on The First and The Last has reversed. While Ends are clear, Beginnings are shrouded and alluringly mysterious. Distant objects please, William Hazlitt said, because with their "not being obtruded too close upon the eye, we clothe them with the indistinct and airy colors of fancy." People who wrote me didn't hanker to recall bohemian or rantipole days. They thought more about mortality than morality. The rosebuds and daisies they might have gathered had long blown. Nevertheless, they were gardeners searching for taproots and hints of continuance. Not only were they nostalgic, but they hankered for nostalgia. To use another metaphor, they escaped for a moment from the downstairs lives of their presents, and climbing into attics opened forgotten trunks and broken-backed suitcases. For me the memories and feelings they evoked were not those of the gospel song "Precious Memories." Their letters were not delivered by "unseen angels" but by Eric, the mailman. But yet, when I read the letters "how they lingered, ever near me." They brightened days and made me simultaneously melancholy and happy. Henry talked for an hour. He was joyous. He described his retirement and the successes of his children and scrolled through the lives of our college classmates. As he talked, I noticed a catch in his voice—the onset of Parkinson's I realized later. Ian said that he escaped worry by imagining errands and walking around "full of determined bewilderment which dissuades interruption since I seem to know what I am doing." After saying that he thought the virus might be a hoax, Corky asked my opinion. "It's real," I said. "Well, if it is," he replied. "We'll get though it with God's help." Corky's peace of mind was too important to him, his family, and to me, not to lie. "You are right," I said then quickly shifting the subject, told a story about a sheep that meowed, chased squirrels and chipmunks, and nested in a tree. "What kind of tree?" Corky asked. "A yew," I said.

Doug wrote that at the beginning of the epidemic he drove to a nursing home in Ohio to see his ninety-six-year-old mother "before they closed it down to visitors." To insure the home was not already closed, Doug telephoned before making the eight-hour trip. "Of course," he wrote, "they closed to visitors twenty minutes before I arrived." Doug persuaded the head nurse to wrap his mother in blankets and wheel her outside for a handful of minutes. "Her dementia had gotten worse, and I suspected this would be the last time I saw her. Even though I didn't have a fever or any symptoms of the virus, I worried that I was a carrier and might actually introduce her to the virus, becoming the agent of my own worst fear." Doug recounted that he said all he planned to say and that he thanked his mother for her loving kindnesses to him. "I'm not sure how much she understood," he concluded. "By the time I said good-bye, she had forgotten most of what I said. There are things worse than this virus."

Former students whom I taught decades ago also

wrote me. Now in their upper sixties, they had aged beyond place hunting and the deceptions of ambition. For most the past seemed more beguiling than the future. "I remember taking your essay course," one man recalled. "After reading my scribbling to the class in which I used my first car as a vehicle to navigate between different narrative destinations, you asked me repeatedly to describe what was in the glove compartment when I bought the car. I told you the truth, nothing other than a driver's manual, which prompted you to ask again and again, until I said, 'A breath mint, a half-spent pack of Trojans (the Pleasure Pack), and a spent shell casing from a 357 magnum.' That day you taught me how to lie and made a writer out of me." Among my younger correspondents was a woman who graduated from the university thirty years ago. She mailed a picture of herself holding three of my books: *Still Life, Trespassing,* and *A Continuing Education.* Her son, the woman said, would enter the university in the fall, and she was sending the books with him in hopes that I'd sign them. "I wasn't a memorable English student," she said, "and what I wrote for your class was pretty awful. But you made an impression on me, and through the years I have written a few things, the subjects always something small and mundane, ants, for example. I could write about ants for hours! And trees—I remember going outside after your class and looking up at trees for inspiration."

The correspondences mitigated the bituminous effects of the virus. They also made me aware of happier days. The brains of oldsters work by association. Places and thoughts that come to mind do not appear alone. They come coupled to a miscellany of things. Often relationships between the items are clear.

Other times they are inexplicable, bound by a word, an event, a mood, or objects and thoughts buried and irretrievable. While listening to a phone call, I remembered a man saying to me on Crete years ago, "Give me a suitcase and a Hilton, and I'm ready for adventure." While reading a letter from a friend in West Tennessee I recalled that once while driving through Memphis I listened to a radio program called "Supper Time with Christ" in which the head waiter promised a "delicious, nutritious, tasty, and wholesome meal." As could be anticipated, many resuscitated memories had to do with education. When my son Francis was a freshman, he came home from college to attend the funeral of his closest friend's father. Because he was in Storrs, Francis couldn't apply for his next year's room in person at the housing office, as rules required. Instead, Francis faxed his application to the university then called the housing office. An official instructed that on his return to school, he should appear at the office and produce proof he attended a funeral. To fix the matter I wrote the office. "I assume," I stated, that this letter will be "sufficient proof of my son's attendance at a funeral." "Only the mad," I continued, "fill their pockets with souvenirs at funerals. If you wish to discuss defunct corpses, Chicago overcoats, earth baths or general matters necrophiliac, you may contact me at home at the following number."

"That was bold," Vicki said after my recalling the letter and describing it to her. Vicki was wrong. I was humorous not bold. I have rarely been adventuresome as another recovered memory illustrated. In 1963 I sailed from New York to Southampton on the *United States*. I was twenty-one years old and headed for Cambridge. At a meal one evening, I met an older woman, no more than thirty-five I now suppose. She was smart. Wine flowed, and our conversation effervesced. Both of us ordered chocolate cake and vanilla ice cream for dessert after which she urged me to skip Cambridge. She owned a ranch in Kenya, and she invited me to accompany her to Kenya and live with her on the ranch. "I'll pay your way and show you things in East Africa that you won't find in books," she said. Obviously, I went to Cambridge. I was so naïve that I didn't think to sample "ranch life" with her on the boat. That particular memory startled me when it inexplicably popped into mind during a chat about classmates who attended Parmer elementary school in Nashville in 1955. When the call ended, I sat still and wondered why I hadn't gone to Kenya. Although such thoughts were indulgent, they were also therapeutic and broke the tedium of virus days. Eventually, Vicki called me to diner, and I pushed up and out of my chair, having concluded that if I had gone to Kenya the Mau Mau would have gotten me.

Since schools were closed and students had excess recess time, some emailed and asked questions. Because I wrote books, they assumed I had "answers." The moving finger which writes moves on to obscurity. In the preface to an edition of *The Purple Land*, W. H. Hudson opined that the "sleep of a book is apt to be of the unwaking kind." Students were too young not to be bruised by truths as I now saw them. Virginia Wolfe defined the art of writing as laying an egg in the reader's mind. Suppose the eggs I laid were not simply addled but were "addlizers." I didn't want to explain that the paragraphs which appeared on my pages were often there not because of belief but simply because the words worked. I didn't quote Robert Jefferies' *The Story of My Life* in which he said that "in human affairs everything happens by chance—that is, in defiance of human ideas, and without any direction or intelligence." I could not tell an ambitious young man eager to attend college that I'd never set goals.

How irresponsible it would have been to write, "Intellectual growth that starts in college resembles death-bed repentance: it doesn't take the converted very far." I dared not say that I thought the best way to live was without goals and that I meandered through the years much as I composed books, almost without direction. When asked about achievements, I wanted to quote Robert Lynd's remark, "The man of inaction has preserved many fine buildings, many fine institutions, many fine gardens." I resisted the temptation. My correspondents had not aged into toying with platitudes. Such pleasures are a playful part of passing and cause the elderly to chuckle. Oldsters recognize their insignificance and don't take them seriously. Upon the unformed and impressionable, people not old enough to appreciate wit, their effects might, I worried, be destructive. "I taught school for forty-five years," I said to Vicki, "but I wrote for adults."

In an email a boy quoted three sentences I wrote eight years ago, "the wisdoms appropriate to and which guide age and youth are different. The muscles of youth are too firm. Years have not softened them into strength enough to shoulder the burdens of experience." The boy said the sentences were "uncomforting" adding that they puzzled him and asked if he were missing "something crucial." "At what point do my shoulders become strong enough to carry the burdens of experience?" I admired the paradox I fashioned, but I wasn't sure what my lines meant. In my answer, I eschewed playfulness and tried to make my reply appear helpful and honest. I told the boy not to take anything I wrote to heart. "I didn't." "Mull, ponder, and push on." I said that for me to tell anyone off the page how to live would be presumptuous and dangerously arrogant. I explained that I looked at the world, "sometimes aslant and other times straight on." I recounted what that had remained constant during my life since childhood were wonder and curiosity and a desire to love and appreciate. I advised him to read Charles Dickens. "His world is rich and marvelous, sad and joyous." "Once upon a time," I concluded, "I urged students to ignore the reading assigned in my courses and instead read *David Copperfield*. You do the same, and when you finish *Copperfield*, open Henry Fielding's *Tom Jones*."

Writing students exhausted me. I'm not calloused enough to bear the thought that anything I wrote influenced someone. How much easier to talk to an old timer and scoot glibly pass requests for direction, quoting, for example, a statement like that made by Leigh Hunt in a critique of *Twelfth Night*, "Dig a well, plant a tree, write a book, and go to heaven." In any case the elderly never ask advice. They tell stories. Immediately after sending my reply to the boy, I turned with relief to subject I'd been considering before I received his email: how growing up next to a pond affected a person differently than growing up beside a river. "Ponds," I'd written, "were still and fostered contemplation and nurtured the familial. They resembled eyes wide in awe. In contrast, rivers rushed and blinked continually." "Does riverside life," I asked, "produce wanderers and explorers, frenetic people attracted to a multiplicity of experiences rather than to domesticity and calm of mind?" Along with letters and calls, such small thoughts occupied my hours and mitigated concern about the coronavirus. Of course, the respites were temporary. "Our romantic and itinerant character," Hazlitt wrote, "is not to be domesticated." Escaping the sense of "being caged," as a letter writer put it, was difficult and at times frustration erupted cankered making me sound like self-pitying Job.

"You and I," I said to a friend on the telephone, "are out-of-the-nursing-home elderly. If we get the virus, we'll die or be so maimed that both we and our families will wish that we had died. Ending the lockdown and restarting the economy won't change the way we live. Until there is a vaccine our lives will be static. We won't be able to board an airplane, take a cruise, attend a concert or sports event, enter a library, eat in a restaurant, exercise in a gymnasium or visit family and friends. Our imaginations will be immured, and we won't dream of traveling light and rough to a better old world like a hobo, our troubles in a bindle at the end of a pole slung over our shoulders. Our days will pass with our not doing and probably not thinking until we say, 'to Hell with it' or worse. And that will be goodbye to all that, and us."

The sooty spell dissipated quickly. The next day a wind storm tore through the yard. The following morning, I got up at five and spent two and a half hours picking up sticks and dragging fallen limbs to the woodpile behind the house. I returned to work that afternoon and carted wood for another hour and a half. Easter came, and Vicki gave me a chocolate bunny. She discovered it in the icebox in the basement. She bought it a year ago, but because the bunny was a kit, only four inches tall, she overlooked it when decorating the dining room for last year's family meal. Normally chocolate bunnies don't survive long in my presence. Before Easter ends, I've usually bitten the ears off every rabbit in the house. Although my kit will feel neglected and grow stale, this Easter I did not behave like Farmer McGregor. I spared the bunny and returned him to the warren in the icebox, and if the year goes, simply goes, I'll bring him out again next spring.

The day was sunny, and Vicki and I decided to drive around Mansfield and look at flowers. Forsythia bloomed in ragged yellow balls and hedges. "Like happiness," Vicki said. On the way home she wanted to pause at McDonald's and pick up a breakfast sandwich, hash browns, and coffee, proposing to eat them sitting on the grass above Mansfield Hollow Dam. I've never ordered food at or for that matter banked at a drive-thru window, so I stopped driving and Vicki took over the wheel. McDonald's didn't have any breakfast sandwiches and we returned home where Vicki cooked eggs and bacon and toasted homemade biscuits. We buttered the biscuits and blanketed them with blackberry and strawberry jams Vicki made last summer in Nova Scotia. Later we walked the dogs through the university woods along the Fenton River. Among the few people we saw was a small Chinese girl dressed in a pink bunny suit. Over the rabbit's nose and mouth was a mask which she'd decorated with blue and yellow flowers. Earlier in the week my friend David turned 84, and the next day Vicki baked him an après-birthday carrot cake. We drove to his house, rang the doorbell, and put the cake on the stoop. When David opened the door wearing a mask, we sang "Happy Birthday."

Sometimes July Grasses were hard to find, Richard Jefferies wrote, but if a person searched "in corners and out-of-the-way places and not in the broad acres," he'd discover them. They lurked, he said, by waysides, on banks, "at the back of ponds," inside the enclosures of woods, in the angles of corn fields, and especially in "uninteresting places." Jefferies directions are good hints for living in and without a virus, Milton's Satan was deluded when he proclaimed that the mind could transform a Heaven into a Hell and a Hell into a Heaven. No regime of demonic positive thinking can change Hell into Heaven. But in great part the mind actually is its own place, and if one looks and thinks carefully, the neglected and the uninteresting become satisfying. In "Summer Moods," John Clare wrote: "I love to muse o'er meadows newly mown / Where withering grass perfumes the sultry air, / Where bees search round with sad and weary drone / In vain for flowers that bloomed but newly there." Yes, memories linger. The flowers may no longer bloom and recollection of them may sadden but the whiffs that drift through the years invigorate. Moreover, I can't escape chores. Yesterday a late spring snow dropped four inches on Storrs, and my yard is again a brush pile. Still, the bare limbs of cherries have become racks swaying with shawls and gowns of flowers. I also have a sensible prophylactic reply ready if anyone reads one of my books and writes seeking guidance. When Pelham left home intent on becoming a gentleman and a dandy, his mother wrote him in London. Her letter was a conduct book of suggestions. Among them was a mystifier that I intend to appropriate. "You may also pick up a little acquaintance with metaphysics," she wrote. "That sort of thing is a good deal talked about just at present." Or I could demur explaining that I'd lost confidence in all advice, especially that proffered by me. If I worked on the refusal, perhaps I could conclude with a quotation that has lurked in my desk for a decade. "'We all have our little foibles,' as the cannibal said when he tossed his grandmother's head into the stew pot."

Terrible Sanity

Terrible Sanity

The price of living dutifully and responsibly is high, often costing life itself. Days devoid of madness are often terrible, desolate, and in their sanity truly mad. At my age a person scrolls back through his decades and ponders the innumerable occasions on which he betrayed himself in order to be true to others or true to the expectations of others. However, Time salves, and the regrets one fancies he feels rarely inflame and are always fleeting. In assessing what his months at Walden Pond taught him, Thoreau said that he learned "that if one advances confidently in the direction of his dreams, and endeavors to live the life he has imagined, he will meet with a success unexpected in common hours." Most of my aged friends are half in love with easeful death and are not susceptible to seborrheic optimism. Dreams don't determine the direction I'm traveling, but if my druthers could be answered, I'd like to slip back into dust quickly and painlessly.

Of course, dreams sometimes break my sleep. In them celestial cities surrounded by jasper walls never appear. Occasionally, the dreams are mad, compensating perhaps for my having lived placidly and rationally. Last week I dreamed I owned a small home-furnishings store. I specialized in selling blood-stained floorboards. My clientele were the jaded wealthy for whom exotic pleasure had lost its savor. They purchased the boards as conversation pieces and fitted them into parquet floors, generally in foyers but sometimes in libraries and music rooms. The most expensive boards were associated with notorious murders, the cheapest domestic abuse. I also sold blood-stained comforters and sheets. The more intricate the pattern of spillage the higher the price. Mounted behind clear glass, these served as wall hangings. They were especially popular with postmodern mothers keen to adorn their progeny's playrooms with "decorations more emotionally stimulating than Mary Poppins or Winnie the Pooh wallpaper." "It's astonishingly therapeutic for a repressed little girl to see blood and imagine being trapped in a room with a madman," a commercial child psychologist declared.

No longer do I ask "what's the news" or speculate about what the news will be. Instead I ponder "what was the news?" In part I do so because washing old news is easy whereas the unscrubbed present settles on the skin and clogs pores. The hagiography evoked by the death of President George Bush was, for example, macabre and underbred—Egyptian in its pyramidical vulgarity. How repellant to Fed Ex his shell back and forth across the country to be gabbled over by the political class. He deserved a quick, decorous burial in Texas, refined and soothingly proper, muted recognition attesting to his common humanity.

The truth is that I am not comfortable in every minute of the present hour. When a stranger addresses me and says, "Have a blessed day," the words are as unpleasant to my ears as a crop duster is to the nose. No long-term wife is a cloister unto herself. Unable to retreat into a verbal nunnery, Vicki has been tainted by my linguistic distastes. Like me she reacts more strongly to the manner of speech than to the matter.

Last month after hearing an announcer on National Public Radio say "irregardless" three times in fifty-one minutes, she telephoned the station in Amherst, Massachusetts. "Curdling illiteracy does not go well with breakfast," she said, urging the woman who answered her call to inform the announcer that *regardless* was standard English.

I react stronger than Vicki to the insignificant, especially lardy uplift. In December during examinations, signs appeared atop the circulation desk in the university library. The signs were modest, only eight by ten inches. One morning a sign simply said, "You Can." Underneath the words appeared a bloodless Valentine heart. The next day "Eat, Sleep, Breathe. Good Luck" replaced "You Can," and the heart became a Rosetta Stone of emoji's: a five-pointed star, an empty circle, a smiley face with a curl swinging across the forehead like a pendulum, something akin to a croquet mallet, and then another something resembling a mitten with the thumb jutting out as if the wearer were hitching a ride. "Such signs should say, 'Study. Only Nitwits Rely on Luck,' 'You Can't If You Don't Work Your Ass Off,' and 'Distinguish Yourself from the Lazy Herd and Make Your Fee-Paying Parents Proud,'" my friend Josh said to me.

Pasted on a balcony inside the atrium of the Shea Entrance to Windham Hospital in Willimantic are four large pictures. In one a kindly Asian police woman leans over preparing to roll an overweight man in a wheelchair into a hospital. In another a smiling African-American woman wearing a sunny orange blouse hands a tray of food to a bedridden patient. In the middle of each picture appears a sandwich of words. The upper and lower crusts are "Every" and "matters" respectively. The filling between varies: heartbeat followed by language, meal, and ride. "Bonehead sentiments, mayonnaise," Josh fulminated. "No one thinks every heartbeat matters, not even folks whose doctors have signed their sailing orders. Try ordering a pizza in Gothic or Brygian. How important is a ride to the 7-Eleven to buy chicken tenders and *People* magazine? As for every meal—people who believe that should eat dinner at my house. Abyss [Josh's wife] is a cordon noire cook. The food will not be memorable." More to Josh's taste was the attitude of a woman who recently bought all the yellow potatoes for sale at a local farmer's market. "Yellow ones," she said, "make the best mashed potatoes. All my husband's relatives are coming to my house for Christmas dinner. If I stuff their mouths with potatoes, they won't be able to talk so damn much."

The present irritates Josh more than it does me, probably because age tranquilizes and I am four years older than he. After reading an article by a newspaper divine which mentioned Resurrection of the Body, Josh wrote a response and sent it to the paper. In it, he asked what sort of body he could expect to receive: "an old one tried and true but withal suffering from a stiff crankshaft and diverticulitis in the fuel line or a model straight from conception with fashionable bells and whistles all of which exceed the capabilities of new corpses and which the quick never learn to use and as a result cause more wrecks than communion wine." Josh criticized the latest models in part to appeal to me, explaining that he knew that the past interested me more than the present or the future. As might be expected the paper did not print Josh's letter. What I wanted to know and Josh neglected to say was whether recent models included the current new-fangled safety devices, and if so, why such gizmos were needed in heaven. Had the divines who created heaven inserted malware into their programs guaranteeing that the Saved would be forever tempted by Mephistophelean spam?

During fall Vicki and I saw three puppet shows at the university: Sarah Nolen's "The Fairy Tailor," "The Gingerbread Man" staged by Wonder Spark Puppets, and "The Fairy Circus" by the Tanglewood Marionettes. The shows were magical. Not only did they effervesce and buoy my spirits but they also transported me back to childhood, to the Children's Theater in Nashville and performances of "Peter Pan" in which I whistled and clapped to save Tinkerbell and laughed as Tick Tock the crocodile pursued Captain Hook eager to add the rest of the Captain's savories to the hand he swallowed. On leaving "The Fairy Circus" I imagined having skin as soft and glossy as satin and wearing a scarlet top hat, purple elfin slippers, and a green silk robe speckled with silver stars. I was, if not a puppet, a fairy of my own making, a transformation possible only in the long-ago past.

I thought about dress because recently I'd viewed an exhibition of Ellen Emmet Rand's portraits at the university art museum. I needed a thorough transformation. To the museum I wore gray cargo shorts, a yellow fleece my son Francis wore in middle school twenty-six years ago, a green and red, hummus and paint-splattered plaid shirt, white socks, and a pair of running shoes retired from the track and which I don when I dig compost. In my hands I carried a bicycle helmet so old that the midnight-dark plastic had faded into day. As Mother would have put it, I "looked like something the cat sucked." Rand's portraits made me feel unfinished and forced me recall a time when I didn't look far from society born and wore dark suits, regimental ties, and wing-tipped shoes. The men depicted by Rand looked like the fathers and uncles of my childhood friends. They sat sculpted in heavy suits and vests topped by starched collars. "Woolled over" and insulated from the transient, they appeared reassuringly substantial and at their immovable best embodied stability and reliability. Most of the women depicted wore dresses that gathered about them ornamenting and separating them from thoughtless spoilage. Several dresses were collared, and when dresses lacked collars, sitters often wore pearls. The women were more than decorative. They were formidable. Not only would the young girls among them grow into the stays supporting the armchairs which confined the men, but they would inherit their wealth.

Few people smiled and only in two portraits were teeth visible, one depicting a mezzo soprano in full song, the other an informally dressed sporting socialite holding a small terrier. When I was young, my father urged me to resist the importuning of camera addicts and not to expose my "bones" in public. When translated from the picture tube to domestic life, the television command "Smile. You're on Candid Camera" was particularly abhorrent. Father believed candid photographs resembled gossip. As a good life required discipline and, indeed, acting, so Father thought photographs should not blunder into privacy, but instead should be distant and posed. Times change. Instead of revealing a person's foolish, precipitate character, the smile now signifies humanity, naturalness, and unbuttoned oneness with the good, the true, and the democratic.

"A little paper big on community," *Neighbors* is

published monthly and distributed free throughout northeast Connecticut. Advertisements, announcements, and well-intentioned articles fill its pages, the headline above a typical article reading "Friends Can Make the Cold Seem Unimportant." For the record I found the most recent number beside the check-out counter at Price Chopper. I read it while waiting for Vicki to pick up a few items. The few, as I expected, became legion, resembling the ants magically transformed into Myrmidons. In the issue's sixteen pages, twenty-three people were smiling and showing their teeth, seven of whom appeared in an advertisement for the Hope and Wellness Center and Salon in nearby Ashford. Several other neighbors had zipped-lip smiles while the mouths of a couple of old guys were open. They gapped like dark caverns, and the men's teeth had aged so far beyond yellow that I couldn't distinguish incisors from palates.

Before *irregardless* entered radio speech and the possessive of I became *I's*, before words galloped across punctuation into run-on thought, and before composition became a jargon-ridden aspic lumpy with theory, pre-writing, and portfolios, English teachers taught writing by teaching classes to diagram sentences. While at the Rand exhibition, I recalled a statement a teacher made sixty years ago at Montgomery Bell Academy in Nashville. "The appearance of thought," she said, "is as important as that of the body." In sentences perceptions are determined by skeletal interiors, not by exterior fabrics. Unfortunately, remembrances of curative things past are short-lived, except in the minds of people like me who consciously turn from the present to mull the past. Almost no one remembers the person frequently celebrated as the most effective composition teacher of his generation. For thirty years beginning in the 1920s he taught English at a small Southern college. In freshman composition courses he used Tinker Toys to teach diagramming, parts of speech, and sentence structure. In each class he distributed an assortment of Tinker Toys. While green spools were transitive verbs, violet ones were intransitive. Nouns were smaller spools, subjects red, direct objects orange, indirect objects gray, and objects of prepositions white. Connecting the spools and framing sentences were sticks. These ranged in length. Prepositions measured one inch. Conjunctions were one and a quarter lengths, those separating items in lists three-quarters of an inch, and those linking compound sentences two inches. Adjectives also varied in length, most about one and a half inches. All, however, were longer than adverbs which the teacher discouraged students from using. The course was popular because classes were fun, and effective, transforming high schoolers who stumbled over the parts of speech into competent analytical writers. By the end of the course almost every student was able to frame readable paragraphs.

Murder will wear a reader out. No longer do I read contemporary crime novels. In fact, I read few newly published books. Instead I wander the university library and pull forgotten books off shelves. Not knowing what I will find satisfies my residual hankering for mystery. In this century, E. B. White stated in *The Points of My Compass*, "things move with lamentable swiftness." Tinker Toys, pleated trousers, old-school speech, and dusty books put a hitch in the giddy ups of the moment. Last week in the stacks I found Robert Wood's *How to Tell the Birds from the Flowers*, "A Manual of Flornithology for Beginners." Published in 1907 the book consisted of a bouquet of light verse. In linking birds and plants, the poems were heavy with puns and too rooted to soar into an abstract lyrical empyrean. "A Sparrow. Asparagus" declared, "The Sparrow, from flying, is quite out of breath, / In fact he has worked himself almost to death, / While the lazy Asparagus,—so it is said,—/ Spends all of his time in the 'sparagus bed."

On a nearby shelf I found *Sunshine; or, Cures for All Ills* by Mrs. Prosser, that is, Sophie Amelia Prosser who wrote some 35 books in the latter half of the 19th century. "Religion—the sunshine of the soul that flows from love to Christ," Mrs. Prosser explained, "is a cure for all the ills to which man is subjected on earth." The Religious Tract Society of London published Mrs. Prosser's books. The American Tract Society in Boston reprinted the volumes in the United States. No publication date was printed on the title page of *Sunshine*. However, on the free end paper appeared a dated inscription: "Presented to Miss Mary Augusta Barney as a token of Respect and Regard by her friend Bob. May 19th 1872." The contents of *Sunshine* were familiar. I've read hundreds of religious tracts, and in three academic studies I wrote about them. Mrs. Prosser's stories didn't startle, but they brought to mind my library life of fifty years ago, a happy time spent sitting at tables, reading, marveling, and taking notes. The single line in *Sunshine* that I jotted down was spoken by Sir Herbert Carteret, a worldly man who misjudged Christian forbearance as weakness. "These weak-brained men are sometimes the happiest," Sir Herbert said when pondering an impoverished Christian's refusal to allow his low station to provoke divisive dissatisfaction.

I have long enjoyed byways—shady overgrown paths apart from interstates—in books not simply neglected volumes like religious tracts but also odd trails in the volumes themselves, in *Sunshine* the inscription and then at the end of the text eight pages advertising other Christian books. On each page appeared an illustration four inches wide and six and a half tall. *Children of Many Lands*, for example, cost 65 cents. In the illustration, Ching Wang, a Chinese boy with a long pigtail, was skipping while simultaneously juggling two balls. The plate from *Link and Other Stories* showed "Link Saving Jamie." Link resembled an Irish setter more than a St. Bernard. Nevertheless, he was a life saver bringing a canteen of water to Jamie who lay comatose on the ground. The picture advertising *Winthorpes* depicted "The Sewing Class." Six ragamuffin little girls in tattered smocks surrounded their teacher, a neat young woman with a white apron spread across her lap. One of the girls was so poor she was barefoot, and a seventh girl hovered ghostly and tubercular in the background.

With its ever-malleable memories, for older people the past is sweeter than the present. Early in December Anne sent me a watercolor she painted of a sculpture on the grounds Montgomery Bell Academy. The sculpture depicts a teacher standing beside a student. The teacher is gesturing and spreading his left arm urging the student to accept the invitation to life proffered by the world that stretches before him. I taught at MBA for a year before attending graduate school, and a goodly number of people have associated the teacher with me. "With love to my oldest living boyfriend," Anne wrote on the card accompanying her painting. Anne's and my parents were dear friends. She and I were the same age, and in high school we went out together several times. Anne was a glorious girl, beautiful, smart, and faultlessly appealing. If all the stars had fallen out of the constellations and into line, we would have enjoyed life together. I was too young, however. In those years I was terrified of girls, and we never progressed beyond the eternally sweet hand-holding stage of courtship. Moreover, I was a dreamer daily imagining myself an adventurer exploring "far-away places with strange sounding names." Thoreau wrote well, but he knew little about real living. What happinesses, what possibilities, what lives I missed by pursuing dreams. Insofar as success is concerned—in looking back successful people my age often deem their achievements delusions, if not snares, and judge compatriots who jettisoned ambition in their early years to have been preternaturally wise.

Christmas is bookkeeping season. People compute losses and estimate liabilities, that is, track friends who are about to tumble off the balance sheet. Few accounts remain active in the ledgers of most oldsters, so they delve into the past. In his Christmas card, Jensen said he belonged to three clubs: a genealogy club, a Scandinavian club, and the Sons of the American Revolution. "All," he wrote, take "me back to my roots," adding that his genealogy file had "almost ten thousand relatives, almost four thousand marriages described, and seven thousand, seven hundred individuals with descriptive notes." My roots do not spread broad. My parents and my great aunts and uncles as well as all their children are dead. I have one first cousin whom I have not seen for forty years. A couple of fourth or fifth cousins may lurk in some mollusk-filled barrow but spading them up would strain the lumbar regions of my mind and computer.

Jensen is a sui generis antiquarian. Managing a deep-digging genealogy harrow is beyond most elderly people. What some do inadvertently is create friendships that never existed. The sources of these are usually casual meetings that time and failing memories elevate into intimacy. In December I received a mailbox of letters from people whom I'd never met or had met once decades ago. The letters described the doings of strangers. While "Dr. Mike moved his practice to Knoxville," Fred Jr. "married for the fourth time. Can you believe it?" An unknown woman sent a photograph of her and her husband taken in Cozumel on their 62nd wedding anniversary, and an unrecognizable great-grandfather sent a picture of "his littlest little angel" wearing a blue and white Pee-Wee football uniform. Confusing me with someone else or allowing time to transform passing into a substantial moment would embarrass the letter writers if they became aware of their mistakes. For the record I did not correct their misapprehensions. Instead I wrote long appreciative responses, thanking my correspondents for remembering me and sharing their news. If neither they nor I die, they will write again next December and I will reply. In life charm is kinder than truth.

Among the volumes advertised at the back of *Sunshine* was *Netherclift*. The caption under the accompanying illustration read "Missing Papers Found." In the illustration two men faced each other across a table. In front of one man sat a campaign or lap desk. From it he'd extracted a sheaf of papers which he handed to the other man. Many people don't simply confuse their pasts and unwittingly fabricate events and their histories; instead they consciously create pasts, discovering papers that were never missing because they never existed. All people are story tellers, if only to themselves, and inhabit fictions of their own making. This is especially true of the old who are discontent because they've become that platitudinous invisibility the elderly whose hours are pinched and boring, broken only by pills and visits to doctors. "Being totally unexceptional," thought Layeville, a character in Frederic Prokosch's *The Seven Who Fled*, might be "a quality as rare as perfection of face, and perhaps a quality equally desolate and solitary." For many people the key to escaping solitary confinement is lying, especially about the past. "My real life," Prokosch himself said, "has transpired in darkness, secrecy, fleeting contacts and incommunicable delights, any number of strange picaresque episodes and peccadilloes and even crimes, and I don't think any of my friends have even the faintest notion of what I'm really like or have any idea of what my life has really consisted of."

How flattering to think one has never resembled and never will resemble other men. How marvelous to imagine oneself a man of mystery whose days were and still are fabulously provocative. How terrible for a person to reach end time and admit he led a gray anecdotal less life. How wonderful to be someone who didn't waste years buttoning shirts and trousers, taking off shoes and socks, and putting on pajamas. Both Prokosch and his books slipped out of public ken during his last years. But then he enjoyed a resurgent moment on the appearance of *Voices* a memoir recounting meetings and conversations with celebrated people. Over the years Prokosch had met many famous people. He perused accounts of artists' lives and collected gossip about them. He read their books and viewed their paintings and sculptures. But his memories were, as Robert Greenfield his biographer put it, "creative misrememberings … internal monologues designed in ingenious and entertaining ways to read like dialogues." In other words, they were lies but lies which forged a lively past generating the interest both of others and of himself.

Would that while drinking tea with Wallace Stevens as did Prokosch, I'd heard Stevens say, "Delicious tea, isn't it? A friend sends it from Peking. In a diplomatic pouch. I would love to sail in a pouch. If not in a diplomat's then perhaps in a kangaroo's." "That night for dessert we had a Singapore Ice Cream," Prokosch recounted, remembering an evening in Paris. "Gertrude Stein looked very voluptuous as she licked at her spoon, which she did with half-closed eyes and a slow steady rhythm. Her tongue suggested the bow of an expert fiddler who is playing a languid and delicious adagio." During a Chinese meal with Prokosch, Thomas Wolfe "placed his fists on the table, which trembled precariously, and the sweat on his face caught the light from the window. He gave a sudden gasp and clutched at the air triumphantly. He looked like a swimmer rising from the bottom of a whirlpool. His wild eyes, squeezed in fat, gleamed like a boar's, and the bubbles on his lips shone with a wild exultation."

I have never dined with a famous person. Nor can I imagine such a meal. Perhaps if I cooked up then published the menu of a misremembered banquet attended by the famous dead, I would receive first-class mail other than Christmas cards. What Duško Popov the most famous double agent during World War II and the man responsible for convincing the Nazis that the Allies D-Day invasion would take place at Calais, revealed one night when we were in our cups drinking 1928 Krug would astonish military hangers-on. His words would cause the ashes of A. G. P. Taylor to rise from the floor of the crematorium at Golders Green in a whirlwind and rewrite his history of the Second World War. But I am, let me assure readers, discreet, indeed well-bred. I certainly would not reveal everything confided to me in imaginary conversations. Only a big, big check could tempt me to repeat what Jane Austen disclosed in the parlor at Chawton after bolting down a couple of stiff ones.

I have been to Capri, but despite the propensity to imagine myself a fairy I didn't see Curzio Malaparte dressed in "a scarlet silk shirt and black velvet trousers and red leather sandals with big gold buckles." I don't drink spirits, and so I also missed watching his hand crawl "like an adder" around a "blue-veined highball glass." No one has ever "stared at me grimly, like a big spotted toad" as Somerset Maugham did while talking to Prokosch. Perhaps I wouldn't be an insignificant belletrist if I'd accompanied Prokosch on his visits to the literati. On his asking what she thought about Gogol, Virginia Woolf answered, "I have no thoughts today." To his inquiry about Dostoevsky, she responded, "I have no feelings about Dostoevsky." Of Pirandello, she said, "I feel no kinship for Pirandello." About *Ulysses*, she replied, "I have no sentiments about *Ulysses*. At least none that are worth mentioning. When I read it, it struck me as a wild miscalculation." "She suddenly looked ten years older," Prokosch observed. "Her hair was tinged with gray. Her eyes looked strangely bloodshot and her cheeks were streaked with weariness. She stared at a fly which was clinging to a light bulb. Then she tilted her head, as though posing for a photograph. 'A catastrophe,' she murmured. 'A veritable catastrophe of the critical faculties.' She lowered her eyelids, which looked like wilted petals. Then she pressed her hands together in what looked like a prayer. She sat motionless for a moment. She seemed to have turned into an effigy."

Francis Bacon was wrong. Rarely does reading make a full man, but reading *Voices* made me want to tickle the dry bones of the past. The only literary person to whom I ever chatted regularly about books was myself although I would have enjoyed talking to Bobby Shafto had he not been heavier and sweatier than Thomas Wolfe or Hannah Bantry had she stopped gnawing on her mutton bone long enough to be more talkative than Virginia Woolf. Clothes don't interest me as much as they did Prokosch's Curzio Malaparte, but I'd like to know the pattern of the trousers and the brand of the shoe Son John of nursery rhyme notoriety wore to bed after a night of carousing and diddling. I hope the former was not a pair of lime-colored golf slacks blotched with bouquets of bachelor buttons and daffodils, and that the shoe was a two-toned wingtip and not, oh horror, a Nike trainer.

Prokosch inscribed copies of his books to famous people. Although he did not present the copies to the people, later he sold them. He enhanced the provenance of the books by claiming they'd once belonged to the people to whom he inscribed them. In the basement are remaindered volumes of my books. I lack the gumption to dedicate books to and afterward claim the acquaintance of celebrities. But recently I inscribed several books to myself from myself. Instead of selling them, I donated them to the fifty-cent and one-dollar book sale at the Mansfield Library. "For Sam Pickering," I wrote typically, "a wonderful companion, a man whose presence I cannot and don't wish to escape, a grand fellow who brightens my days and whose conversation makes barren moments blossom. From your great, greater, and greatest admirer, with best wishes, indeed with love and more, Sam Pickering." Or "For Sam Pickering, whose vast breezy reading keeps the wind in my jib and me out of the Doldrums. Who else would have found an article in a Dixiecrat medical newsletter describing a plastic surgeon whose New Year's resolution was to perform four hundred breast augmentations during the coming year? 'Georgia's females are God's glory— Lord love 'em,' he explained. 'But sometimes our ladies sip a little too much sauce and become frisky. By performing implants and creating DAR chapters of majestic stuffed shirts, I intend to temper those improprieties. Moreover, I hope my patients will become role models for our precious youthlettes as they rise into the confusions of puberty and are tempted to become high school cheerleaders.'"

"Thank you, Sam, old buddy, for having a mind like a caliper," the inscription concluded, "and for not allowing me to forget that our age has its own Galens and Sushrutas. Your research has kept me from plunging into the wake kicked up by the breast and crawl strokes of so, so many television pundits, saving me from drowning in a Sargasso Sea of bluster and gagging ignorance. Your friend, morning and evening and tea time, too, as always, Sam Pickering." This second inscription irritated the purchaser of the volume, and she emailed demanding that I apologize to medical fraternity and sorority pledges. As I am studiously polite and responded to the Christmas cards from strangers, so I answered the email.

"I'm always willing to recant a verbal infelicity," I wrote. "Pride is the begetter of all sins, even the delightful ones, and chewing humble pie is good for the internal organs. It facilitates virtue and improves sleep

hygiene besides removing facial freckles more effica-
ciously than lemon juice or honey and sugar scrubs.
Moreover, its main ingredients are words, and they
cost so little that Piggly Wiggly does not stock them.
Nevertheless, to demand an apology for a dedication
penned by a title page me is stunningly naïve and presumptuous—an anatomical impossibility that should
be obvious to all competent followers of Herophilus. I
can only assume that you have not yet earned or have
recently lost your medical license. Nonetheless thank
you for writing. Your opinion is important to me, and
have a Happy New Year."

"Who sent you the email? Vicki asked later. "I bet
it was Galumphy Dumplesop." "You're right," I said.
"Of course, I'm right. She's a silly bang snap and snuf-
fles about like an upholstered gray rodent. No one else
would have written you, and why didn't you tell the
truth: that even if ripeness is all her opinion doesn't
matter a road apple to you?" Vicki said. "I value equa-
nimity," I answered. In *Voices* Frederic Prokosch, I
continued, "recalled listening to Edith Sitwell discuss
Milton at a cocktail party. As she sat on a sofa talking,
a butler walked past holding a tray of hors d'oeuvres.
Cradling a drink, Edmund Wilson stopped the butler,
plucked a shrimp from the tray, and dipped it into
a bowl of mayonnaise sauce. He held the shrimp in
the air as he sipped his whiskey," Prokosch reported,
concluding, "I watched with frozen horror as the
shrimp slid from its toothpick and gracefully landed
on Miss Sitwell's coiffure. But Miss Sitwell ignored it
and continued with serenity."

During December friends sent newsletters in
which they recapped their year's activities. They
were elderly and flush with spare time and money.
Most traveled living for months in Surinam, Ecuador,

Malta, New Zealand, Mali, Uganda, and Southeast Asia. In Asia, a woman recounted, she and her husband spent weeks roaming jungles and "exploring temples in Cambodia, Laos, Thailand, and Bhutan." My correspondents did not wander the past. But they sojourned in places appointed so differently from their homes—in Massachusetts, Washington, Oregon, Tennessee, and Virginia—that in a sense they escaped the present and their everyday lives and might as well have been roaming the past, that of actual memories or that of fond imaginings. Perhaps their journeys were genuflections to dreams buried under the detritus of responsible living. For my part I spent Christmas in Greenville, South Carolina. Parked on South Main Street on Christmas Eve was a convertible. Its body was red and molded into the shape of a sled. Behind the wheel sat a man dressed like Santa Claus, chortling and offering to take families for rides. "What uncomplicated joyous fun," I thought, but then I noticed a sign painted on the car's right front fender: "Jesus is the Reason for the Season." A Lexus SUV, the LX model, then backed up near Vicki and me and parked along the curb. The price of the Lexus started at eighty-six thousand dollars. The license was a South Carolina vanity plate. Stamped across the top of the plate was "In God We Trust." "In God We Trust Fund," Vicki said. "The corporate religious complex—churches have become malls of money-changers."

"Yes," I said, after which I drifted out of the unappealing present into the past. During the previous week I'd read the Romantic poets, and suddenly I found myself far from Vicki and South Carolina and in Italy with Shelley and his wife Mary's good friend Maria Gisborne. "Let's be merry," Shelley wrote in his "Letter to Maria Gisborne," "We'll have tea and toast; / Custards for supper, and an endless host / Of syllabubs and jellies and mince pies, / and other such lady-like luxuries." After eating, Shelley said they'd talk. "We'll make our friendly philosophic revel / Outlast the leafless time; till buds and flowers / Warn the obscure inevitable hours." Then "tomorrow," he continued, "to fresh woods and pastures new.'" Yes, but in my case to old growth forests and pastures long fallow and brambly with blackberries and alders, to forgotten places where the wild birds sing and the yellow potatoes grow.

On A Siding

Because people know I have written essays for forty years, they suggest subjects to me. Actually, matters are more complicated. Imagined people suggest more topics than do flesh and blood acquaintances. That's probably because my writings interest the phantoms wandering my dreams more than they do bowel-bound mortals. Earlier this month a ghostly couple visited me just before sunrise. While the woman urged me to write about the color brown, the man told me to consider the railway flatcar. "Think about all you could pile on it," he said, "and if the car is on a siding, you won't have to stray from your study. You can avoid straining your mind while you stack experiences on the deck." In William McFee's *Spenlove in Arcady*, Frederick Spenlove, a retired naval engineer, explained his sedate existence to thirteen-year old Dora Pagett, saying that "when people get on in life, they haven't your resources for amusing themselves."

What they have is the capacity for enduring idleness. In *The Way of the World*, Nicolas Bouvier opined that although travel provided "occasions for shaking oneself up," it didn't expand a person's freedom. Instead, it involved "a kind of reduction." "Deprived of one's usual setting, the customary routine stripped away like so much wrapping paper, the traveler," and by implication the active seeker, "finds himself reduced to more modest proportions." Travel could, however, Bouvier noted, make a person more receptive to curiosity, intuition, and "love at first sight"—not matters that appeal to the elderly whom life has taught to distrust intuition and eschew curiosity. As for love at first sight, cataracts, thankfully, temper that irrational disruption. Instead of busily searching for ways to amuse themselves, oldsters allow amusement to find them.

In past years the telephone calls I received were perishable and natural. Friends and relatives called pregnant with news and cheer. Now only robocallers telephone, and the calls I receive are artificial and so light weight they take up no emotional space on the flatcar. Callers fret that I might have chronic leg pain and want to give me a motorized wheelchair. They are eager to enroll me in an investment club that pays 14% interest a year after a modest outlay of fifty thousand dollars. "We do cleaning of air vent and gutter," a man said whose English had been short-circuited by the wearying number of calls he made every day. "I know you need burial insurance," Robin began dispensing with the usual salutation of "How are you today?" "Perhaps she called because she knew a great deal about your health—how you are now or how you won't be tomorrow," Vicki said. We have received "a suspension notice" lodged against "your Social Security number by the Federal Crime Investigation Department," a concerned woman said, instructing me to return her call and supply sundry banking and identification numbers so that the suspension could be lifted and the payments resumed.

My friend Josh loathes callers who prey upon the progressive gullibility of the elderly. "If you ever get an actual woman talking about Social Security," he told me, "tell her that if you discover her name you are going to break into her house, rip out her heart, and feed it to your Rottweiler." "That sounds like Greek tragedy," I said. "No, the Old Testament," Josh replied. "Josh goes too far. We don't live in Texas," Vicki said. "Just this morning I received a letter from a well-intentioned woman, Mrs. Bridggie William. She wrote from the Ivory Coast proving that kindness is international and not parochial like Josh's anger." Mrs. William was humble and her salutation began, "With Due Respect and Humanity." Because she had suffered, she sympathized with the misfortunes of others. Her husband of forty-six years died "after a Cardiac Arteries Operation," and she herself had "cancer of the liver and stroke." From her husband she inherited 15.8 million dollars. She did not have children, and because her death was imminent, she wanted to give the money "to any good God fearing brother or sister" who would use it "to help Less privilaged (sic) people, orphanages, widows and propagating the word of God." The letter contained a primer of misspellings, idiosyncratic grammar, and garbled sentences. "My, God, you're insensitive," Vicki exclaimed when I mentioned the errors. "The poor woman is dying," Vicki replied. "She cannot help making mistakes. They are insignificant anyway. Only a retired prig would notice them. Don't you have sick friends who are losing their minds and no longer can spell or write clear prose? You are always telling me that much of what your friends say doesn't make sense."

Before I responded to Vicki, the telephone rang and interrupted our conversation. "Wall St" was raising money again, this time for fire fighters not for disabled veterans or a police benevolent fund. The truth is that inconsistency is both human and divine, and Vicki can be short. Because she donates to a souk of charities, importuning calls disturb every meal. Two weeks ago, I overheard a conversation with a telephone solicitor. "Hello, Victoria, my name is Greg," the man oozed. "How are you today?" "Greg," Vicki answered immediately, not allowing the oleaginous concern about well-being to cause her to slip into pandering politeness, "you didn't give me your last name, but don't say anything. Let me guess. Could it be Smith or Brown or maybe Jones?" "No, no, don't tell me," she ordered before Greg could reply. "Wait! I've got it. Your last name is Asshole. Orsaholdt in the old country, but Americanized to suit your family." "Nice," I said after Vicki slammed down the receiver. "Maybe not so nice," Vicki said, "but learned and damn satisfactory."

Would that there were more humanity in humanity and that miscreants without consciences didn't roam the hours preying upon enfeebled age. It's too bad that the magic lantern once celebrated as curing personality flaws by beaming light upon people proved a fraud. While a regimen of orange light purged fractured thoughts from lamebrains, enabling them to scamper through the thorniest ideas without being impeded by a single syllable, bathing in blue light expanded the sympathies and eradicated self-centeredness. In a broadside urging individuals to buy his "Bluebird Lantern," one snake-oil salesman suggested that blue should be the dominant color in newly installed stained-glass windows in churches. Like Baptism, light shining through the windows onto members of congregations would "reform hearts and souls," expelling grit from the former, the world from the latter.

In the carton containing robocalls I laid a bundle of emails. Swindles that came around inevitably come around again, and again. From Jim Ovia, chairman of the Board of Directors of Zenith Bank located on the Gulf of Guinea, I recently received an email entitled "Zenith Bank / United Nations Scam Victims Compensation Payments." "This is to bring to your notice that I am delegated from the United Nations," the email announced, "to pay 48 scam victims $9,000,000 USD (Nine Million Dollars) each. You are listed and approved for this payment as one of the scammed victims to be paid this amount, get back to us as soon as possible." "Once hoodwinked always hoodwinkable," I thought. When young I occasionally drifted from the starched and hidebound. In fact, if I had been incapable of straying, I'd be unmarried today. Never, however, did coveting money discolor my better nature. Of course, Vicki and I have fiduciary foibles, and occasionally we purchase lottery tickets. We do so, as Vicki puts it, "not because we lust after unearned wealth, but because we are well-intentioned. As Connecticut residents, we feel duty-bound to help lower the deficit of the state budget."

We also buy tickets because they are conversation starters. Last month Vicki bought a three-dollar Megabucks ticket. The prize was $1.6 billion if spread over twenty years. If taken all at once, the loot was $900 million. Federal and state taxes siphoned off another $400 million leaving the lottery winner with $500 million. Vicki and I spent many hours discussing how we'd disperse our prize. We decided to split the money four ways, we and each of the three children receiving an equal share. "Not the treasure of the Knights Templar but not a pittance," I said. "Not the Golden Fleece either," Vicki replied, "but certainly a golden scarf, an amount of little interest to a hedge fund manager camping in splendid vulgarity in Fairfield County but suitable to the modest ways of a retired English teacher." What we quickly realized, however, was that the money would disrupt the sensible tenor of our days. Even if the lucre did not corrupt us, ridding ourselves of it would be difficult as we differed over the charities to which we'd donate. Moreover, we suspected that we'd calculate our taxes incorrectly and soon be in hock to the government. "Worry would shorten our lives. We'd ignore the simple things that matter, and we'd waste away losing sleep and becoming tubercular," Vicki said one afternoon as we sat on a log beside the Nipmuck Trail, thumping puffballs. Later in a nearby field we spotted a bedstraw Sphinx caterpillar crawling through low gray grass. Neither of us had seen the caterpillar before. "A natural piece of eight," Vicki said. The caterpillar's head was red, and its body brown almost black. A series of oval yellow spots ran along its sides like small windows backlit by holiday candles. We walked home through the university. A pair of red-tailed hawks perched atop a light pole beside the hockey field. On noticing us, the hawks sprang off the pole and began to soar and dip, putting on a Thanksgiving-Day show for us, lifting our sight above the gelded, artificial turf.

As might be expected, we decided that like most extravagant good fortune winning the lottery would be ruinous. To be endowed with extraordinary looks, brains, athleticism, indeed any great talent or skill, was a curse. It imprisoned a person in the expectations of others. People do not shape their identities; they are forged by what others say about them, by the adjectives and phrases pinned on them. Such phrases cling to individuals for their entire lives, no matter the experiences they weather, through green spring and summer, browning fall, and cold, cold winter: an amazing football player, fabulously wealthy, a genius, a star, gifted beyond compare, legendary beauty. How freeing to be a Professor of Nothing and a Student of Everything, to be the invisible occupant of an unnamed chair. Living modestly and anonymously enables a person to enjoy the actual riches of life. At least this is what Vicki and I decided—a self-congratulatory conclusion that made us think well of ourselves. "No one in his right mind would want to win $500 million," we said repeatedly.

Of course, we won, not fabled gold of Lost Dutchman's Mine, but twelve dollars. "A nine-dollar profit on a three-dollar investment, a return of 300%," I told acquaintances, not one of whom had ever purchased a lottery ticket. "Eat your hearts out," I said, fanning nine singletons out across my palm after which I solicited advice on choosing "my team," a lawyer, an accountant, and an investment counselor. Losing is better for one's health than winning. The financial success made me feverish, and one day shortly after the drawing I found a dollar in change on the campus: two quarters on the indoor running track, another by the front entrance to the library, a dime and a nickel under a bicycle rack, and then a dime on the sidewalk circling Mirror Lake. "Clearly lucky money," I told Vicki. "I am going to Price Chopper and buy a Lotto ticket. Luck breeds luck. We are bound to win." The prize was $4 million before legal fees and actuarial adjustments for taxes and immediate disbursement. "Is a million and a half worth the effort?" Vicki asked. "Not really," I said, "but—what the Hell—figuring out what to do with the leavings will give us something to talk about at dinner during dessert." In matters of luck, ritual is exceedingly important, the sine qua non of success. Because I found all the coins while afoot, I walked to Price Chopper to buy a ticket. I did so despite a rainstorm. Indeed, I enhanced our chance of winning by ignoring the risk of hypothermia and walking home.

Surprisingly we did not win the lottery. Perhaps I overlooked a crucial part of the purchasing ritual. I simply don't know. No matter, numerology is working in our favor and before long we will bound out of the house covered with frog skins like Botticelli's Venus when she rose from the sea. In the drawing, none of our numbers matched a number on the winning ticket. But one of our numbers was only a single digit off—28 rather than 29—and two of our numbers missed being selected by three, that is, on our ticket appeared 35 and 36 while 32 and 39 were on the winning ticket. On Thanksgiving morning, I ran the Manchester Road Race. Even more propitious was my race number 3795. The 3 and the 9 were both on the winning Lotto ticket. And yes, there is more. Last week on the campus I found sixteen pennies, and when I accompanied Vicki to pick up a prescription at CVS pharmacy, I discovered that the prices of Halloween miscellanea had been reduced 90%. Floating in a translucent rubbery ball three inches in diameter was a smaller ball—a haunted eyeball, its vitreous fluid white, pupil pink, and lens black. Bouncing the ball caused the eye to blink red, green, and blue. The ball originally cost $1.59, but the markdown reduced the price to sixteen cents—the sixteen cents I found on the campus and which Vicki carried for me in her purse. "Bounce it sixteen times before you buy the next lottery ticket," Vicki said, "that'll do the trick."

Of course, we don't need to win the lottery. Good news is always coming pulling a chariot loaded with bullion. Last week I received an email from Mrs. Lisa Robinson. "You have a Charity Donation of $1,200,000.00 from Lisa," it read, "For full details contact her now via E-mail." Because I am old, sometimes I treat money cavalierly. By mistake I deleted the generous Lisa's notification. However, I'm accustomed to losing lolly on the stock market and have learned that what goes down usually comes back up. Consequently, I'm certain Lisa will contact me again. By the time she does, the pot will have sweetened as interest will have added another hundred thousand to her donation. Vicki has urged me not to respond until Lisa promises two million. "We are not cheapskates and shouldn't ruin our reputations by selling ourselves short," she said.

Among the emails I stored on the flatcar were several invitations. The two organizers of TED talks at the university invited me to speak at a conference in April (TED being an anacronym for Technology, Entertainment, and Design). At their best the talks stimulated "learning, inspiration, wonder, and conversation." This year's theme was Crushing the Comfort Zone. Comfort Zones, the email explained, "are where we feel at ease as individuals, organizations, or as a society at large. They are familiar places; however, nothing grows there. Those who are most successful constantly challenge these comfort zones rather than letting their familiarity define them." Hectoring does not come naturally to me. Recently I wrote that so long as people did not harm others they were "entitled to their lies and comforting vanities." Pride cometh before pushing strangers into falls, I wrote; "ignoring truth's cruel sanctity, zealots uproot the illusions that make life bearable, while simultaneously applauding their own actions, convinced they are selfless and virtuous." "Reformations," Josh once said, "are rarely bloodless and never bruise less."

People should be free to write the novels of their lives. Most write dime novels "but what is wrong with that?" I asked. How nice to dream of love and adventure while blowing and raking leaves, to imagine island days while mowing grass or shoveling snow, or in the shank of an evening to write a memoir sumptuous with fabricated encounters with the famous and influential? From comfort zones reduced to embers by the ardent and well-meaning, green new worlds never rise blooming with lasting decency, tolerance, compassion, honorable truth, and love. Of course, I didn't write that to the students who sent the invitation. They were young and in an optimistic time of life, capable not simply of hoping but also of believing that change could better rather than only change. They believed in the ameliorating effects of learning and had yet to realize that although learning will make them more capable, it won't make them wiser. Their "devices" hadn't informed them that during the last quarter of a century while machines had grown smarter, people had gotten stupider. Alas, time will eventually slice the uncut pages of their lives. Would that it causes them to appreciate and worry about the fragility of the social order.

I wondered wistfully if I believed in the mitigating powers of change when I was a child. Probably not, I concluded. I wore blinkers and was too busy delighting in the world as it was, catching and roaming, not mulling ideas but accepting the home truth that manners made man and society. In cloudy moments nowadays I realize that to predict the future all a person need do is swivel his head around and look backward. The future is the past. Man will repeat the mistakes he has always made in peace and war, in love and politics, in education, in books, in predicting the weather and the winners of chess matches, in everything under the sun and the moon. He will sell his integrity for zirconium. His tears will dry, and he will behave like the Levite and avert his gaze from the painful and the unjust. He will genuflect to leftover men. He will be a team player and do his part to continue the madness of the world. If instructed to do so, he'll steal Jesus's binoculars and never raise them to his eyes or raise his eyes above the secular.

But then, or so I want to think, midnight is never completely dark. Sometimes above the horizon glitter gentling experiences like that described by Leigh Hunt in "Jenny Kissed Me."

> Jenny kissed me when we met,
> Jumping from the chair she sat in;
> Time, you thief! who love to get
> Sweets into your list, put that in!
> Say I'm weary, say I'm sad,
> Say that wealth and health have missed me,
> Say I'm growing old, but add
> Jenny kissed me!

A scrapbook of such light duets staves off the hardening of feelings and arteries, be they sung with Dotty or Sally, red-headed Alice or brown-eyed Nancy. They are the gel of loosening melodies that flow through the hearts of the elderly softening callouses, engendering benevolence, and making Jenny's old friends, good, cheery companions, no matter that frost heaves have so corrugated the Yellow Brick Road that walking, much less skipping, on it is impossible.

"I and friends my age," I wrote the students, "long for stability and the comforts of health and the familiar. When I am comfortable, I am a kinder, gentler, more charitable person than I am when my life is out of balance and I suffer from vertigo." "But enough of this sermonette," I ended. "I am too old-school for you. Thank you for the invitation. I appreciate it—really appreciate it. You are well-meaning decent kids who haven't lived my eight decades. In the same moment we inhabit different cultural worlds. I've never used a cell phone and am so out of step with you that I might as well be a club-carrying devil-worshipper. But in any case, may you both enjoy good fortune in the decades ahead." Instead of *good fortune* I almost wrote *comfortable* lives, but that would have been passively arrogant. They could not know that in fifty years they'd think less about the future than about the past. Imperceptibly their imaginations will drift into Almost-Was Land and its garden of forking paths. Like me they will prefer the wisdom of their ancestors to that of their progeny. Moreover, I did not raise the specter of habit. I resisted quoting Robert Lynd who said that life would be intolerable if a person had to choose his behavior instead of having it chosen for him by custom. "No one but a lunatic," he wrote, "could really make a habit of having no habits."

"Another temptation to embarrass myself publicly avoided, another blood-pressure raising speech dodged, and another night free for popcorn and a movie on Netflix topped off with a bedtime book," I told Vicki. "You better hope you never need a blood transfusion," Vicki replied. "A college student will probably have donated the blood, and before his erythrocytes settle into common sense, you'll have purchased a cell phone, signed up for Facebook, learned to Twitter, bought ear plugs in order to listen to Lady Gaga and Bebe Rexha, and given umpteen nauseatingly inspirational TED talks."

On the flatcar I also stored cartoons of books, the contents reflecting the miscellaneous nature of my reading. Among the volumes in the most recent box were Jerome K. Jerome's *Novel Notes*, John Masefield's *The Bird of Dawning*, *Race* by William McFee, Colin Thubron's *In Siberia*, and Eugene Field's *Poems of Childhood*. Field led me "Over the Hills and Far Away" where I heard the Dinkey-Bird singing. Afterward in the Garden of Shut-Eye Town, I climbed the Sugar-Plum Tree. With Dervla Murphy I rode *Full Tilt* from Ireland to India on a bicycle, and I explored *The Secret City* with Hugh Walpole. "It's not the business of fiction to teach us anything," Agnes Repplier declared in *Points of View*. "Nor," I thought, "is it the office of a retired English teacher to tell moppets how to behave." Oh, how I enjoyed the company of Hazel, a character in *Race*. "The trouble with Hazel was her entire lack of conscience when she began telling anything," McFee wrote. "It was not that she told lies so much as that she was unaware of the existence of truth." Hazel was my kind of gal, no trouble at all, but sensible and imaginative, blooming and fecund, a storyteller not inhibited by the xeroderma of wintry fact. Earlier in the year, she told literary acquaintances about an article she spotted on the front page of the *Clarion-Dispatch*, a newspaper popular in northeast Louisiana. "Fiendish Liberal Professor Caged" the headline stated. Responding to complaints from a state representative, police at a public college removed a teacher from class, and when he became obstreperous, incarcerated him in cell that resembled a chicken coop. "The man is a rabid socialist," the solon declared; "his lectures are hydrophobic. He's not like us. He's from Massachusetts, and not only is he unmarried, but he doesn't have a sweetheart and probably never has hidden a hot cross bun in a corner. He doesn't watch football, and Agnew the butcher in Dovetown says he is a vegetarian. He drives a small French car, detests our holy American capitalism, and wants to repeal the 2nd Amendment to the Constitution." Even worse, and these words, Hazel reported, were said sotto voce and printed in pale, almost invisible, ink, "he's turning right-thinking, right-leaning, rightly-raised students into Democrats."

Clarence Day's Father was another character of my kidney, to express matters in anatomical words understandable to out-of-fashionista seniors. Father, Day wrote, "paid no attention to the prejudices of others except to disapprove of them. He had plenty of prejudices himself, of course, but they were his own." Quite right, Father probably had prejudices like mine disapproving of and avoiding smokers, speeders, intensely nice people whose presence makes rooms stuffy, strangers who on meeting me assume our acquaintance to be on first-name basis, mathematical illiterates who say "no problem," pomposities who speak as if they were reading poetry on public radio, "deeply affected" mourners who send condolences by email, and, the most grating of all, religious hustlers who mount podiums and claim to be spokesmen for faith-based communities. If asked to give a TED talk to oldsters rather than to youth, I'd read Stephen Dunn's "A Postmortem Guide." "The truth is," Dunn wrote near the end of the poem explaining not needing God, "I learned to live without hope / as well as I could, almost happily, / in the despoiled and radiant now." In Frederic Prokosch's *Nine Days to Mukalla*, a sayyid observed that old people abandoned the "impetuous tastes" of youth and embraced poetry. Poetry, he said, "is like rain. It cools and strengthens and makes things grow. It softens the glare of reality. It draws us back into solitude."

In *Travels with a Donkey*, Robert Louis Stevenson testified that "For my part I travel not to go anywhere, but to go. I travel for travel's sake." Similarly, I read, not to learn or pillage books for inspirational opioids but simply to read. Like the sayyid's poetry, reading deflects the harsh light of reality and transforms grueling loneliness into agreeable solitude. Of course, reading can startle, but for people my age the startling is usually armchair startling. Certainly, books may awaken but generally they quickly slip out of hand, the pages that stirred thought distinguished by a bookmark not by up-and-about, pajama-less actions. Among the volumes on the flatcar were two of Prokosch's novels, the *Nine Days* and *Age of Thunder*, both phantasmagoric, the latter describing traveling through eastern France at the end of World War II, the former a magical Odyssey across the Horn of Africa. Prokosch was a skilled wordsmith, and his prose was luxuriant. From the perspective of an airplane high over the Indian Ocean, waves, he wrote, steal "over the sea with a lazy damascened pattern, like a great white web drawn over a sheet of blue glass." Often his pages resembled night-blooming gardens, the flowers hot housed, their scents simultaneously seductive and repulsive, for me evoking memories of pasts led and not led: eastern Europe in the early 1960s and the Levant forty years ago. After reading the books, however, I didn't forswear the comforts of home and dropping the potato chips I was munching race out the kitchen door lusting after adventure.

Instead I walked to the university library and borrowed two more of Prokosch's novels *The Seven Who Fled* and *Night of the Poor*. I moved slowly. Three weeks earlier Vicki and I had gone for a stroll along the Fenton River. After a short distance, the big toe on my right foot began to ache. I thought a coupling nut had unaccountably become lodged in my boot and was pressing down on my toe. When I removed the boot, the bolt turned out to be a hickory tussock moth caterpillar. The caterpillar was crushed and its poisonous hairs had sliced through my sock. By evening my toe was scarlet and swollen, and the metatarsal throbbed as if being pounded by a small mallet. Pustules formed, broke, and formed again. Soaking my foot in hot water did not loosen the hairs, and after two weeks I milled the skin off the top of the toe with a razor, hoping that the hairs would be swept away in a wash of blood. The barbering was only partly successful and after three weeks, the bone still hurt causing me to walk gingerly. The previous day had been rainy, and as I walked to the library earthworms crinkled across sidewalks drying in the sunlight. For years I have plucked earthworms from walkways and placed them on dry ground. Because I moved slowly going to the library, I saved more worms than usual. While doing so, I found two pennies. "Lucky pennies, a reward for rescuing worms," I told Vicki. "Ninety-eight more will make a lucky dollar. Once I have all the pennies, I'll buy a lottery ticket. My solicitude for the vermiform will be rewarded. The numbers on our ticket will be drawn, and we should start thinking now about how to dispose of the money."

After dinner that night Vicki and I watched a travelogue depicting Australia's Kimberley. "Do you remember Windjana Gorge and the Bungle Bungles?"

I asked. "Slightly," Vicki said. "Gosh," I said, "I'd like to go back." "Why don't you?" she answered. "Once we win the lottery, we'll have a bakery of dough." "Cassidy doesn't think I could make it, at least not without her help," I replied. "She called yesterday and urged me to let Medicare buy me a back brace— before 'it is too late,' she warned." "Do robocalls ever end?" Vicki exclaimed. "No, they'll continue after I'm beyond Medicare's help and my Social Security stops. They are the fallen world's way of cursing people with immortality," I said. "After I die," I continued, "ignore the professional mourners who'll promise a candelabra of foot candles in hopes of persuading you to take out burial insurance on my corpse." I then stood and picking up *The Seven* climbed the stairs to bed. Despite dreaming of roaming an outback again, I knew practically every experience I now put on the flatcar would be inhouse and papery, the sedentary remnants of desk and study.

On my bedside table lay a birthday card. "For your birthday," it read, "Thought you would like a trip down Memory Lane." The lane was a hive of shops with signs jutting from doorways or displayed in windows. Most advertised things ripped away by age: Hair, Pain-Free Joints, 8 Hours Sleep, Firm Skin, Good Knees, Hearing, and on an oval lens-shaped board Eye Sight. Before falling asleep, I recalled a conversation Patty and I had with Carey earlier in the week. In June Carey learned he had cancer. "Fast-moving," he told us, "a real sprinter." Because his car was sixteen years old and rattling to pieces, Carey was considering purchasing another car and solicited our opinions. Since people our age don't drive much each year, Patty observed, buying a new car was not a good investment. "Purchase a three-year-old used car with all the safety devices," he suggested. "I don't think I should worry about safety," Carey replied after pausing for a moment, "and I suppose buying any car doesn't make financial sense. I'm sure to run out of gas before my present car suffers a terminal breakdown." "What did you and Patty say to that?" Vicki asked. "What could we do?" I replied. "We are Carey's good friends and love him dearly. We agreed."

If they live long enough, organizers of the TED talks will learn that familiarity defines age. The elderly live repetitious lives. Free spirits and originality don't attract them. The songs of the past are the melodies of their presents, and they approach the margins of comfort zones only on tiptoe. Even when they stray almost out of character and behave differently from the habitual, they inhibit variance by describing their actions in familiar terms. This fall Vicki and I attended a men's basketball game at the university for the first time in thirty years. The tickets were free—promotions modeled on the entrepreneurial tactic of baiting the hook: "Whet the appetite. Dangle a freebie in front of them now. If they bite, chances are that sooner or later they will return to the lure." Play on the court proved incidental to advertising. Signs flashed, shifted, and jangled turning sight into robovision. Before I shut my eyes, I counted some forty advertisements—Coca Cola, Chevrolet, Nissan, Connecticut Acura Dealers, Laz Fly, Frontier Telephone, UCONN Health, Delta Dental, Select Physical, Subway, Dunkin' Donuts, Cheez-It,, Ticket Galaxy, Mohegan Sun, Citgo, Key Bank, Wells Fargo, State Farm, Travelers, Ameritas, Geico, AAA, UPS, Connecticut Business Systems, Bob's Discount Furniture, Lippincott Van Lines, Nike, Fox 61 News, on and on from one end of the court to the other, from the roof of the gymnasium to the floor.

During basketball games, bands play, crowds caterwaul, and announcers roar. The noise reaches eight on the Intolerable Scale violently shaking the eardrum. Throughout the next day, Josh forewarned me, aftershocks reverberate through the inner ear, and the tremors don't stop until a week has passed. Consequently, Vicki and I wore earplugs. They muffled the clamor preventing our auditory tubes from collapsing and rendering deciphering advertisements megaphoned through the gym's amplifiers impossible. In an oasis of quiet during halftime I suggested that we leave. Vicki, however, watches more television than I do. She has absorbed the jargon of newscasters, and said we had to remain until the game ended. "For closure," she explained. She may have smiled as she spoke, but the barrage of advertising had strained my eyes, and I could not see clearly. For my part I have never used closure. The word is popular with short-order cooks who bake cakes using mixes and afterward take them to church bazaars and assure prospective buyers the cakes are homemade—as if blending chemicals on a kitchen table makes a cake homemade. In any case few irritations end on the temperate bank of the river Phlegethon.

The telephone was ringing when Vicki and I got home after the game. On the line was a robocaller peddling beauty aids, including a purse-friendly tool kit of instruments, one of which was a blackhead extractor. While we were at the game, a blackmailing email arrived. The sender said he possessed a video which depicted me watching a rude film. He threatened to mail the video to everyone in my computer address book unless I sent him a thousand dollars in bitcoins. "I've found a United Nations of coins on the campus—French, British, German, Greek, Egyptian,

Syrian—but I have never found a bitcoin. What is it?" I asked Vicki. "I don't know," she said. "But certainly, it's filthy lucre and isn't lucky. If you see a mysterious coin, don't pick it up. But if you do succumb to greed and discover it to be a bitcoin, toss it in the garbage immediately then hurry home and scrub your hands."

No matter how far I travel, waking or sleeping, I cannot escape roboshysters. The elderly are con men's favorite prey. That night I dreamed I was in Sochi, the Russian resort on the Black Sea. As I stood in an open beachside pavilion a man approached and stopping in front of me asked, "Are you Dostoevsky?" Later I concluded that the man recognized me as being foreign and likely American because I wore a Bermuda-shorts-length bathing suit and not the parts-hugging speedo popular with Slavic males. I don't know what led the man to guess that I wrote. I wasn't taking notes. Probably he addressed the same question to all potential gulls, thinking that appearing to assume that they were literary and thus interesting was a flattering conversation-starter. In any case the truckling, assertive tone of the experienced grifter "rang a bell," and before the man could dig into his spiel and my wallet, I hung up on him and strode off across the rocky, bastinadoing beach. Escaping the criminal or the fear of crime are impossible and darken living. Every day thieves clamor out of the telephone and cavort across the computer screen. For my parents life was different. Crooks did not soil their hours. Clamorous greed did not poison the air. Only friends telephoned, and email did not exist. For them sunny optimism marked living. They thought well of people. They trusted others and believed that innate goodness was possible.

In the mail the next afternoon I received a brochure from a contractor who must have thought I won the lottery. Pictures of the lavish houses the contractor built in Darien and Greenwich filled the brochure. The contractor was especially proud of his drawing and billiard rooms, great halls, and bathrooms. Almost all lavatories in the new homes the man constructed were large, and the most extravagant featured two toilets. In these bathrooms bouquets of flowers decorated the porcelain bowls, the most popular being violets and apple blossoms, marigolds, roses, and peonies. Such lavatories were not water closets but water living rooms. Usually the toilets were paired side by side, separated by a coffee table, both facing a distant wall on which hung a flat-screen television. No photograph showed a telephone on the coffee table, the builder assuming that owners of the houses would be engrossed in watching Antiques Roadshow or America's Got Talent and would resent having their pleasure disturbed by barracking telephones. On the other hand, the rooms were so large that if the owners so desired, they could bring in a rack of chairs and a couple more tables and host a Canasta party.

The items I put on the flatcar paradoxically made my days bumpy. When I was young, I raced so effortlessly through weeks that hills seemed level. I noticed but didn't pause to mull. Now that I move slower, I see less but observe more closely. For its part close observation doesn't increase understanding as much as it makes one aware of oddity. Decades ago, two-hole outhouses were common, and once behind an abandoned country school, I saw an eight-holler. But the updated fashionable indoor version appointed with a television startled me. My domestic Comfort Zone includes a pantry, a 1940's kitchen, and a dining room that time and a retiring life have transformed into a storage closet. My zone is small and doesn't have enough space to include a bathroom transformed into a playroom. I, myself, am too old and too old-fashioned to be remodeled. The advertising and incessant robocalls—for four days in a row Ray has telephoned practically begging to clean my rugs; each time he calls from a different town close to Storrs, from Vernon, Lebanon, Hebron, and Ashford—such things may intrigue but they are also dislocating and tiring.

Last night I was too weary to go to bed at a reasonable nine o'clock. When I finally went upstairs at 10:15, I brushed my teeth with athlete's foot medicine. Tubes of Colgate's Total and Equate's Antifungal Cream lay next to each other beside the sink in the bathroom. I squeezed a dose of the cream onto my toothbrush and started scrubbing. "Gosh," I thought, "this toothpaste has gotten stale. It doesn't taste at all like 'Clean Mint.'" Thinking paste farther down the tube might still be fresh, I rinsed my toothbrush and anointed the bristles with another dollop of cream, a real whacker-doodle, an amount that would transform ringworm into a straight line. "Not a bad thing," Vicki said later, "Tomorrow will be peaceful. You won't be itching to give your opinion about every damn thing under the sun and on the page."

Four days later the board of trustees at a prominent university in Massachusetts released the name of the school's new president. Acquaintances so busied themselves telling me what they thought about the choice that I had little opportunity to voice my opinion. "He is a man about whom the only thing that can be said is that nothing will ever be said about anything he says," McFee's Hazel reported. "Before he became a gear in the corporate-educational complex," she continued, "he was a grand undistinguished man. His first wife said he was the nicest bald-headed man she ever met. He was kind and gentle and wouldn't swat the flies that swarmed the top of his head on hot days. He said that the flies were probably mommies and daddies and that he didn't want to be responsible for throngs of orphaned muscidae."

Until he concentrated his energies on laser engineering in order to scurry up the stalk of STEM studies, his research was vital and fanciful. His world wasn't academic, and every day he spent hours behind his house cultivating a private garden. The results of the work did not appear in learned quarterlies, and the only records of his studies exist in his former spouse's memory. For two springs and summers, she told Hazel, once week at dinner he ate a salver of butterfly eggs. He hoped the eggs would hatch and that the caterpillars would thrive and pupate in his cecum or ascending colon. "He dreamed that when he spoke his words would be winged and butterflies would swarm swallow-tailed from his mouth, or, if not from his esophagus, would flutter from the far end of his colon, transforming an inelegant digestive process into something so flowery that it seemed perfumed."

In those days the president was a meticulous gastronome and fed his caterpillars responsibly, never forgetting to include helpings of their favorite foods on his dinner menu. Thus, after seeding his stomach with the eggs of great spangled fritillaries, for dessert he ate a bowl of violets. To accompany the eggs of mourning cloaks, he tossed a salad composed of mulberry, birch, and willow leaves. While the caterpillars of spring azures thought horse chestnut, maple, olive, and honeysuckle leaves particularly toothsome, the favorite savories of black swallowtails were dill, celery, and Queen Anne's lace. For their part cabbage whites preferred salmagundis of mustards and cresses, kale, broccoli, cauliflower, and cabbages themselves. The president dined so often upon leaves that he almost became a folivore. Moreover, he ate so many vegetables that he was a closet vegetarian, "not something he revealed to the feedlots of carnivores who dominate administrative search committees."

The additions to his diet were salubrious, and both his BMI and blood pressure decreased, lowering the risk of diabetes, an ailment that bedeviled his immediate family. Unfortunately, he failed to create an interior butterfly conservatory. His words did not take flight, and his celiac disturbances remained all too human. Because of an especially vigorous sneeze, Hazel related, he once expelled a tineid or clothes moth from his nose. This resulted from an accident, however, not from intention. "While ridding his attic of his grandmother's furs, he inhaled the egg of the moth. The egg lodged in his left nostril where it grew through several instars until it pupated." "The shortcomings of his lepidoptery experiments aside, he will likely prove to be a deft administrator," Hazel said. "Early in his career he published an article in which he suggested ways in which people could save time and increase their efficiency. Instead of idly waiting for the water in their showers to heat, people could, for example, use the minutes to get dressed. By the time they tied their shoelaces, the water would be hot and they could bathe in comfort."

"You have spun off the tracks," Vicki said when I repeated Hazel's remarks. "Perhaps," I said, "but no matter his age or vigor a real man occasionally stokes his boiler and goes on a toot." Actually, the truth is that Vicki and I rarely steam far from our roundhouse on Hillside Circle. Moreover, we don't shovel coal. Firemen climb out of distant tenders and come to us scruffy and scamming, smudging hours. Vicki donates money to animal rescue and conservation groups. Recently a lady swindler wrote her. Initially the woman praised Vicki's humane concerns, calling her benevolent and compassionate, "a lover of the living earth." The woman said she could tell that Vicki was an "adorning mother to her pets" and volunteered that for a fee her organization would clone "the forever darlings of your heart." "Never again would your best friends disappear across the Rainbow Bridge." To entice Vicki to "immortalize" her memories, a decal depicting a cartoon dog bone accompanied the letter. The bone was ten inches long, and printed along the tibia in capital letters was "I love my granddogs."

Sharpers monitor cultural developments closer than other people. Cloning has left Trending behind and moved into Happening-Now. Zoos of creatures have been cloned: mice, sheep, cattle, and polo ponies, so many animals that the mass cloning of human beings is inevitable. Vicki did not respond to the solicitation, but the letter unsettled our temperate Comfort Zone. "Suppose," Vicki said, "that an admiring son had his parents cloned after their deaths and raised the babies as his children. If he reared his son and father and daughter and mother as brother and sister would the attraction between them smolder then burn as it did before they became his parents? Would they fall in love and marry again, and if they did, would the marriage be incestuous?" "Perhaps they'd behave modishly and shack up together. Then their lives wouldn't be incestuous, only indecent," I interrupted. "Maybe," I continued, "that as the man studied the children, he'd discover terrible things about his parents, things which he didn't imagine before they became his offspring, and which decades earlier affected his life. On the other hand, he may have hated his parents and had them cloned so he could exact revenge."

"Enough," Vicki said, "these are the thoughts of a devil-worshipper. Put my letter on the flatcar then convince The Little Engine That Could to pull the car into the mountains and push it off a trestle before it reaches good old boys and girls like us for whom the despoiled present remains radiant." "Should we go to a second basketball game, this time a women's game?" I asked, changing the subject. "Admission is pricey, $25 a head. But Josh tells me that in the future we might be able do better." "What's the price if the team loses?" Josh asked the woman at the ticket office last week. "$10 seems fair or $5 if the loss is one-sided." "What did the woman say?" Vicki asked. She repeated the $25 price. "But shouldn't losses be discounted?" Josh asked, "there's always a discount for damaged goods: moth-eaten, water-stained, moldy, bruised, pre-worn, that sort of thing." "I don't know," the woman said. "How can anyone know beforehand that the team won't win?" "That's easy. Consult The Power That Is," Josh said, pointing upward, "and we'll continue this conversation next season." "Oh," the woman said, surreptitiously glancing at the ceiling, "next season, yes, by all means, next season"

"Good Lord, the poor soul," Vicki exclaimed. "Forget sports. Buy a Lucky for Life lottery ticket. Pay for it with bitcoins." "Okay," I said, "and after we win, we'll move to Corfu. Routine will unravel. We won't have a telephone; mail won't reach us, and Hazel will forget about us. Our lives will be simpler. We'll enjoy 'the charms of seclusion' and behaving like the Lawrence Durrell of *Prospero's Cell* rent a fisherman's cottage—'a white house set on a rock.' Cypress will hang over our roof; our door will open onto olive and ilex. Gatekeepers and silver-washed fritillaries, commas and scarce swallowtails will flutter through branches and dangle from twigs like Christmas ornaments. We'll doze on the small bumpy terrace next to the house. The wind will lift our thoughts over the distant hills and blow them into the blue, blue sky where they'll shimmer for a moment then vanish like mirages." "And when winter comes," Vicki said, "I'll turn milk into hot chocolate. After dark we'll light a fire inside the house and bake bread and dip it in olive oil. Nonexistent strangers will visit. They'll snuggle down next to us in front of the fire and tell wayward lies. We'll catch a white unicorn, and we'll listen to the highwayman riding, riding, riding. We'll visit woodlands dark and dim. Then we'll hear the sound of waters and sail to sleep in a junk piled high with stories of 'apes and ivory, skulls and roses.'"

Not Much Longer

"How long do you want to live?" the doctor asked. "Not much longer," I said. "I think I can manage that and maybe a little more," the doctor replied, and we both laughed. Behind my laughter lay truth. I had written more than thirty books and hundreds of articles. I didn't have a great deal to say twenty books ago, and now I had less. Vicki's and my children had grown up and into distant lives. Despite their protestations to the contrary, I'd reached the medical age beyond which I'd deteriorate into a nuisance then become a burden. Moreover, I did not have to worry about Vicki. I'd sacked away enough money to keep her comfortable through old age. As for friends, I had only a couple and they had tottered into their premortem decade.

I spent most of my life in universities. Teachers toss the word *colleague* about because the people with whom they teach rarely become friends. They don't share a cultural background. Their ages vary, and they come from different castes and distant parts of the country, if not distant countries. The classroom experience is the only experience they have in common. At best professors smile and speak to colleagues in the building that houses their department before hurrying into their offices and shutting the doors. In passing they sometimes ask about their colleagues' research, a politeness no more sincere than the reflexive "Have a nice day." "We mortal millions live alone," Matthew Arnold wrote. Because university teachers are mobile and nomadic, the buddies of elementary, high school, and college drift out of acquaintance. Memories of football and crew, of dances and dating, of camp and summer homes linger, but actual presences disappear or become so hazy they are fictions. They reappear only on the obituary page. Instead of warming the mind, such obituaries chill the heart and foster regret for life not lived. Paragraphs memorializing friends who settled in the towns and cities in which they grew up describe years spent as stewards of others, charities run, and service clubs managed—selfless participation in societies which at first glance seem smaller than the university world but which are, in fact, much greater. Academics are, in Matthew Arnold's words, enisled in the sea of life. They don't join; they are not "hail fellows well-met," and if they resemble me, and they do, they live cloistered lives.

Age exacerbates the "not much" of life. Conversation no longer interests me. Years of living have taught me that talk never leads to the meeting of minds, and I avoid people who think differently from me. Moreover, the words of people my age are often more rehearsed than spontaneous or argumentative. Their conversations consist of exsanguinated anecdotes repeated so often that they are as lively as the danse macabre. Thank goodness the Great First Cause blessed the aged with hearing loss. If not, the talk of their peers would have led hordes of elders to forsake the faiths of their fathers and worshipping Ixtab to convert their garages and basements into make-shift temples.

In one sense, perhaps, people don't think or actually talk radically differently from one another.

They mourn, make love, console, and sentimentalize, Edwin Whipple lamented, "in cant phrases." This was aggravated, he judged, because most men passed their lives attempting to misrepresent themselves, "everybody being bitten by an ambition *to appear* instead of *to be.*" Whipple was a perceptive critic, and no one escapes Procrustean conformity whether it rises from within or is imposed from without. Last winter a doctor trenched the back of my neck in order to remove a growth. After stitching the cut, the doctor covered it with a voluminous white bandage. "An elderly man just released from a walk-in clinic," Vicki said when I returned home. "All you need to complete the identity are crutches or if you can't manage those then a wheelchair." Despite Vicki's seeing me as stereotypical, I'm not sure I agree with Whipple. Although just being takes effort, occasionally folks succeed in alleviating the pressure to falsify their appearance. Oftentimes it takes a lifetime of undoing to become an absence or, better, to disappear. Recently I have enjoyed some success. On Friday I didn't receive an email or a letter. Moreover, the telephone did not ring. On Saturday the mailman drove pass the house without pausing, and Saturday and Sunday, the phone only rang once, the call a mechanical reminder that I had an appointment to have my teeth cleaned. For a person to misrepresent himself is difficult if no one is aware of his presence.

If asked to list my present interests, the page would be bare. I think sports beneath the concern of an adult. I do jog five days a week with my friend David, but he is deaf, and conversation falters. Sometimes jogging jars my brain and forces words out of my cerebrum which I am compelled to repeat to David. "Do you know," I shouted last week, "that if penicillin had not been discovered, you'd be running alone?" Despite being asked to stand for Congress, I believe political talk unbecoming. Conversation about lunatics and the ego-maniacal poisons inclinations toward elevated thought and deed. I don't subscribe to newspapers or magazines. To me automobiles are not objects of tactile veneration but only devices for moving flesh. I have never worn rings on my fingers or bells on my toes. I spent forty-five years teaching, but nothing I said in a classroom ameliorated my sense of the sanguinary reality of man's inhumanity. I doubt that education ever brought about any enduring, contagious altruism. Certainly, religions have failed. Long have I turned to art in pensive moments. But now I doubt art. Instead of broadening vision and awakening ways of seeing, perhaps art denatures and distracts a person from actual beauty. Does it undermine appreciation by treating the palpable as inferior to the inner and imagined? In any case my taste has always been limited. The paintings on the walls of my suburban house are windows into 19th century landscapes, impressionistic farmlands, and into the aviaries and reptile houses of zoos. Paintings depicting people don't appeal to me, and only family members stare from the walls. "Renoir's women," an acquaintance remarked echoing my judgment, "look as if they are either going to or returning from a barbeque, the latter plump and red in the face from overeating, the former on their way to being drenched in habanero sauce then spitted and cooked."

When I was young, Easter was an effervescent convivial day. Peter Cottontails frolicked across the fronts of cards sent to me from relatives in Virginia. I hunted eggs and bit the ears off chocolate bunnies. Family and close friends came for lunch, and the old mahogany dining-room table sagged, weighed down by, among others, legs of lamb, country hams, green beans, sweet potatoes, stewed tomatoes, pickled peaches, and platters of biscuits. This year I spent Easter in the basement reading room of the university library. All the other people in the room were Chinese graduate students silently studying computer screens. In the library I read *The Hawbucks* written by John Masefield and published in 1929. A compendium of fox-hunting scenes and country vignettes, the novel followed the pattern of Henry Fielding's *Tom Jones*. Although the main characters galloped through chapters, the narrative only rose to a canter at the conclusion. At the start George Childrey returned from years in the colonies to take over the family manor after his older brother drank too much and broke his neck while jumping his horse. George was an attractive prodigal son—feckless but warm-hearted and spontaneously charitable. In contrast his younger brother Nicholas who had managed the property until George's resurrection was a "red-lipped, somewhat loose-mouthed" businessman, unattractive, calculating, and self-centered. The female lead of the novel was Caroline Harridew, the daughter or a roughhewn country squire. While Squire Harridew was the book's understudy for Squire Western, George was a lineal descendant of Tom Jones, tempered by later-day Victoriana, making him, alas, not so gloriously lecherous. For her part Carrie resembled Sophy Western, luscious with golden hair, deep violet eyes, and exquisite skin. Her mouth, Masefield wrote, tongue in-cheek, "was of singular beauty, both at rest and when smiling; within it were splendid white, regular teeth which (the dentist said) could crack coconuts."

Living on an island in a mill stream surrounded

by paradisiacal forest was Mad or Maid Margaret, the squire's by-blow by a "woman from Corselaydead." Although Margaret was her half-sister's double, the squire ignored her existence, as did the country gentry, including George who met her only three or four times. Despite being poor Margaret cared for a niece and nephew, trying unsuccessfully to nurse the girl to health and nourishing the boy's artistic ambition. Margaret made cameo appearances in the novel, almost all of whose 336 pages focused on Carrie and the pack of males she infatuated. George had known Carrie when she was a girl, and on seeing her after his return home was besotted. Carrie and George were handsome, high-spirited, and good-natured. They enjoyed one another's company, and a marriage like that between Sophy Western and Tom Jones seemed inevitable. But when George proposed and the reader expected to hear a wedding anthem ring out, Carrie turned him down explaining that she was engaged, happily so, to Nicholas, George's brother and the book's Blifil. George went literally and metaphorically to pieces. Riding recklessly, he tried to jump Stonepits Old Quarry. He failed. While his horse landed safely into water, George fell on rocks knocking himself out.

When George regained consciousness on page 335, he thought the person bending over him was Carrie despite the woman's being "tanned by the wind and stalwart-looking." Instead it was Maid Margaret who suddenly thrust through the hedge of pages devoted to Carrie in order to nurse George. "You keep still," she instructed; "don't talk. We'll soon have you to the hospital." "'Don't throw me away,' he moaned in an agony of sudden pain. 'I'll not throw you away,' Maid Margaret said. 'I've only just found you. Now shut your eyes and don't talk.'" Three asterisks then appeared followed by the book's final sentence. "She was the woman whom he married; but it had cost him some pain to find her." In part the novel was a shaggy-dog love story, well, perhaps an absence-of-love-depicted story. The surprising brevity of the ending appealed to me. Masefield behaved like a narrative sans culotte and decapitated the tale with a giggle.

Not only does a long life kindle the pleasure one takes in foolishness, but it also goads a person to act, if not foolishly, at least embarrassingly. Embarrassment isolates, and at its blushing best makes a person momentarily imagine himself an individual. For a time, I've wanted to take a "Grand" European River cruise, beginning in Amsterdam and sailing down the Rhine to the Danube and on to the Black Sea ending after an excursion to Bucharest. I was last in Bucharest in December 1963. Between terms at Cambridge, I bounced around eastern Europe by myself for six weeks, cadging reduced rates for hotels and trains by telling people I was a young American Communist. The next summer I escorted twenty-four college girls through western Europe for ten weeks. During the trip I saw Amsterdam for my first and only time. Probably the most expensive and certainly among the best grand cruises were operated by Tauck, a tour company headquartered in Wilton, Connecticut. Shipboard, the cheapest rooms with balconies ranged between just under $17,000 to slightly over $18,000 per person, sailing dates determining the differences and air fare being additional.

English teachers are penurious by inclination and necessity. I fit the pattern. In stitching my wallet together, I didn't employ silver threads and golden needles. Because their moneys are limited, teachers are forced to be resourceful. In past years I bartered talks for reduced rates on ships and airplanes. To obtain them I wrote smarmy, flatteringly letters. Vicki always held her head in her hands and implored me not to mail the letters. "Have you no self-esteem?" she said. "Not any I can afford," I answered. Three or four times the letters succeeded. "I am surprised and pleased," Vicki said on the occasion of my last success, "but this is excruciatingly embarrassing. Promise me you won't do this again." "Never again," I promised and for the most part kept my word. Nevertheless, despite the preaching of the General Confession, if a person does not err and stray from well-beaten paths, he'll become wolf-meat. The wolf knows where the sheepish can be found, and when he hankers for mutton, he'll leap the railings surrounding the fold.

After talking to the doctor and reckoning that "not much" interested me except rattle-pated novels, I decided that a dose of embarrassment would buck me up. And so, despite Vicki's chagrin, I wrote the head of Tauck. "In for a nickel, in for thirty-five thousand," I said. The prescription worked. Since mailing the letter, I have been preternaturally alert. For five or six days I skedaddled when the postman knocked and left the room when the telephone rang. My letter was strong mortifying medicine. Few people would have had the stomach to write it, reread it then mail it. The first paragraph established a wheedling, genuflecting tone. "A moment after I mail this letter," I wrote, "I will cringe in embarrassment and spend the rest of the day letting some terrible Russian film on Netflix smother consciousness. But, still, the old adage that Pride cometh before a Fall is incorrect. The Fall comes before Pride, and your 2020 River Cruising book is very seductive." Afterward I waffled though 780 words tickling and cajoling, smoothing all my callouses with Pond's Word Cream. A month has passed since I wrote the letter. I have not heard from the company, but the side effects of writing have been marvelous. I have spent hours roaming the university welcoming spring and transforming the "not much" into "almost too much."

What I noticed was commonplace. Yet, instead of appearing humdrum, everything exhilarated and dazzled. Blue and green oilcloths of periwinkle rumpled brightly across shady backyards. Stringy branches of weeping cherry suddenly swelled into bobbins of lace. Overnight demure cornell azalea blossomed brazenly rouged and powdered. Neglected forsythia hedges gathered in powerful tows, swelled, then shattered into yellow spume. Settings of flowering cups on saucer magnolia glowed magenta, and blossoms on star magnolia were so profuse they turned limbs into constellations dangling from the Milky Way. Unexpectedly, in light of the ebullience induced by embarrassment, my favorite magnolias were yulans, the branches of which were spindly and adolescent. Moreover, their yellow flowers were pale and demure. They looked sad as if they were delicate only children, flowering for a moment, then sinking tubercular, their petals doomed to age rapidly into brown senescence. As trees budded so did I, albeit in my case not so interestingly. On golden larches needle buds initially looked like tiny fluted glasses, a caramel froth beading their rims. Later the froth broke apart then melded into multiple round balls. The balls resembled minute scoops of ice cream transforming the glasses into cones. Of course, I busied myself with more than plants, one afternoon with an armful of black racers. On another I sat on a bank beside a pair of Canada geese. They had finished courting and were resting. I talked to them. They didn't reply, but until the warming sun made them dozy, they seemed interested in what I said.

Initial doses of embarrassment invigorate, but they don't convey permanent immunity to world-weariness. Booster shots are necessary, the efficacy of the treatment dependent upon a person's age and his disenchantment with quotidian fervor. The loosening of bodily functions including the tongue become so common that most embarrassments bring the elderly no vivifying discomfort. To benefit the old, a booster must "pack a punch," its content an antigen clotted with stupid remarks or behavior, the former more salubrious if voiced before strangers. Recently I drove Vicki to see an ophthalmologist. The doctor's office was in a building hived with cells. Patients and technicians scurried about in a buzzing frenzy. "Have you ever thought," I said to the doctor in my best business consultant voice, "that if you treated only the one-eyed you could move into a smaller building, reduce your staff by half, and have more time for hobbies like stamp collecting and skate-boarding?" "What?" the doctor said widening his eyes. "I've never been on a skateboard."

"That's the last time you accompany me to a doctor. I can do without the embarrassment. I don't care if my eyes are dilated, and I'm half blind, I'm driving myself," Vicki said on leaving building. "Okay, babe," I replied, feeling energetic, eager to return to Storrs and to spend the afternoon wandering the university farm, watching newly born colts stagger about as if they were on crutches. "You shooed me out of the office before I could finish," I continued. "I intended to advise the doctor that if he wanted to augment his income, he could focus his practice on the three-eyed.

The surplus eyeballs would enable him to inflate his charges without necessitating a corresponding increase in staff or office space." "What next?" Vicki said, her tone not admiring, but nevertheless making me think about the colts and causing me to kick up my heels and mutter yea, not neigh.

What came next distracted me from visiting the horse barn. Waiting for us at home was an email from David my jogging companion. The previous day David, too, had an appointment with an eye doctor. "The trip to the ophthalmologist was a near-death experience," he began. "The average age of us patients must have been ninety. We all gimped and quivered and bulged out in surprising places." On arriving patients went "to a large waiting room" and stayed there until a technician fetched them. The technician tested "visual ability" and asked "a host of apparently meaningless questions, for example, 'what time last evening did you use this particularly eye drop?'" Then he led patients to a much smaller waiting area where they bided their time before being seen by "the grand ophthalmologist himself." Around the room were a dozen straight-backed chairs pushed against the wall. The chairs were so close together that their seats touched. When David entered the room, two seats were available. He sat on one, and a tall old man leaning on a walker took the seat next to him. "I have been here ninety minutes," one woman said. "My appointment was scheduled for 1:15." "Mine was also at 1:15," a woman sitting nearby remarked. "So was mine," David recounted, "but I didn't say anything."

Eventually the technician escorted the patients to the doctor. Finally, David and the man were the only people left in the room. "Should I get up and move to a different chair? Perhaps the old man would take offense at my move. Also, moving would be admitting that I was not comfortable sitting next to him," David mulled. "But then my joined-at-the-hip companion began to discharge a fusillade of aromatic rousers. The need to find a new seat became pressing. However, my changing seats now would tip off my companion that I had noticed his discharges, of which he, in his senility, may have been unaware or which he may well have hoped had escaped my notice. What to do?" "The only appropriate thing you could have done," I wrote back, "was to reply in kind. As the Bible preaches, an eye for an eye, and a gust of wind for a gust of wind. Of course, the possibility of this response would depend upon your diet and the state of your alimentary canal." Although Vicki thought the suggestions I made to her doctor "off-putting," she embraced the spirit of David's question. In the future, she suggested, if David found himself in the company of a redolent companion, he should address the man or woman, and say, "Thank you so very much. That cheese is a little too strong for my taste, and you need not cut off another hunk for me. I do hope you won't mind my passing on the offer of additional wedges. Don't waste them though. Save them for home and serve them at dinner. Apple pie and cheese are such a good dessert."

The biblical springs of King Solomon are gone. However, the voice of the turtle can still occasionally be heard, and grapes continue to attract bees. But no one my age has teeth that resemble a flock of sheep even shorn. No one's forehead looks like piece of pomegranate. Instead it looks like a remnant of mosaic, newly dug from a gravelly ruin, the surface uneven and ridged with moles, warts, blood spots, and mysterious liverwurst-colored crusts. No one my age believes his bed is green and the beams of his condominium are cedar. Even when doctors' appointments don't darken the horizon, the elderly cannot escape physical matters. Once upon a time taking off underpants was dangerous. Now removing them is safe, but putting them on is dangerous. After jogging and taking a shower, I sit on a bench and pull up my underpants one leg at a time. I don't stand because I worry that a foot will get hung in the fabric, and I'll slip and fall, smashing my pelvis into arrowheads. The most effective method of ejecting such worries from the mind is to reduce them to foolishness. To accomplish this a person should say something odd or embarrassing. For over a month in the university gymnasium a table blocked the top of the stairs which I and my ancient jogger friends climbed every day. Behind the table sat three students assisting a hydration study. All day they dispensed and collected large and small containers of urine.

Like most men of a certain age watery matters bedevil Josh. As a result, he plans excursions so that he never strays far from a lavatory. The necessity exasperates him, and he banishes urinating from thought until impelled to think about it. For two weeks Josh ignored the "waste water treatment plant" atop the stairs. A mature man, however, can endure "only so much provocation." The study collected specimens only from male athletes. "That's ridiculous," Josh said one morning after catching his foot on the top step of the stairs and knocking over a case of empty urine containers. "The amount of time in which a person participates in athletics is only a fraction of his life. All the informed, significant, and engaging parts come later. Who beside college presidents ever celebrates the wit and wisdom of athletes?" The following morning, he urged the research assistants to revise the hydration protocol. Instead of collecting "wee-wee" from boys, he suggested that "much" could be accomplished by soliciting water from "the old and the wise, male and female." Afterward the specimens should be sent to a laboratory. There a spectrometer ought to study the liquid. Analysis would, he declared, identify the elements responsible for the wisdom of age. Once that was done, scientists could brew "a refreshing, stimulating, and intellectually-vivifying urea-based tonic." By stirring the proper chemical ingredients into distilled water, they could create "a pick-me-up guaranteed to clear plaque from the brain, remove bunions, dehumidify dropsy, and reduce the bron in bronchitis to temperate coughing." The tonic could be bottled and sold to "students of all ages under the label of An A in Every Class." "I expect," he said, "that it will be a stunning commercial success, and Bud-Wiser will vault over all competitors and seize the opportunity to become the distributor." "Huh?" the most alert of the whiffets said. "A brilliant, but wasted suggestion—too practical for academia." I said seizing Josh's arm. "Let's go. David is already on the track."

Jogging invigorates. Running a ten-kilometer road race animates entrepreneurial inclinations more effectively than two-years at Harvard Business School. David has run more than three hundred and fifty races. As a result, he is a font of creative enterprise. His latest project is sartorial, "modest and elegant, appealing to the fastidious and the chic, to wearers of the bespoke." Recently he wrote several haberdasheries on London's Saville Row suggesting replacing the "difficult-to-manage-at-a-crisis" button and metal zipper flies on men's trousers with Velcro. The response was enthusiastic. Several tailors urged him to expand the notion and include men's undergarments. "Little could be more efficacious and sanitary," one tailor wrote, "than eliminating the elusive slits above the forks of boxer shorts and installing hands-down simple Velcro sealers."

Although "what next's" don't necessarily inflame, they usually quicken. During the past year I've mulled dramaturgy. Perhaps I'll write an article on the subject. On fashionable stages thespians that produce motile gametes are endangered. Casts are routinely all female, and women appear in roles that in less enlightened times were played by men: Hotspur, Hamlet, Romeo, Richard II, and Falstaff among a runway of others. In an assertively revisionist dramatization of Shakespeare a Caucasian woman played Othello. As could be expected the show was short-lived despite being staged in a summer stock theater noted for experimental presentations. Josh predicts that in the future, not the immediate future, and certainly in a far-off-Broadway, hitherto unheard-of theater, that a male lead will be played by a man. Of course, only an aggressively sexist director would pick a man to play a man—indeed only a courageous, devil-may-care director, the owner of an umbrella strong enough to shield him or her from the ensuing typhoon of criticism, from, as Vicki is fond of saying, "a gigantic shit-storm," an all-American combination northeaster and southwester. But, as Josh assured Vicki, "That's all right. Better to be the cynosure of a manuré hurricano than to snooze eyeless and tongueless in Gospel, Georgia."

When a booster begins to weaken, I question the prescription and consider switching medications. Sometimes I mull becoming serious. To establish a suitable solemnity, I go to the library and read literary criticism. Alas, articles that celebrate "transparency" are inevitably opaque. "Reimaginings" don't initiate beginnings but cause sleeping sickness. The authors use lumbering phrases like Affective Spaces and Relational Bodies, "rank flatulencies," a popular novelist dubbed them. Why, I wonder, is literary language colorless? Must academic writing deoxygenize and stifle? Do the writers segregate themselves behind the incomprehensible because they detest the incoherence of corruptible social realities? Are they purists who long for empty defined spaces in which they can function undisturbed? As their prose shuns the approbation of the general reader, so the reader dismisses them, if he notices them at all. Do the neglect and rejection garnered from being excluded by common readers pander to critics' egos by convincing them that they are singular, thus transforming neglect from a sign of failure into one of success? Of course, the truth is simpler; many literary critics write poorly.

"No critical mouser," I thought recently as I closed a book describing universals, "calls a bat a flittermouse." Not a postmodernist but the novelist, Frederick Marryat introduced me to the "celebrated Doctor Appallacheosmocommetico," a man of vast learning and experience who'd fandangoed with the Spanish, tarantellaed with the Italians, and "swung the Cherok pooga with the Hindoo." On meeting him, I learned that he'd had "one hundred and forty sets of teeth one after another" and was expecting "a new set next Christmas." What would a structuralist say about the man I saw last summer at Coventry Lake who had a chest tattooed on his chest, the full torso complete with nipples, brambles of hair, and a large paddle-shaped skin tag? No deconstructionist ever transforms an ending into a beginning and kicks off a high-stepping lecture with the music hall song that concludes:

A man received this wire one day,
"Your mother-in-law has passed away."
So the torment of his life had fled.
Then farther on the message read,
"Will you please instruct, which do you prefer,
Shall we embalm, cremate or bury her?"
So he sent them back this answer brisk,
"Do all three at once. Please take no risk."

This week my visits to the library have been brief. Across Mirror Lake needles are emerging from baldy cypress. They are yellow and stick up from branchlets looking like the heads of minute mud eels. Beavers have thickened the walls around the pond below Horsebarn Hill. By doing so, they doubled the size of the pond and transformed it into a formidable moat protecting their lodge. On Norway spruce new cones are red and look like wild strawberries not quite ripe enough to pick. Wheat chains of catkins have turned European hornbeams into jewelry stores, and the branches of carmine crabapples smolder muffled in carbuncular flowers. The ground under Yoshino cherries are snowdrifts of pink and white, and shadbushes are knots of blossoms, the petals bending and tying into one another then slipping and dangling loose.

As the Dane said, "there are more things in heaven and earth, Horatio, than are dreamt of in your philosophy." One moment a spoiled child shrieks. A cappuccino machine wheezes. Floaters blow across my sight like a flock of starlings rolling over in the wind, and Vicki announces, "The color green is essential to me."

"Life is amazing," Lieutenant D'Armagnac states in Paul Bowles's *The Sheltering Sky*. "All your philosophic systems crumble. At every turn one finds the unexpected." D'Armagnac was right and wrong. At every turn a person finds both the unexpected and the expected. Tomorrow or the next day, I will inject myself and say or do something embarrassing or ludicrous. I will ignore the temporizing advice proffered by Mr. Pleydell, the advocate, in Walter Scott's novel *Guy Mannering*. "There are folks," he said, "before whom one should care how they play the fool—because they have either too much malice, or too little wit." After the booster, sanity will return quickly, and I'll jettison all inclination toward seriousness.

Despite any intentions I have to appear earnest and project a consequential persona, words will out. Can I resist commenting on the social imperative urging people to refer to boyfriends and girlfriends as human-friends? Should I remark on Connecticut Public Television's addressing its latest fund-raising letter to "Ms. & Mrs. Pickering"? Do I say anything about going to the indoor track the morning after a rainy commencement and finding 98 abandoned umbrellas? When I left the building after running five miles, 96 umbrellas remained. Sitting on a bench in the locker room under the basketball court were 17 pots of white chrysanthemums. After I showered and climbed the stairs to my bicycle, 16 pots were left. That night on the Discovery Channel I watched a discussion of the relative merits of nurture and nature. During the final minutes of the show, the moderator solicited comments from the audience. "Heredity can't be discounted," a man said. "My father was extraordinarily handsome and intelligent, and I have been told that I am just like him." All genealogies are suspect. "Your literary ancestor," I said addressing the screen, "was Joseph Scaliger, not your father and not a progenitor recognized by the host."

Ought I to accede to the request from a folklore journal and write an essay describing "regional differences in colloquial speech, specifically phrases that refer to untoward doings of the intestinal tract?" All people who have grazed through decades have heard such expressions making them amateur dialectologists. For example, in the South when a person breaks wind, someone nearby will exclaim, "Peugh! Who pooted?" Almost always the commentator speaks in a falsetto voice. In New England matters are different. Only silence marks the passing of brassy eruptions. People standing close to the trumpeter raise their eyes to the heavens and stare into the distance looking as if they were studying the moons of Jupiter. Across the nation in California, a ripsnorter elicits camaraderie and the robust salutation "Greetings from the Interior."

Don't write the article, Josh advised me, paraphrasing Dr. Johnson who believed books should elevate and teach "the art of living." I doubt I will follow Josh's considered advice. I'm not an artist, but the way I endure living is by writing about it. However, recently I have decided to refine my speech. Never more will I call a person *fat*. When confronted by looming obesity, I will use *pinguitude*. No feelings will be bruised. No carking verbal censor will be offended. Because the word is known only to linguistic resurrectionists, my reputation for sensitivity will not be besmirched. In passing let me reassure concerned auditors that I will not alter my speech so radically that I become one of those tiresome people who limp through books trailing clouds of passives.

Rhetoric is a hand mirror reflecting social fashion. Like tracheal mites disrupting the production of honey, political speech now infests literary chit-chat, denaturing appreciation and beggaring the imagination. Courses focusing on words in which the content is simply, and fancifully, celebratory have become catalogue rarities. Of course, beyond the textbook all people stitch sentences together and compose stories celebrating their lives. "The number of gals who seduced me while I was mowing grass would astonish you," a neighbor said in July. "It certainly startled me. The blades the mower spun across the yard became the mulch of daydreams. I thought the tufts looked like hems on square dance dresses do-si-doing over the ground. Now a landscaping company tends the lawn. I write a check, but I don't dream. Sally [the neighbor's late wife] repeatedly told me she hoped I'd never stop mowing. She said the exertion was good for me, and after spending three hours cutting grass, I was in high spirits and was great fun to be around."

Among the most content individuals are inventive people who shape life by creating words, most commonly the baby talk of affection. For a little while such words enable them to slip wooden convention and the expediently appropriate. In January I read Robert Paltock's *The Life and Adventures of Peter Wilkins, Cornish Man,* published in 1751. After being shipwrecked near the South Pole, Wilkins was swept through an underground cavern into an undiscovered world. There he met and married a gawry or flying woman with whom he had a litter of children. Wilkins enjoyed countless adventures, unmatched today by any excursions advertised by cruise lines or by any celluloid experiences featured on the Science Fiction channel.

On a merry swangean gone astray, Wilkins' wife Youwarkee crash landed on his apartment. She was a native of Normbdsgrsutt. Because he couldn't pronounce the name of her country, Wilkins dubbed it Doorpt Swangeanti, the land of flight. Wilkins's new world was a thesaurus of verbal delights. Wilkins himself was Youwarkee's barkatt, that is husband, and their first baby boy was a yawm. The outfit that enabled Youwarkee to fly was a graundee and resembled the offspring produced by breeding a cape to a Venetian blind. In order to sweeten her prayers when she was young, Youwarkee baked rappins, marmalade cakes, for the ragams or priests, in her native Normbdsgrsutt. Her father, a colamb or governor, lived in the town of Arndrumnstake. He had long believed Youwarkee dead and was still mourning her loss when she suddenly visited him. He was in his dotage, and on hearing a family member say her name, he exclaimed, "I have heard a name spoken that will never be out of my heart till I am in Hoximo," the place where "the dead are buried."

To sustain me while I explored Youwarkee's homeland, I ate several slices of watermelon. Would that I could have sampled a crullmott, the melon popular with grocery shoppers in Doorpt Swangeanti. Man is covetous, even a person delectating in chilled watermelon in a quiet book-lined study, and I longed for a colapet, that is, the carryall that Youwarkee's neighbors wore around their necks. The bags were more capacious than present-day backpacks and not marred by tattoos of decals, pins, badges, and trashy branding inscriptions. When Vicki's and my children were small, we invented pages of words. We were enthusiastic neologists, and words were a staple of dinner conversation. I even complied a dictionary, listing words and hinting at their definitions, not all of these being unanimously agreed upon. So that I would not lose the words and the children's, and in a sense Vicki's and my own, childhoods I stored the dictionary in a safe place. Of course, the children have grown up and into occupations. They have forgotten their good first years, and I can't remember where I secreted the dictionary. Occasionally when mortality is too much with me, I recall writing it and long to see its pages. I wish I could don a graundee and fly back into memory and discover the dictionary. Sometimes the loss seems ineffably great, and I feel so sad I almost humhumhum-m-m-o, Normbdsgrsuttian for weep.

Words don't necessarily teach. But sometimes, particularly if they are embarrassing enough, words dispel sodden melancholy—not so well, perhaps, as the song of a wood thrush wafting from a wood and fluting into sunshine and likewise not so well as a gingko in May, golden-green, blooming with male cones and feathery with leaves shaped like rice-paper hand fans. Or maybe simply the familiars of spring itself—beech leaves, maidenly soft and green, brown deer mushrooms atop roots trailing from beneath a stump, and hay-scented ferns spreading in spindrifts across shadowy hillsides. If a person listens, he will hear the rapping of woodpeckers, the sound not animating pale shades but bringing to the eye the vivifying colors of springs past, and present. In truth, maybe I say embarrassing things to escape the eternal notes of sadness that toll throughout the days of the elderly. Two months ago, Ron's closest childhood friend Albert was diagnosed with brain cancer. "Three months at the most," a doctor said. The doctor was right. Last week when Ron talked to him Albert responded in syllables. Only once did he say a sentence. "This ends soon," he said. Two days later he died.

"You are so a serious writer that you are practically mole-eyed," Vicki said recently. "Saying embarrassing things creates a wrong impression." The wrongs and rights of my words matter much less to me now than they did forty years ago. In fact, getting things wrong may be the best way to get things right. In the famous tale of the "The Forty Thieves" from the *Arabian Nights*, Ali Baba was a poor woodcutter. One day he saw a band of thieves ride into the woods. After they dismounted, they pushed through bushes until they reached a pile of rocks in front of which their captain said, "Open Sesame." The rocks parted revealing a door to a cave filled with fabulous riches. In the cave the thieves deposited the bounty from their most recent crimes. Afterward they left the cave. Their leader then said, "Shut Sesame," and the rocks closed behind them. Having heard the passwords Ali Baba entered the cave, saw the treasure, and loaded several bags of gold on the backs of the asses he employed to carry wood.

Ali Baba had a rich, selfish brother named Cassim. When Cassim observed his sibling's new opulence, he became jealous. He forced Ali Baba to disclose the source of his wealth and compelled him to reveal the location of the cave and supply him with the magical passwords. Initially all went well for Cassim, and his covetousness appeared rewarded. He entered the cave and gathered jewels and coins galore. Unfortunately, when he decided to leave, he realized he had forgotten the password which would reveal the door and open the rocks. He said, "Open Barley" and "Open Wheat," then a silo of other grains. Nothing worked, and later when the thieves returned to the cave, they found him inside. To discourage other looters, they turned the cave into an abattoir, quartering him and nailing the cuts of beef to the wall.

Not only was Cassim greedy but he was also unimaginative. On the page wrong words open the temporal lobe and reveal chests filled with glittering memories. "Open Black-Eyed Peas and Stewed Tomatoes" unlatches the door to the past and enables me to leave my study, attend Parmer School, and romp with Heinzie and Fritzie my dogs. "Open Fried Clams" transports me to Maine and Nova Scotia, to summers at Camp Timanous and at Four Winds, the house Vicki and her brothers own. "Open Country Ham" finds me barefoot in Hanover, Virginia, exploring pine woods and bottom lands, dashing about like a dragonfly, catching cicadas and snakes and, alas, poison ivy. If Cassim had not been greedy and hadn't been seduced by the gilded, who knows where "Open Barley" might have taken him? Maybe to a better tomorrow and "fresh woods and pastures new." Does always saying the correct thing rather than the wrong actually cost a person his life?

Most embarrassing remarks are not spicy but tasteless. David's sight has deteriorated badly, and in July he is scheduled for a cornea transplant. I urged him to ascertain the provenance of the cornea. I warned him against corneas the previous possessors of which had led untoward lives, advising that the new eye might skew his vision and cloud morality. "You do not want fleets of piratical motes sailing across your sight. How unsettling it would be if you started ogling the nubile. What would your poor children think?" I said. "The character you established and nurtured by living carefully for 83 years would vanish in a blink of the eye. Astigmatism would stigmatize your reputation and create a permanent sty on your escutcheon." I also warned him that a cornea from a man who'd been favored with catamitic inclinations might disrupt our long, fruitful friendship. "If you began glancing fondly at my backside, our jovial after-jogging showers would probably end. Instead of running together, we'd run apart. How lonely we'd be."

I won't repeat those remarks to strangers. "That would be folly," Vicki said, "not just embarrassing but likely to attract the notice of bat-eared social-crats." In *The Peal of Bells* Robert Lynd analyzed the dilemma he confronted when selecting a collar to wear to a dinner. Choosing between a collar with butterfly or square-angled wings required analytical mulling. Because butterfly wings were no longer in fashion, Lynd eventually chose a collar with square-angled wings. According to hindsight, he dressed correctly. "When I arrived," he wrote, "a moment's glance told me that every other man present was wearing exactly the same sort of collar as myself, and I felt that peculiar joy of being dressed like everybody else which is known only to the civilized races." "Great as are the pleasures of being odd," he stated, "the pleasures of not being odd rival and probably surpass them."

I will never thrash about in Lynd's sartorial quandary. To apply a slang expression appropriate to my gourmandizing, I have not attended a formal dinner in donkey's years. On my table the most elaborate dish is a veggie burger topped by a pesticide-free garden of lettuce, tomatoes, mushrooms, and onions. That culinary observation aside, however, I think Lynd incorrect, at least from the perspective of my informal now. Lynd is a marvelous writer, but on the matter of collars he was wrong. The pleasures of oddity or, expressed another way, saying the unexpected and embarrassing outweigh bolted convention. When the rocks roll apart, one may see a cave littered with rubbish, but then amid the refuse he might find fool's wondrous gold. As a person ages, his skills diminish and his talents atrophy. His wants decrease correspondingly, and his contentment swells. When I was a boy in Virginia, I explored country dumps. Once I unearthed a small drum. It was battered, but, holy cow, could I make noise with it, or at least I did so until Grandmother banished her little drummer from the house. Reader, when convention weights as heavily as the nightly television news, try saying "Open Sesame." If that does not bring a change, and it may not, follow the lead of Adam and say, "Open Apple." After that start, you should be able to progress swiftly to "Open Butterbean" and "Open Beefsteak Tomato." If said in a loud voice in the presence of others, doors will swing on their hinges. I am not sure if they will shut or open, but certainly people around you will move.

Exhilarating Things

In Elissa Grodin's *A Handful of Worldliness*, Edwina Goodman stretched out in bed, head on a pillow, eyes closed, and pondered love. "Life," she thought, "was not much more than a spark bookended by darkness, but it was full of the most exhilarating things." During my life such things have usually been small, ignored by people around me and at the time unrecognized by me. It was probable, Robert Lynd wrote in *The Peal of Bells* that no one saw more than a few details of the world surrounding him at any time. If the world were "re-created" for him, it was always by something little and to others scarcely noticeable—"a woman's face, a harbor of fishing boats, a thrush's song, a pair of white bullocks ploughing under olive-trees." "Any of these things," Lynd ruminated, "may be clues to that happier world into which the imagination is always trying to escape. Or it may be that they prove to us that the happier world is already about us and that we had only to open our eyes in order to see it."

As a person grows old, darkness begins to lower. Once I knew a lot about many things. Now I know a little about few. The lonely long-distance runner grows lonelier and turns into a short-distance walker. His muscles sag, and remembrance becomes almost all. Recently I read *Staff Picks*, a collection of George Singleton's short stories. In one story a man takes his twelve-year old son to meet women who could have been his mother. In part the story is a "What If" or "Love's Labour's Lost" tale. Singleton is in his sixties, and although fiction, his stories reflect the nonfictional concerns and doings of people his, and my, age. In a person's later years, escaping the rule-less play of memory is both impossible and exhilarating. What oldster does not scroll through his past and wonder about the people whom he might have married and who might have married him? Inevitably memory tells things slant. Or, as Jim Barnes puts it in "Skipping," "Something never quite returns when you want / the facts the way you'd like them to be." Happily, the misremembered are the wondrous fool's gold of age, the coin of smiles and contentment. Suddenly the sun shines, imagination greens, red calves trail their mothers through high pasture grass, and pondering love, a person experiences the joys of lives he never lived. For a few moments the lotus blooms. In "dreamful ease," one hears lost voices no longer silent under mounds of grass, but beckoning, calling, plucking petals off daisies and handing old friends cherries that have no stones.

"Life's a journey," a doctor said after a mutual friend was diagnosed with a fatal illness. On his last legs, a person becomes increasingly sedentary. When an acquaintance telephones with bad news, the person doesn't race to the door like Mary Worth reassuring the caller, saying, "I'll be right over." Instead, he mumbles "Oh, dear" and sinks deeper into his armchair. No longer does he force fancies into deeds. Neither does he pursue ideals. Instead he mutters elegiac, energy saving remarks explaining that life has taught him that ideals are unattainable. He testifies that his years have exposed the flaws in "so-called" accomplishments. "The sad truth is that every saint led an imperfect life." "Shoddier and more blemished perhaps than the commonplace life led by an ordinary individual," he adds, shifting in the armchair, seeking a more comfortable seat. Such thoughts make it difficult to breast the dank wave of cynicism that inevitably chills one's final years. Unless a person exerts himself, he will become corrosively critical and exhilaration will vanish from his days. Instead of acting, he dissects, justifying his inaction and discovering reasons for condemning others. Milton understood this dolorous progress. Where God "set us in a fair allowance of way, with honest liberty and prudence to our guard," Milton wrote in "Doctrine and Discipline of Divorce," "we never leave subtilizing and casuisting till we have straightened and pared that liberal path into a razor's edge."

Books cannot lift a person out of a chair, but they can blunt edges and awaken memory. They can elevate spirits and cause days to sparkle. In May I read Reese Witherspoon's *Whiskey in a Teacup. What Growing Up in the South Taught Me about Life, Love, and Baking Biscuits*, a spring-time coffee-table and cookbook printed on glossy paper with at least one bright picture on every other page. The pictures were pastel and spread ruffled and expansively like peonies or square-dance dresses. The book's end papers looked like wallpaper, soothingly yellow and alight with magnolia blossoms. Throughout the book appeared "lite" essays giving Witherspoon's thoughts on sweet tea, family, dinner parties, and gardens. The essays were soothing and forgettable, momentarily alluring like light sliding through an ornamental Victorian stained-glass window and dappling the floor of an entrance hall.

"Whiskey in a Teacup," Witherspoon explained, describes Southern women who are combinations of beauty and strength. For the most part the women Witherspoon portrayed lived in affluent Belle Meade a city in West Nashville. I grew up in Belle Meade. My life there was astonishingly happy. Now that I am an old man, I think often about childhood friends and wonder why I left Nashville. I bumped into Witherspoon's book, literarily so, as it lay on a display table in Barnes & Noble. The corner of the table jabbed my thigh and made the muscles jump. While my muscles bounded in spasms, I picked up *Whiskey in a Teacup* and by chance opened to a page celebrating "Big Hair." On the opposite leaf was a photograph of an oil painting of Barry, the wife of my friend Wentworth. Barry is extraordinarily kind and thoughtful and was warmly loving to my mother. My heart leapt up, and sharp analysis softened into malleable golden memories. Like Edwina Goodman, I closed my eyes. I didn't ponder love, but instead followed will o' the wisp traces of myself in Nashville. Among the familiar places to which Witherspoon referred were St. George's Episcopal Church where I was confirmed and my son Francis was christened, and Montgomery Bell Academy the country day school I and Witherspoon's father attended. For her part Witherspoon went to Harpeth Hall as did every girl on whom I had an adolescent crush and some of whom had crushes on me, not something, alas, I was aware of at the time.

To enjoy *Whiskey in a Teacup*, a person has to be a sap. And why not since being a sap is both a privilege and the saving grace of age? "Where have all the monograms gone?" I thought as I read. "What happened to wallpaper blooming with peacocks?" Nothing I own now is monogrammed. The wallpaper in my house is peeling and was grimy when I bought the home in 1983. Witherspoon's house is clean and well-lit. Her sconces and doorknobs shine. I own a couple of scones, but I don't know where they are—probably in a box lost in the basement. Witherspoon's dogs are handsome and well-mannered. As a girl Mother owned beautiful English setters. My dogs are rougher and were rescued from the mongrel side of the kennel. They are gloriously affectionate tail-waggers, but their manners are doggish, and they misbehave. Last night Suzy lost her temper and upset waste cans in the television room, the kitchen, and both bathrooms.

Although Witherspoon's recipes are tempting, I no longer eat fried chicken or pecan pie. My heart discriminates. It tolerates grams of seasoned memories but not those of freshly cooked fat. I accompanied Witherspoon to the Iroquois Steeplechase. However, I did not sit with her in the enclosure but on the hillside with boyhood friends. Unlike Witherspoon we didn't wolf down pork sliders doused in bourbon. In the medieval age of my youth, sliders had not been invented or at least we hadn't discovered them. Moreover, we were underage and too young to taste bourbon. Popcorn and Mounds bars were delights enough.

There is more method in inaction than in action. Delectation flourishes away from noise and bustle, and the active person is often too busy to savor exhilaration. Quiet lends itself to appreciating striking remarks. On learning that a zealot who wished to see him refused to give his name and only identified himself as "a servant of the Lord," Charles Spurgeon, the acclaimed minister at the Metropolitan Tabernacle in London in the 19th century, responded, "Tell him that I am busy with his Master." On hearing me lament that remembering people's names had become difficult, my friend Josh said that forgetfulness reflected sophistication. Names of people and things, he elaborated, evolved arbitrarily and varied from language to language. "Your carelessness with regards to nomenclature reveals that you are not a rote learner or rote liver. You have refused to allow pedestrian mores to restrict your freedom. You are not the slave of custom but are in effect a beacon—the guiding light whose beam illuminates paths for the way-worn to follow."

Not everything Josh says is so appealing or perceptive. "Southerners," he once declared in a speech in Birmingham, "claim to be Christians, but don't live Christian lives. In contrast New Englanders say they are atheists but live according to the Sermon on the Mount." "If the I, Now Movement tolerated dissent gracefully," he said recently, "it wouldn't attract so much toxic criticism. Of course, that would diminish attention and in effect be social hari-kari." "I have read too many mesmerizing books to be enthralled by intimate histories," Josh continued. "The testimonials are supinely uninteresting. At every word an undergarment falls to the floor, and I fall asleep. I am too old to be interested in the discoveries of gossip mongers. They are small game hunters, the more decayed their prey the more appealing it is. They unearth rotten stories, skin them, and then stretch the skins on a rack. Afterward they transform the skins into trophies by inflating them with hot words. If their taxidermy is good, the trophies will balloon and from a distance seem prodigious." "Isn't that a little harsh?" I responded. "Truth is harsh," Josh replied. Silence is the better part of reason, and I started to urge Josh to temper his speech. Before I spoke, however, Josh quoted two lines from *Showboat*, "No matter what you say, / I still suits me."

Obviously, Josh is tendentious and perhaps excessively learned. However, I have known him for too many years to break with him over ideas. For twenty-five books, he has rubbed my mind the wrong way from tail to neck, but I have adjusted to his contentious ways. In part I frequent his company because the inhibited social consciousness and the spiritless conversation of tamed people like me sometimes becomes unbearable. Vicki urges me to spend less time with him. She says he is "monstracious," a two-edged neologism, one margin of which is sharper and more disapproving than "monstrous." The opposite margin is less censorious because it focuses attention on the word itself rather than the object of criticism. After quoting *Showboat*, Josh cited Macaulay on the Doctrine of Correctness. "It would be amusing," Macaulay wrote, "to make a digest of the irrational laws which bad critics have framed for the government of poets." "Worse," Josh continued, "are bad laws framed by the governing caste not by and for people but to control them. To the New World the *Mayflower* brought the Puritan Taliban, self-righteous and armed with deadly rectitude. Weren't your ancestors Quakers?" he asked. On my saying "yes," he responded, "Then read about their treatment in Massachusetts and weep."

Would that my mind worked like a switch engine and had torque enough jerk quotations off sidings and assemble them quickly into trains of persuasive arguments. Alas, I am an afterthought man. In analyzing the motivation of divines who railed against dancing, Robert Lynd wrote something with which I agreed but remembered only after I left Josh's presence. Criticism of dancing, Lynd stated, "is merely an exaggeration of the prevailing sense of mankind that sex is a wild animal and most difficult to tame into a fireside pet. It is upon the civilization of this animal, nonetheless, though not upon the butchering of it, that the decencies of the world depend."

Still, I am not so supine as Josh's harangues imply. Occasionally an injustice prompts me into action. Last Thanksgiving while driving to New York, I stopped at the Greenwich Rest Stop on the Merritt Parkway. While there was no line outside the men's lavatory, that outside the women's extended from the bathroom itself along a hall and out the front door. Inside the men's room were two stalls and two urinals. The stalls were empty so I took the private matters of females in need into my hands and became their usher. For twenty-five minutes I escorted women in and out of the men's room. "Women coming through," I said to men using the urinals, "continue facing the wall, lads." Because my ministrations embarrassed Vicki and Eliza who was home for the holiday, they refused my aid, giving me time to become a polished escort. I received many compliments. These ranged from "the last gentleman," "you're a doll," and "my personal St. Bernard" to "if all men were like you, the war of the sexes wouldn't even be a skirmish." I received a Whitman's sampler of thank-you's. "God! Was I desperate! Thank goodness, you were here," one woman said on leaving the lavatory. "I know you," an older woman said taking my arm as I led her to a stall, "You are Sam Pickering. You spoke in my town in 1987. What fun that was." For the record no man objected. Indeed, two said "good for you." "That was easy," I said later. "Yes," Vicki said, "easy because you were wearing a suit. You didn't look like an official but a man of consequence, someone to be obeyed and not trifled with."

A fortnight ago Josh complimented the mayor on the selection of a new slogan for the town, "Mansfield—Your Place to Grow." "It was," Josh said, "the perfect accompaniment for high-in-preservatives, ageless onion dip, Doritos, and six packs of Budweiser Lite in cans." Unlike many oldsters, Josh enjoys disruptions to his somnolent retirement. Recently he has received a legal brief of telephone spam masquerading as fund-raising for the ACLU. No matter that the crooks calling didn't know the difference between the American Civil Liberties Union and the YMCA, Josh's response was always the same. "I appreciate your thinking about me and praying that I'll have a nice day. Let me assure you that my legs don't suffer from any shinbone or soft-tissue deformities. You should know my ACLs are healthy, but if I ever tear a ligament, I will immediately let you know. However, I suspect my knees will remain sound as I don't play basketball or football. I do, however, frequent the local Senior Center. Are there any activities that you think I should avoid—perhaps games of Trivia or Name That Tune? I have already given up Bingo because the tension causes heart palpitations and the shouting and screaming strains vocal cords and leads to pharyngitis."

When in my armchair I read, both fiction and nonfiction although I think differences between the two imposed and more artificial than real. Only rarely do I peruse a newspaper. What corporations think newsworthy seems unworthy. Accounts of personalities are dead zones. Never are the doings of celebrities seductive enough to vex me. Even in the flesh, famous people exist in name only. In any case I'm not sure what constitutes fame. In fact, I have never met a famous person, and I doubt a famous person has ever met me. What separates bookends, exhilarates, and makes me appreciate life are accounts of the wondrous real. The wife of my Internet friend Dave is gifted cook. Each Christmas she hosts "an annual giveaway for friends and family." Last year she baked 43 varieties of bars and cookies. During the holiday people came to her house bringing boxes which they filled "with whatever looks good and as much as their box can hold." When illness or seasonal plans prevented people from picking up cookies, Dave and his wife packed boxes and delivered them. Oh, yes, happy, happy days—"God rest ye merry gentlemen."

Paper truth distorts. To set the margins straight, let me acknowledge that my family is renown. We have long been notable First Responders. In 1918 Grandma Pickering used artificial respiration to resuscitate a piglet that appeared dead. In 1919 an account of her success was published in the record of *American Duroc-Jersey Swine Breeders* volume 42. For over a hundred years the family has followed Grandma's example and saved or rescued countless creatures. Last week Vicki plucked a ladybug and a green-striped darner out of the dogs' water bowl on the back steps. For my part I shooed a shiftless northern water snake out of the path of a riding mower, and despite being weary after jogging six miles, I chased an English sparrow out of a closed hallway in the gymnasium. I did so by opening a window and by flapping my arms like wings and skipping up and down peeping reassuringly.

Exhilaration is mercurial. It quickly changes from bull to bear after which it growls and turning back to bull bellows. Hanging on the wall behind my arm-chair are a cluster of academic prints and woodcuts. Measuring fifteen by twenty-two inches, the largest is a page from the *Cambridge University Almanack* of 1814. On it appears the Main Court of "Catherine Hall," the college I attended at Cambridge now known as St. Catharine's College. Walking across the lawn in front of the buildings are three dons wearing gowns and mortar boards. In a triangle formed where roofs of two of the buildings pitch downward and join can be glimpsed the roof another building. Built in 1634, the building was torn down in 1966 because the hard soil beneath it dried and its foundation shifted. I was the last student to live in the building, and I remained there only after petitioning the college's governing body. When I notice the bit of roof, the evanescence of everything comes to mind, not merely that of bricks and wood, but of books and of people and their memories. Suspended close by is a smaller print of Catherine Hall, this colored and published in 1809. On each side of the entrance to the Main Court are three trees, their trunks masts, their tops sails billowing with green leaves. At Cambridge I read a library of books, but my years were not academic. Now they are the stuff of sentimental and exhilarating memory and, certainly, of regret. I punted on the Cam, but never did I take a sweetheart with me. I did not have a sweetheart. Would that I'd had a girl to whom I could have introduced my children as someone who might have been their mother. While young fools are dangerous, old fools are foolishly fond. What bothers me is not knowing how to dispose of the prints. They have some value, but their real worth is sentimental not monetary. To my family they are decorations and mean nothing. I'd like to give them to people for whom they'd have emotional value, but I don't know such folks.

The same is true of the other prints on the wall, one

of Dartmouth College looking across the green toward Dartmouth Hall in 1832, and two of University College London, both colored and facing the columned classical front of Senate House from Gower Street, the first of "London University" in 1828, the second of "University College." This last print isn't dated, but the people strolling along Gower are wearing regency attire, the men in top hats, the women in dresses that sweep the sidewalk. The men carry ornamental canes, and approaching up the street from town is a barouche pulled by two horses. Also, on my wall are a woodcut and an etching. In the etching are the Ball and Carter Buildings at Montgomery Bell Academy, not only the high school I attended but also where I taught in 1965 and 1966 before leaving Nashville. The etching was done yesterday in 1991 and the woodcut in 1977. In the woodcut are "The Barns & Herb Gardens at the University of Connecticut." Two cows and a sheep graze on a hillside. The barn is the old milking barn; adjoining it is a small building which housed two or three Holstein bulls when I came to the university. The bulls were huge—natural forces beyond the imagination of people syringe-fed artificial insemination. Outside the barn, flowers resembling Easter lilies are blooming, and a woman and a man are working in a garden. The man is leaning over, and the woman is carrying a wicker basket filled with plants that look like onions.

In Singleton's stories, divorce is common. For my part I'm divorced from the places where I taught and from various classroom me's. Schools and teaching were not all my life, but they illuminated the dark. "Dear King Bee," an almost-forgotten graduate-school buddy wrote from Florida at the beginning of the new year, "are you still buzzing around? Remember the Halloween on which you pretended to be a corpse and painted your face white, taped black crepe paper on your clothes, and danced about singing 'Get me to the crematorium on time' instead of 'Get me to the church'?" "Nowadays I'm a drone," I answered. "As for dancing, I've retired the old black and white slippers. I worry that I will trip and break a hip. Besides no one jitterbugs nowadays. Actually, I am so darn cold here in New England that I wouldn't mind a little fire in and on my belly."

But, that aside, reader, what can I do with my wall hangings? Who knows? But are you aware that according to an ancient story birds marry on St. Valentine's Day? Or that when the fruit of the monkey no-climb or sandbox tree dries and explodes it can hurl seeds a hundred and fifty feet? You'll be startled to learn that when Henry James began dictating his novels in the 1890's he stipulated that his amanuensis use a Remington typewriter, and by the way don't swim the river Styx. Its waters are fatally corrosive. But stay, I'll bet you don't know that Witherspoon's book contains a recipe for pickled red onions. I'm going to try it. At my age red onions are better for the skin than a cosmetic scrubbing with turtle water. Moreover, a culinarian told me onions go splendidly with potted lampreys. However, I probably won't serve prunes. In 18th century brothels, prunes were dispensed as prophylactics against syphilis. Imagine the gossip if guests noticed a sweet old or young thing gorging on prunes. Oh, well, untoward thoughts aside, time garbles. No friend knows I went to Cambridge, and my children can't name the college I attended. For my part I remember so little about the year I spent at University College London that I wonder if I was ever there. In December when

I bemoaned not remembering people who sent me Christmas cards, Josh remarked that as a man ages the attic vanishes from his brain, taking with it armoires, steamer trunks, and scrapbooks, all cluttered with memories. "Eventually," Josh said, "the second story of his house disappears, and until he honks out, he will live on one story and in one story, this last repeated interminably."

In April Raymond recommended that Vicki and I watch *Quicksand*, a six-part Scandinavian series on Netflix. The series was dark and violent. After we saw the last segment, Vicki said Raymond should be prosecuted for entrapment. That night I dreamed I was the caretaker of a golf course in northwestern Russia near Scandinavia. Groundhogs bedeviled me by digging burrows in sand traps. "Don't you get it," I said to Vicki the next morning, "*sand* and *trap* and just a traipse across Finland to Sweden and Norway and a short sail down the Baltic to Denmark?" "Yes," Vicki replied, "a hodge-podge like everything—memories and souvenirs and conversation." In one of Singleton's stories, Marvin an aging gardener shakes his head and says, "It's not like I can't remember anything anymore. It's just that my head's filled up. It's overflowing. I mean, I always had a head full of possible hybrids swirling around, but now I have memories, and guilt pangs, and wishes. If my mind were a grinding wheel, you wouldn't believe the sparks I'm producing nonstop."

The danger comes when the wheel breaks, the sparks stop, and exhilaration ends. Happily, daily life does its surprising best to keep the machine oiled. In March a friend from summer camp days in the early 1960s telephoned to wish me "Happy Birthday." He confused me with someone else and got the month slightly wrong. My birthday is in September. But that's just an insignificant matter of days, and we had a nice chat. He asked about my health, and I asked about his. We concluded that we were both in "pretty good" fettle aside from the expected scrapes and bruises of age. He volunteered that he had a "touch of palsy" in his left hand and that his "you-know-what" had gone into permanent estivation. "Every once in a while," he said, "it gets a little plump, but it's hardly noticeable and doesn't last long enough to be a nuisance."

My birthday shares an umbilical cord with Humpty-Dumpty's "un-birthday." In May a former student sent me a reprint of Monk Lewis's *Journal of a West India Proprietor; kept during a residence in the Island of Jamaica.* "Happy birthday," the student wrote. "I suspect your birthday occurs in another month, but exact dates don't matter to people who refuse to allow the calendar to fence them in." "You will like this book," the student said. "The pages are alive with curiosities like those you described in class—anecdotes that brightened our linoleum days and made our schooling quirky and real—remarkably useful if a person works for a hedge fund as I do. See pages 32 and 33, the entry for December 16, 1815." Lewis was a novelist, a diplomat, and the wealthy owner of estates in Jamaica. In the entry, Lewis testified that he was "particularly fond of conjugal attachments between animals," noting that because such attachments were "so universal" in the human species he set no store by them. While the boat on which he was sojourning lay in Jamaica's "Black River," two sharks were observed "playing about the ship." When the female was killed, he recounted, "the desolation of the male was excessive." "What he did *without* her remains a secret, but what he did with her was clear enough; for scarce was the breath out of his Eurydice's body, when he stuck his teeth in her, and began to eat her up with all possible expedition."

"So peculiar a mark of posthumous attachment" excited the "sensibility" of the sailors, and to help the shark perform his "melancholy duty the more easily," they lowered a boat and becoming his "carvers" used their hatchets to chop his better half into masticatory pieces. While the sailors butchered, "the widower opened his jaws as wide as possible, and gulped down pounds upon pounds of the dear departed as fast as they were thrown to him, with the greatest delight and all avidity imaginable." "I have no doubt that all the while he was eating," Lewis concluded, "he was thoroughly persuaded that every morsel which went into his stomach would make its way to his heart directly! 'She was perfectly consistent,' he said to himself 'she was excellent through life, and really, she's extremely good now she's dead!' and then unable to conceal his pain, 'He sigh'd and swallow'd, and sigh'd and swallow'd, / And sigh'd and swallow'd again.'"

Lewis doubted that "the annals of Hymen" could "produce a similar instance of post-obitual affection." Lewis is probably right. Vast numbers of marriages become lifeless, and as a result matrimonial chronicles are usually jejune. Even graveside declarations rarely warm marital recollections. Annals of the mail are odder and more exhilarating. I don't think my teaching harmed students. It may have contributed to some becoming less conventionally ambitious, but that is not necessarily bad. On the other hand, perusing my essays hasn't always had notable salubrious effects. Because reviewers inevitably overlooked the "astonishing" power of my prose, I often quoted testimonials praising the beneficial, often miraculous, results of studying my books. I modeled my endorsements on advertisements for patent medicines popular in the nineteenth century. On Monday the mail brought two items. The first was a letter from a man in Missouri. "I have long been a close reader of your books, and I thought the following observations copied from a column which appeared in the weekly community paper here in Koshkonong would please you," the man wrote. "The anecdote may appear familiar, but nothing is original. Words are raised on words, and even miracles are derivative."

According to the column, a man and his wife were picking daisies in a field behind a firecracker emporium when suddenly the building exploded. Unfortunately, the detonation blew the man into bits, well, to be more accurate, into "twenty-six pieces." Because a large oak tree stood between her and the building, the wife was unhurt, aside from being deafened and a splinter's shredding from the tree and impaling itself in her bottom. Fortunately, the woman was generously padded, so despite the velocity with which the wood took flight, the splinter did not penetrate deep enough to reach any of the new widow's vital organs. On her back the woman carried a bag containing a jug of home-brewed mid-western comfort and two of my recent volumes, *Parade's End* and *One Grand, Sweet Song*. She and her husband planned to sit under the oak, pluck "she loves me" and "she loves me not" petals from daisies, sip the comfort, and read heart-warming excerpts from my essays to each other.

The splinter spurred the woman into quick thinking. She hobbled onto the lawn of a house bordering the field and borrowed a rake from a dead yardman. At the time of the explosion he was currying grass. For a moment heat from the blast created a kiln. The heat reduced the yardman to embers, except for his right hand which it baked and sealed to the rake. The woman could not dislodge it, but mustering "more strength than she knew she had," she managed to slide the hand down to the head of the rake. There it stayed because "it wouldn't let go," no matter how hard the woman tried to bend the man's fingers back and peel them off the handle. She then returned to the field and raked her husband into a pile. For eleven straight years she had been the jig-saw puzzle champion of Oregon County. In fact, she met her husband at a regional competition in Doniphan. After extracting twigs, fragments of wall board, crab grass, and an unexploded ashcan from his remains, the wife arranged the parts in a grid of interlocking pieces.

The shock wave from the explosion shattered the jug in the bag, and the liquor soaked the books. The skills of one generation are not always passed to the next, and although the dead man's father and grandfather had been celebrated moonshiners, the son did not inherit their talent. Not surprisingly, mistakes often become blessings. The liquor in the jug contained so much methanol and lead that had the couple dallied away the afternoon under the tree sipping and reading sweet nothings they would have been poisoned and died. Happily, however, the chemicals spread through the books making their pages adhesive. The woman was an unsnapped and semi-nude dresser. She liked going barefoot and wearing pink halters and short shorts with twirly hems decorated with polka dots. The thought of widow's weeds nauseated her, and she resolved to remain single for as short a time as possible. She tore the pages out of the books and wrapping them around her husband glued his parts together. The pages dried quicker than plaster of Paris, and, not only, the weekly reported, "did the laying on of words heal the man's wounds but like plastic surgery they eradicated a collection of frightful scars and drained a sump of moles." "Pickering's essays are practically sanctified. Amen!" the column stated. "They always impart a kindly warmth and quicken the circulation of the mental juices. They widen the nostrils and drive the little flies of bad grammar and scrofulous constructions from the mind. For four decades his paragraphs have raised the eye lids of the blind and uncaked the ears of the deaf. They have goosed the chair-ridden causing them to kick aside their foot stools, hop on to their marmadukes, praise God, and sing 'Pack up your troubles. Sit at your old wooden desk, and read, read, read.'" Three hours after Pickering's words oozed into his bloodstream, the husband rose like a Roman candle from the ground and shouted, "I've done seen Beulah Land and Osage Beach and Cross Timbers, too. On my next vacation after Honey Bunch and I visit Sam Pickering, we are going to Beersheba and Ava and Theodosia."

With that the Lazarean tossed off his glad adhesive rags and started walking home. "And he didn't walk long neither," my correspondent reported. "Soon he started jogging. Only once did he stop and that was at the pharmacy to order your newest medicinal *The World Was My Garden, Too*. That night he ate a fine dinner of chitterlings, scrambled eggs and brains, corn bread, okra, and cabbage fried in bacon grease. Afterward he belched as usual, as if the explosion had not occurred and he hadn't been blowed up." In truth things appeared almost unchanged. However, in reassembling her husband, the former widow now reborn wife committed a small error. That morning the couple had not been alone. A jackass was also grazing on daisies. The Big Bang did not discriminate between the four-legged and the two legged and distributed the fragments of both creatures randomly across the field. Hurry made the widow careless, and in fitting her husband back together, she attached the head of the jackass to his neck. "Maybe I should have noticed," she told the reporter who wrote the clipping. "But there won't much change. The new head made him handsomer, and his voice was more musical. But his appetite and conversation remained the same, and, hellfire, none of his friends noticed any difference. The next afternoon he and his buddies drove over to West Plains for the annual donkey softball game. I suppose they should have observed something then because for the first time in eighteen years they won the game."

Fiction is longer winded than truth. While truth is usually expressed in declarative sentences and short two-penny nail paragraphs, fiction rambles unhinged though compound and complex sentences into unending paragraphs. The second exhilarating item in the mail was actual and brief: a membership application from the Starling Breeders of America, "the Massachusetts Chapter." Accompanying the application was a schedule of suggested donations. Simple membership cost $20. From this the Feather level the schedule fluttered upward past Nest and Feeder to Box Builder at $250 and Aviary at $500. By the by, three years ago, I received a solicitation from the Turnip and Parsnip Growers of Ohio describing their goal to introduce ROOT Studies in college curricula. "Leave STEM to wilt in the smog, and dig deep into the springs of life with ROOT studies," the solicitation urged. Following the example of universities that are more athletic than academic, the organization had already started a branding campaign changing the familiar catchphrase "Root hog, or die" to the command "ROOT capitalists, or starve." I should describe the organization in more detail. But although my readers have hearty appetites, they tend to be people of little faith and to their detriment don't always believe everything I write.

Besides I want to take the bit or, better, the pencil out of my mouth. The day is hot and too exhaustingly humid to continue writing. Thunder is rumbling in the west. Soon the sky will turn gunny. Wind will shake the tops of the trees and rain will fall freshening the air. The first drops will be small and cool and tickling. I'm going outside and sit at the edge of the driveway under a canopy of red oaks. Earlier in the afternoon I ate half a watermelon. I haven't drunk a Coca-Cola in two years, but I'll fill a tall glass with ice and sip the Coke. Suzy will accompany me outside. She'll crouch under my chair or sit in my lap. Together we'll watch lightning flash and leaves dance and glisten. I'd like to see the two fawns who live in the wood behind the house, but they will be sheltering in the anonymity of the trees. Almost no people will pass on the road, perhaps a shirtless jogger kicking up his heels and almost singing in the euphoria of youth and then an older Chinese graduate student bent and shrinking under an umbrella. Suzy and I will remain outside until the thunder drifts away, the rain thickens, and the drops start hopping off the drive like bull frogs. People like Edwina Goodman who have spent their lives out of sight among exhilarating small things appreciate littleness. Almost never do they, or I, feel deprived.

Obit.

Preface

To forestall sugary recollection and inoculate wailers against gagging superlatives, I'm publishing this obituary before Bermuda grass grows on my stomach. Moreover, the obituary will not appear anywhere else. No account of my life will share column inches with recipes for mud pie and pickled onions, Mary Worth's "have a nice day" club, and Chamber of Commerce fruit cocktail patriotism. It won't advertise crematoria fire sales or expose herculean cupidity. It won't mention doddering swine, sanctified cads, and prehensile lunatics. But hold, that's enough. I must change my tone. These words are too truculent for lovers of obituaries. Because pessimism draws attention to itself, the phrases appear vain and self-approving. To lessen their acidity, I need to dump a bucket of leavening consonants and vowels into my previous sentences. The best way to ensure that lime spreads evenly though my necrology is to describe today.

The morning was lithe and lovely, and as we do every spring, Vicki and I attended the Memorial Day parade in Mansfield Center. While Vicki accompanied the marchers to the new graveyard and listened to the speeches, I wandered nearby woods and scrubby overgrown meadows. My America has always been beautiful for weedy places and tangled roots. Along the hems of woods celandine and spurge were chartreuse and amber. Carillons of lily of the valley patched the eroding edges of garden paths, and around still pools pink azalea bloomed, the fragrance almond and soporific transforming busy muscular walking into benign carelessness. A hatching of pearl crescents swirled near the ground kicking up then falling into the grass like orange confetti. Although flowers had yellowed and begun to drizzle from autumn olive, the perfume lingered in fence-line corners. A groundhog kinked across an abandoned pasture and bundled into a den. A pileated woodpecker shrieked, and a mockingbird hopped through the air above a rail fence and disappeared behind a massive sugar maple. Three turkey hens hurried along a dirt road swaying and lurching. A divergent beech beetle landed on my shirt. Almost an inch long, the beetle's body tapered to a point, and in the middle rose tented. Coppery and brassy, the beetle appeared plated. It reminded me of a narrow lapel pin, not one proclaiming allegiance to a lodge or nation, but instead announcing membership in the web of life. Nailed to trees growing on the shoulders of Echo Road were wooden signs eight inches tall and twenty wide. Pained on them in green letters were two lines. "DO NOT MOW," the first commanded. "SLOW—TURTLES," the second warned. "How fitting that would be for my tombstone," I thought. "Nothing could better that."

Obituary

Samuel Francis Pickering of Storrs died on.... He was born September 30, 1941, in Nashville, Tennessee. His parents were Sam Pickering of Carthage, Tennessee and Katherine Ratcliffe Pickering of Richmond, Virginia. He is survived by his wife Victoria Johnson Pickering from Princeton, New Jersey, and their children: Francis of Southington, Connecticut, Edward (Erica) of Greenville, South Carolina, and Eliza (Travis) of Redwood City, California. He graduated from Montgomery Bell Academy in Nashville and from the University of the South (Sewanee). Afterward he attended St. Catharine's College, Cambridge and received a second B.A. On returning from England he taught for a year at Montgomery Bell Academy. He then attended Princeton and earned a Ph.D. in English in 1970. He taught English at Dartmouth College for eight years followed by thirty-five years at the University of Connecticut.

"To Connecticut I am endlessly grateful," he wrote; "I owe my home and family to the university." During his classroom years, he also taught for a year in Syria and another year in Jordan. He wrote some thirty books and hundreds of articles. The subjects varied, ranging from scholarly studies of children's books and a book on teaching to travel books and collections of personal essays giving his take or non-take on life. He also wrote a memoir that stopped at the end of 8th grade when he belonged to the Safety Patrol. He did not continue the memoir because he said an extended account of his astonishingly happy life would make readers hate him. "No one could enjoy living more than I have," he once said. "Reading Pickering," a reviewer wrote in *The Smithsonian* decades ago, "is like taking a walk with your oldest, wittiest friend." "Now," Pickering said shortly before his death, "I am old, and the friends who thought me witty have fallen off the perch. But that's okay. What

I wrote made me smile and mutter, 'What a guy.'"
During his life, Pickering received honorary degrees
and won awards. "But don't mention them in my obituary," he instructed his family. "Less is more—more
or less." Obsequies will be muted and private.

Afterword

Although unusual, an obituary can have a Preface. An
Afterword or, better perhaps, an Afterward strains the
expectation of readers until they eschew factual pages
and float into the Never Land of their own lives. Albert
Bigelow Paine dedicated *The Hollow Tree Snowed-In
Book* "To All Dwellers in the Big Deep Woods of
Dream," that is to almost everybody. Tastes change,
but Time never weans a person from fantasy. People
enter sweepstakes, play lotteries, propose marriage,
bet on horses, and buy stocks. Who has not imagined his dark hours being Arabian Nights? Who has
not traveled over the hills to Bisnagar and like Prince
Houssain purchased a magic carpet which instan-
taneously transported him anywhere in the world?
Who was not in Shiraz beside Prince Ali when he discovered the ivory perspective glass? When Ali and I
looked into the glass, we saw whatever we wished
to see. More appealing perhaps to aging valetudinarians was the medicinal apple Prince Ahmed bought
in Samarkand. No matter the morbidity of a person's
illness, sniffing the apple cured him and transformed
death rattles into symphonies of hallelujahs. Of course,
practicalities sometimes temper dreams. Taped to
the front door of a local greenhouse and flower shop
six years ago was a sign suggesting that people over
ninety buy annuals not perennials—jocularity probably not appreciated by all octogenarian gardeners.

How does a person behave in the afterword following his obituary? He might become depressed and like Elijah flee into a wilderness and beg God to end his life. Euthanasia has never been popular with the Great First Cause and his minions, Seraphim, Cherubim, Thrones, and Principalities. After imploring God to promote him to Glory, Elijah fell asleep under a juniper tree. Later an angel woke him commanding, "Arise and Eat." Elijah obeyed and not long after set off for Mt. Horeb. Despite the angel's exhortation, it's unlikely Elijah skipped to Mt. Horeb whistling "Zip-a-dee-do-dah." People eventually age beyond the fervor of both optimism and pessimism and become footsore accepting realists. An acquaintance of Sebastian Chamfort who was learned in the ways of society once remarked that "it would be necessary to swallow a toad every morning in order not to find anything disgusting the rest of the day when one has to spend it in the world."

In an afterword, a person goes on, day after day, sentence after sentence, bufonid after bufonid. Although no longer self-deceiving enough to imagine he'll encounter the momentous, one will experience moments. These won't be followed by exclamation points. Instead they will simply catch the attention. Sometimes they'll please and delight, but eventually they will fade and vanish from thought. "Who could imagine that Annie's Auto and Ramsaran Auto Body Works would both be located on Seven Up Avenue?" I said to Vicki last year as we explored Port of Spain. "No one," Vicki replied before pausing and adding, "because they are on different streets and not on Seven Up Avenue." "That doesn't matter. They're close enough for the page," I answered.

Writing, H. E. Bates wrote is "an exercise in the

art of telling lies." If a writer uses art and craftman-
ship to their fullest extent, "he will not only make his
readers believe his lies are truth but that they are in
fact truer than life itself." The writer without a magic
carpet or mirror, that is, "the ability to invent, is not a
writer." Bates was discussing fiction, but his remarks
also apply to nonfiction. Lies are the alpha and omega
of writing and conversation. In any case last month,
I drove Vicki to the Buckland Hills Mall in Manchester and experienced sips of Pepsi Avenue. Vicki
needed new eyeglasses. I hadn't been to the mall in
twenty years, and while Vicki examined frames in
LensCrafters, I roamed corridors peering into shops
and reading advertisements. At the door to the mall
I searched the directory looking for a listing of the
"Disaster Management Unit." I'd seen the unit in Port
of Spain. Disaster Management, however, did not appear on the directory. The building housing the unit
in Trinidad was falling to pieces. Consequently, on
studying the listings I assumed that after Vicki and
I left the island the structure suffered a disastrous
collapse and buried the unit under a ramp of dusty
rubble. Beyond the entrance in the mall itself was car-
bonated entertainment enough, however. American
Eagle Outfitters titillated hormonal teenage customers
telling them "Love is the Message." At Relaxation a
"special" thirty-minute foot massage cost "Just $30."
Goofy Turtle urged children to "trade in your old
toy to get a new one." The expertise of attorneys at
Beek Eldergill extended beyond a single section into
a township of legal territories: real estate, motor vehicle accidents, bankruptcy, will, probate, family, and
"Dog Bites."

"All this universe is God's blessed sacrament,
the channel of His Spirit to your soul," Frederick

Robinson wrote in the 19th century. In the afterward of this after age, Robinson's statement sounds wistfully delusional. Moreover, Wordsworth's assertion that impulses from vernal woods may teach more about life and morality than "all the sages" is clearly bunkum. Appealing more to the me of these latter days is the dispassionate observation expressed by Charles Conrad Abbott *In Nature's Realm*. "Nature does not wear her heart upon her sleeve, but how few have that penetrative vision which sees through the coverings beneath which her real self is busy." "The world is growing old," Abbott declared in 1900. "We hold ourselves as wise, but the crack o' doom will find us ignorant still. The hold of indifference is so powerful, that we cannot wholly shake it off. We are all fog-bound, even when the sun shines."

Prefaces dribble into afterwards trailing themes. The themes don't beget glimpses that make people less forlorn. Instead they occasion other sightings. As a result, amid the fog of an afterword, indifference loses its grip. In my back yard the oriental bittersweet that garrotes the poles supporting the clothesline is blooming. From the small unnoticeable flowers spray nebulizers of perfume. Across the neighborhood the thick stems of iris are heady with blossoms, my favorite this spring pall-white not Grandma Pickering's dark blue. Seasons bring change, and amid the beauty of early spring lurks the ancient recognition of loss. For years until this April when the university blasted nearby ledges and leveled woodlands to "upgrade" baseball and soccer fields, red-tailed hawks nested in the neighborhood. Frequently, they perched outside my study. I waved and spoke to them. I have poor hearing, and I couldn't make out their responses, but my presence didn't disturb them. Their acceptance pleased me and like an eiderdown made me feel comfortable.

I did not ignore the destruction, but the sun shone brightly and so warmly consoling that I avoided stumbling into the brambles of a crosspatch mood. In the lawn below Gulley Hall at the university the huge tulip tree has now become a morning sky flickering yellow, green, and orange. The ancient white ash in front of the old library looms swelling like a green cumulous cloud, its bark corky and darkly fissured. Nearby a lacebark elm is a mottled tapestry, its trunk floral with orange and gray, red and blue. Red-winged blackbirds are nesting in the cattails around Mirror Lake, wheezing and screeching like a flock of drunken smoke detectors out of the house and on a spree. Along Mugwort Lane wrapping the south slope of Horsebarn Hill, fingers of flowers hang jointed and clustered from black cherry, and the racemes of field pennycress transform a gray ditch into a casket of bewitching yellow. Atop the hill bobolinks rise from the grass, and Savannah sparrows perch on fence poles. Last Sunday Vicki and I and our packlet of three small rescue dogs walked across Horsebarn Hill to the Dairy Bar. We sat above the lilac garden on a bench under the shade of a black oak and shared a cup of coconut and chocolate ice cream. Vicki and I ate our helpings then doled the rest out to the "little monsters." Like the world I have grown old, and I no longer delude myself thinking I am wise. But as I sat and rubbed the dogs, the world did not seem old. Nature did not wear her heart upon her sleeve. Instead she wore it on the trunks, the limbs, branches, leaves, and flowers around us.

In two weeks, Vicki and I will have been married forty years. We plan to eat dinner out. Newlyweds would think our celebration a tired afterward, an event worn bare by four decades together. Although we aren't going to Samarkand or Shiraz but only six miles down the road to Willington Pizza, the evening will be magical. We'll forgo 1959 Dom Perignon. More agreeable and easier our palates will be a draft pilsner, probably Workhorse, the alcoholic content of which is five per cent. Lagers are too bitter for sentimental occasions. Besides their alcoholic content is higher, a disruptive eight percent in Sip of Sunrise and a shocking eight and a half percent in Pineapple Cloudbank. For a starter we will split a modest Caesar salad. For the main course we'll share a small pizza, perhaps the Seafood Casino Pizza consisting of scallops, snow crab, and shrimp seasoned with a lemon white sauce and topped off with bacon bits and cheddar cheese. On the other hand, that may be digestively too much, and maybe we'll eat the simpler, less heart-throbbing Shrimp Scampi Pizza. What we won't order is the House Special Pizza, a feed lot meaty with hamburger, sausage, and pepperoni.

Although we will each imbibe an inspiriting twenty-two ounce glass of beer, we won't force any embarrassing declarations. Because a fortieth anniversary is special, I have, however, exhumed an ancient culinary pun to enliven digestion. "What," I will ask Vicki, "prevents a person from starving in a desert?" The answer is obvious, "the sand which is there." On Vicki's looking quizzical, I will forge ahead and ask, "how does a person know he will find a sandwich?" "Because," I will eventually say, "Ham went into the desert and his descendants bred and mustered." To surprise Vicki and distract her from my punning skills, I'll pick a vase of seasonal flowers for the table, probably three or four spires of yellow foxglove, a cane of multiflora rose fragrant with brushes of blossoms, and thin shafts of forget-me-not and blue toadflax. I'll swell the bouquet with a bell tower of shinleaf pyrola, Deptford pinks, a little fleabane, the redder the better, a stob of mullein, and an armful of black-eyed Susans. The floral disks of the Susans will be so swollen and protruding they seem about to pop off the flowers like buttons from the front of a tight shirt. Wrapping the lip of the vase will be a chaplet of hop sedges, dangling over them pink balls of milkweed. Coloring the stems of the milkweed will be herds of orange oleander aphids, the droves corralled by a pair of lacewings.

Insects intrigue Vicki. Years ago, when I complained about the beggarly half-life of the essay, she urged me to write detective novels. "You've read every who-done-it written and know all the plots. You like bugs. Have some fun. Copy Nancy Drew and the Hardy Boys and start an insect series. The first two titles could be *Murder by Beetle* and *Death by Caterpillar*. You might even make a little money, and we could refinish the downstairs floors." The best beetles for gainful malevolent purposes were, Vicki said, African leaf beetles. Because they were not native to North America, a gumshoe couldn't readily discover the fatal blistering mandibles. Ground and stuffed into a spicy sausage and served to a gourmandizing victim, the beetles ruptured red blood cells and caused paralysis. If skirting invasive species regulations and obtaining the leaf beetles proved impossible, she suggested an antipasto paste of blister beetles, preferably made from the striped blister beetle. A Triscuit sagging under the paste increased the heart rate, dehydrated, and triggered depression and urinary tract infections, "ideal for dispatching an elderly, big-bucks, money-bag-clutching relative." Vicki said she did not know as much about caterpillars as beetles. Still, she thought that a Brunswick stew heavy with minced saddleback, puss, and hag moth caterpillars might 'take down the pike.'"

Although I have lost the dexterity of my youth, I still handle thread well enough to tie a container of insects to the flowers. Think of them as anniversary jewelry—buggy broaches and leaf rings. I'll attach insects Vicki noticed this spring, among a selection of others, white spotted sawyers, bark crab spiders, ebony jewel wing damselflies, whitetail dragonflies, and several emerald green spotted tiger beetles, these last particular favorites of Vicki. For a time, I considered secreting a tree frog amid the flowers. Eventually I realized that controlling his appetite would have been difficult. If he hadn't dined before Vicki's and my celebration, he might eat all the insects, so I decided to leave the flowers frogless. In any case I suspected listening to Vicki's and my fond conversation would have bored him despite his being an arboreal cousin of the famous Froggy who went courting. Moreover, he might not have serenaded us. Chances are a millennial frog wouldn't know the words to "Because of You" or "Cruising Down the River." Even worse, suppose he decided to seek more exciting company and hopping from the vase, landed atop a pad of pepperoni in the middle of a pizza or, alas, went for a swim in Vicki's beer glass?

The pleasures of an Afterward are not as considerable as those of a Preface, but they exist and are much more than good-byes. Decades ago, I spurned the puritanical compulsion to reach conclusions. The day when I mourn my children's father will come, but it hasn't arrived yet. Last year no planet-ruler predicted my death accurately, and so far, this year I have resisted the urge to toss a ball of string into the air, and when it unravels, climb it and disappear into the clouds. Moreover, Kathy the pharmacist at CVS did not give me a complimentary bottle of Dead Man's Pills when she filled my prescriptions for Diltiazem and Latanoprost. In the meantime, postscripts have migrated onto my pages and multiplied, as they do in the lives of sentient people strong enough to be indecisive. I realize that some devotees of obituaries will disagree with this last statement. The lure of finality is powerful. But then I expect contention. Today I erased the fact that Father was from Carthage, Tennessee, from my obituary. Carthage is the seat of Smith County. Recently county commissioners proclaimed their opposition to gun control by designating the county "as a Second Amendment Sanctuary County." My father was kindly and intelligent. He was fond of Carthage but would have thought the appellation shameful. For Political Christians, my friend Carey said, "the Gun is the New Cross of Jesus."

Repetition

Sprayed across the side of a ruptured building in the Pietermaai district of Willemstad in Curacao was, "Once you break the walls that have been holding you captive your journey to explore the world can begin." The words staggered drunkenly, and their letters bled clouts of paint. More often than not sloganeering marks the end rather than the beginning of a journey. The successful don't besmirch place with uplift. They are too busy, and when contentment slips away, they do not lean upon the argot of self-help. Ours is, however, a rattling, aphoristic society. Stamped on the front of a T-shirt I saw recently was "Old Guys Rule." The elderly have dominion over little, certainly not themselves, and instead of ruling they are often warehoused by family and society. A declaration so patently false does not generate interest. Instead of encouraging acquaintance, it isolates. Who wants to talk to a deluded oldster prone to espousing silly affirmations? In any case what sort of conversation could a person have with a "guy"? Occasionally, a shirttail statement makes a passerby pause. In Curacao, I saw a tourist wearing a T-shirt that said, "Four Out of Five People Have a Problem with Fractions."

A statement on a shirt is the sartorial counterpart of a filler at the bottom of a column of newsprint. I have long roamed by-ways in woods and on pages, and fillers in newspapers and magazines often interested me more than articles. Only the basketed slip the tether of habit, and although most of my present-day experiences are those commonly prefaced by the adjective "near-death," I am still alive—well, organic—and jogging. Because I no longer subscribe to a morning paper or weekly magazines, reading fillers has morphed into reading shirts. Would that fillers were not so boring proletarian and that they contained bits of startling natural human fiber like the Afghan maxim, "Doing good to the wicked is like doing ill to the good" or the English saying, "Flies always devour people sweeter than honey." Time has almost turned me into a vegetarian, and anthologies stringy with excerpts now appeal to me more than meaty volumes thick with indigestible ideas. Democracy, a snippet from the writings of Auberon Waugh stated, "can work as a form of government only in conditions of general apathy. Where there is a greater commitment, it is a recipe for conflict, not to say civil war. Why should ten voters abandon their fondest wishes because eleven voters have a different preference? Democracy works perfectly well in an atmosphere of indifference and cynicism, but only so long as practically nobody is interested in politics." Quite right—the best way to make the world safe from democracy and democracy safe from itself is to discourage voting. Dozy electorates do not mount barricades and throw firebombs.

My attention span has attenuated, and as fillers appeal to me more than articles, so I prefer overheard tidbits to lectures. Bits are seeds. They have brief life spans or in the language of the green world are microbiotic. Rarely do they grow into tangles of thought and burden the mind. Sometimes though, they glimmer and lighten passing. "Daddy," a small boy standing in front of a urinal in an airport lavatory said to his father, "Daddy, this is too high for me." "Shoot up," his father replied. "Please do not wash feet in sink," read a sign in a changing room on St. Thomas's Coki Beach. "Lordy," a man washing his hands exclaimed. "Only a someone whose mother was a giraffe could wash his feet in the sink. A normal person would lose his balance, fall backward, and hitting the concrete floor split his skull like a coconut."

This March on Aruba the observation of a tourist standing next to me watching the carnival parade tumbled groundward—if not in a literal physical sense then in a vernacular sense. For over five hours men and women traipsed through Oranjestad, most bejeweled and spangled. Music blared and plumes waved. Resembling feathers, some of the plumes transformed marchers into exotic birds; other plumes looked like petals turning participants into hot house flowers. After a club of young women shook past wearing pink tights and dancing the Soca, the man leaned over and grabbed my right arm, his fingers pressing hard into my triceps. "My God!" he exclaimed, "I've never seen so much tail!" "What?" I said. "Tail," he repeated, "and I know tail. I'm a Holiness minister. If I'd grown up here rather than in Georgia, what a life I'd have led." When I pried my arm free and was silent, he continued. "And I would have made it to heaven, too. The Lord wanted us to be fruitful and love other people." "Lots of other people," I said. "Do you preach fulltime?" I asked, changing the subject. "No," he said, "along with salvation I sell used kitchen appliances. If you're ever in Roswell, Georgia, and need a stove or refrigerator, look me up, and I'll give you a bargain."

He then told me an off-color story of the sort that people who believe they are "holier than thou" feel free to tell. He related the story smoothly, and I suspect that at prayer breakfasts he'd entertained gaggles of elders with it. "The first mention of Adam and Eve," he said, "appears on an ancient Sumerian tablet." According to the tablet, Adam was created the easy natural way from wind and a shovel of mud. In contrast Eve's birth was induced and was painful. Adam was hairier than his present-day descendants and was born with a massive curly tail. Instead of removing a rib from Adam's chest as Gabriel did in several Coptic texts, a maternity angel shaved Adam's backside then chopped off his tail. After unwinding the tail and stripping the hair off, he created Eve. However, the tail was so long that the angel was forced to divide it into bits in order to make a normal-sized woman. If he had not done so, Eve would have been a giantess ten cubits tall. "Waste not, want not," the preacher continued quoting the old adage, "so the angel took the remaining pieces of tail and created a bridge club of more ladies." "That's why," he concluded, "Moslem men have three or four wives." 'What do you think?" he asked at the end of the story.

"Bridge club?" I said, "Tarneeb would be better." I then started walking away from the parade back toward the cruise boat on which I'd been traveling. As could be anticipated, the theological salesman wouldn't allow me to escape easily. He fixed a glittering eye upon me and asked if I'd read the Bible. On my saying I had, he leaned forward preparatory to launching into a sermon, and also, I am sure, into a catechism on the state of my soul. By plucking an ancient literary chestnut out of the ashes of memory I forestalled him long enough to break free. I replied that reading the bible was enjoyable, but that I couldn't pretend to understand all of it. "Still," I said, "I reckon that although the fellow who wrote it wasn't a gentleman, he knew the world as well as any man that ever lived." When his friend Chestnuton asked why he didn't write more, G. F. Abbott responded lightly and revealingly, "Perhaps I have too much to say to say much." I didn't say more. Before the man replied, I hustled into a shop and dematerialized behind a rack sundresses.

The doings of church and school forever entertain. At tea back on the boat, a fellow passenger buttonholed me and praised the spread of "Smoking Allowed" churches across the South. Not only, he said, does allowing smoking, "in fact encouraging it," increase the sizes of congregations, but it makes parishioners feel at home and more comfortable. It keeps them alert during long sermons. They don't doze. "They don't slip the cables tying them to the Cross and becoming derelicts drift beyond the sound of "The Master's Holy Foghorn." The man's remarks startled Vicki. "What next?" she asked me after tea. "Christian swingers' clubs?" Vicki doesn't follow religious trends as closely as I do, and she was not aware that the "next" had already occurred. Christian swingers' clubs were wildly popular in conservative political areas of South Carolina. Many other churches, especially in Georgia and Louisiana, served beer during services. According to a self-anointed bishop, they did so in hopes of palliating parishioners' fondness for stronger drink. Not only did the beer function as a potable contraceptive preventing the "raging thirst for hard liquor" from disturbing God's Day, but by animating people's spirits, it inspired camaraderie and created community. "Now," the bishop declared, "a church picnic occurs every Sunday. People bring potluck meals, and the deacons run raffles and bingo. Children play kick-the-can and hide-and-go seek. We try to keep boys and girls from running off and hiding together, but you know how lively growing Christians are. Once we had a donkey softball game. Finding enough donkeys wasn't easy, but with the Lord's help we were successful." Moreover, imbibing produced educational results. It inspired speaking in tongues. "Not the usual 11 or 12 languages," a Professor of Bible Studies testified, "but on several blessed occasions as many as fifty and once sixty-seven."

The number of coffees with strange-sounding names served at cafés surprises me. On the other hand, nothing that churches get up or down to startles me. Because of the popularity of movies featuring ghost hunters and television shows devoted to the paranormal, no longer do Pentecostal churches in southwest Missouri condemn Halloween and its cast of supernatural beings, particularly the Devil's spawn of witches, demons, and poltergeists. Instead, recognizing the appeal of spectral beings, they now sponsor Haunted House parties in hopes of increasing the number of worshippers. The gatherings are held in abandoned buildings, usually two-story farmhouses. "We haven't found no complete ghosts as such," a minister from Lamar told the *Springfield News-Leader*, "but we've heard footsteps in basements and seen shadows running behind walls. In a kitchen cabinet we discovered a frying pan filled with dried toads, and another time we smelled something bad. A member of the vestry said it was Sulphur fumes left behind when Satan saw us and skedaddled. But a good country woman said it won't nothing but skunk cologne. She ought to know as she is the best cook in the church. She bakes pecan and chess pies for all our picnics. Her pies sustain the heart and smell sweeter than honeycombs. Praise the Lord!"

"The most exciting thing we ever ran across was a petrified foot," the minister continued; "it was wrapped in a bible calendar and stored in a chest of drawers under a pile of chairs and tables in the loft of an abandoned barn. The foot was old, and its toenails had fallen off. Dr. Samson, our local podiatrist and 'Honorary Corn Cutter to the Justices of the Missouri Supreme Court,' reckoned it might have been as much as hundred or a hundred ten years old." "I wish I could tell you if it was a right or left foot," the minister concluded, "but it won't wearing a shoe when we found it." Not all local denominations approved of "hant" parties. Several holiness ministers accused sponsors of doing the devil's work. "Trimming Lucifer's cloven hoof and sharpening his horns," a sanctified sister said. And an Episcopal minister who graduated from Virginia Theological Seminary with a taste for communion wine and common sense and who didn't subscribe to the contemporary fetish for ecumenicism was quoted as saying, "The one ghost those damn fools don't have a hope in Hell of finding is the Holy Ghost. Carved on the arch spanning the entrance to their Wonderland is "Abandon Reason All Ye Who Enter Here."

Eventually people realize that editorializing uplift on shirts or paper doesn't elevate. Although many fillers are impolitic, they are not dangerous. The influence of what one reads is exaggerated, usually by educators who want to believe their assignments have lasting effects. In contrast what a person hears often adheres to the mind like masking tape. On St. Kitts, Peter a taxi driver said that Chinese immigrants owned all the groceries. "The Chinese boys spreads like cock-a-roaches," he said. "They so fast you can't beat them." "What do you think about that?" Vicki asked later. "Nothing. The Chinese and Indians own most stores on the island. What did you think about the man from British Columbia who asked me if I was a socialist?" I replied. "You may be a socialist," Vicki said, "but the ignoramus couldn't explain the difference between a socialist and a cock-a-roach's rectum. Still, I wish you'd showed more restraint and not asked him if he was a son of a bitch. Why do you persist in acting like you forgot your dentures?"

While Turk's Head IPA is called "Down-Da-Road" on Turks and Caicos, the lager is "I-Ain-Ga-Lie." Beer might not induce lies, but it inspires fabrication and exaggeration. Moreover, hypocrisy is a refinement of lying. If hypocrisy, fabrication, and exaggeration became endangered then people would trust their leaders, choose sides, and support causes. If they stopped believing that all they heard or read was a lie, reason would abandon them. They'd become en-thusiasts and social Pentecostals. Ardor would in-flame them. Elections would matter. They'd vote, and civil war would erupt. The best prophylactic against a country's devolving into a dystopia is a regimen of lies. Swallowed not simply at breakfast and after dinner but throughout the day lies foster indifference and sanity. They keep people safely lackadaisical and as a beneficial side effect entertain. Telling the truth is not a suitable pastime for a gentleman or, indeed, for one's brother's keeper. Of course, as a person ages, distinguishing truths from lies becomes impossible as the only events that are clear to oldsters are those that never occurred.

Decades ago, in one of my books a woman showed

me George Washington's glass eye. She said Washington wore it throughout childhood, but she neglected to tell me why he quit wearing it. Curiosity doesn't kill the terrapin because he isn't impetuous. Last year I finally wrote the woman, and inside the Christmas card she sent in December, she explained what precipitated Washington's discarding the eye "although it was pretty and blue and veins didn't pump through it exploding in red clots." It even had an easy-to-reach latch attached so Washington could wink at girl babies. Schooling caused Washington to forsake the eye despite its being a Christian eye and never leading him into sin. In third grade, the woman wrote, Washington's teacher interested him in books, especially Indian stories. Because the stories were exciting and Washington couldn't read them as fast as he wanted, "he growed another eye. There weren't room in the socket for two eyes, and when the new eye got big it rolled its little brother out of the socket like a cowbird pushing another chick out of a nest." After removing a cataract from behind the iris, Washington's father sold the glass eye to a pack peddler. In turn the peddler traded it to the woman's "great-great-great grannie" for a jar of watermelon rind pickles. Every December thereafter the eye blinked at the family from a pool of homemade bourbon atop the Christmas fruit cake. On Christmas day when the cake was sliced, folks around the table pressed their hands together in prayer and said, "Dear Lord bless this heavenly sweetness and this eye which almost saw the things that made the Father of our Country first in war, first in peace, and first in the hearts of his countrymen."

Lying is compensatory and calming. When fret causes a person's nerves to kick up their dendrites, he ought to tell a merry lie rather than swallow a happy

115

pill. I have written books for forty-five years. Occasionally readers send me letters, but mostly "they doesn't." Lying does not fill my mailbox, but it drives moody isolation from my mind. Before thoughts about the lack of letters discourages me, I craft a patented cure-all, usually letters but sometimes telephone calls or more recently book inscriptions. "Dear Billy," Claire wrote on the recto page of *Trespassing*, a collection of my essays published in 1994, "I found this book in a second-hand clothing and junk store on Hunts Point. I know you will love it. Good old Sammy. We always said he'd amount to something. Dear, oh, dear, you and Beth and Sammy and me—I wish we could relieve those scarlet days when we were able enjoy all the pleasures to which flesh was heir to."

"I was so sorry to hear about Beth. I should have written you. But John had recently abandoned me. and how many women have three husbands who walk out the door without a word of explanation and never return, not even to pack their toothbrushes? In case one reappears, I keep a pot of oil boiling on the stove. But all phantasmagoric recipes aside, how fortunate you are to have unforgettable memories of Beth. Do you remember the cook-and-drink-outs at Sea Island and dancing in the moonlight? Those were nights of splendor in the sand. Even the hurricane of time cannot wash them away. And, of course, how glorious it must be for you to have the lovely twins. I heard on the ivy vine that Katie is studying physics at Princeton. Is Bill still exploring the world working on tramp steamers? They must make you proud and happy. But I sure hope you have warned Katie about Southern boys. If you haven't, do so immediately—Ha! Ha!"

"Oh, gosh—how or why I let Sammy slip out of

my arms, I don't know. It just happened. I was young and foolish. I dreamed of—gee, I dreamed about a lot of stupid things—and didn't realize I already held the key to happiness in my hands. Still, I, too, have memories, certainly not as wonderful as yours of Beth. I think of my recollections as flowers. Like me they are dried and blown, and their petals are rusty, but their fragrance lingers, thin on the air, but still it lingers. Well, Billy, if I think any more about the past, I'll weep. Enjoy the book. It will make you smile. Like you, Sammy was a really good fellow, too good, I guess, for my world. All my love, Claire. P. S: I'll bet you don't know what people dub a shorty who lives in a big city, works in the music industry, and is as regular as clockwork in his habits? They call him— Ho! Ho! Wait for it!—a metronome!"

When I finished the inscription, I read it to Vicki. "Doesn't it make you want to thump me on the back and exclaim, 'You're the man'?" I asked. "Not exactly," Vicki replied. That afternoon after I treated Vicki to lunch at McDonald's, I drove to the Mansfield Library and donated the book to the annual one-dollar sale. At the circulation desk a woman was checking out Elmore Leonard's *Maximum Bob*. Printed on the front of the woman's sweatshirt was the statement, "Vaccinations Cause Adults." "What does that mean?" Vicki asked me. The woman overheard Vicki's question. "Kids whose parents don't get them vaccinated for childhood diseases," she said, answering Vicki, "often remain children for all their short lives. Only kids who have been vaccinated live long enough to become adults."

Age is largely responsible for the repetitive nature of my doings. Forgetfulness constricts and determines the lives of "Old Guys." Last week, my friend

David wrote me. "On driving home yesterday," he recounted, "I left my car idling in front of the garage while I fetched the key to unlock the garage door. I carried the key to the door, unlocked it and opened it. Then I returned the key to its hiding place. Next, I walked back to the garage door, shut it, and locked it. Only then did I happen to notice, to my complete surprise, that my car was still idling outside the garage."

People are what others think them. How a person sees himself doesn't matter. How others view him shapes his identity. In February Vicki and I attended the Pride Parade and Gay Street Fair in Fort Lauderdale. Around our necks we hung Mardi Gras beads and on a multicolored ribbon a yellow whistle. We blew our whistles repeatedly practically deafening ourselves. We felt comfortable and thought we were indistinguishable from everybody else at the fair. I was mistaken. Suspended over one booth was a blue banner. Printed on it in white letters was a mysterious phrase I hadn't seen before. I assumed the phrase referred to an exotic intimate matter, but I wasn't sure, so I asked the men manning the booth what the phrase meant. "I'm sorry, sir," the first man said. "I can't tell you." When I looked at the other man, he nodded in agreement and said, "sir, we can't tell you." Once I was too young to know certain things; now I am too old.

Age has moved me into a gated intellectual community, and I rarely stray beyond familiar neighborhood sidewalks. Some days, though, when a Claire or a Billy comes to mind trailing seductive reminiscences, I disconnect the television and reread a travel book. Such books make me wistful for the years in which I dreamed of adventure. Throughout my life bookishness has not been a short-lived flu; it has been a lasting fever, malarial in its reoccurrence. Although antibodies countering the effects of reading practically block my cerebral arteries, once in a while a book influences my behavior. This past spring, I reread Colin Thubron's *In Siberia*, a hauntingly wondrous account of wandering beyond the Urals in the 1990s. Shortly thereafter Vicki and I were in St. Lucia on Pigeon Island. Years ago, we hiked to the top of Signal Peak. Although the path was rocky and steep, the climb was only 330 feet. On this occasion we walked along the shore toward a Carib cave beneath Fort Rodney. We skirted a fence blocking our way and crossing a slide of tumbled boulders reached the end of the path. In front of us gapped the remains of the cave, its entrance shattered by a hurricane. Vicki then stopped and retraced our steps along the shore, but suffering from travel book hangover, a virulent form of irrationality, I decided to beat a path up a cliff face to the fort. I had forgotten my age. The climb was only slightly over 200 feet, initially over the trunks and through the branches of toppled trees. Beyond the trees the ascent sharpened almost to perpendicular. I did not climb so much as pull myself upward, grabbing tufts of lemon grass and bushes. I lodged my feet against rocks, many of which broke loose and fell banging down to the shore. In places I squirmed sideways and digging my elbow into clods of dirt shimmied upward, turning from my stomach onto my back. Two-thirds the way up the cliff face, the muscles in my left arm revolted rendering the arm useless. Often, I lost my grip and slid downward, halting falls by hooking my feet and hands in thickets of bushes. I pondered reversing and descending, but I lacked energy enough to bore back through the broken trees.

When I reached the lip of the bluff, I was covered

with dirt and awash with blood. While branches and sharp blades of grass minced my palms, rocks ground furrows into my legs. I rolled over the top of the bluff onto the edge of a path leading to Fort Rodney. I lay on my back too exhausted to haul myself off the ground. A group of local women suddenly appeared on the path and crowded around me. "Call an ambulance," a kindly woman said. "He needs to go to a hospital." "No, don't call anyone," I said. "Please don't. I'm fine. I just need to rest." When the number of women hovering over me like nurses reached a dozen, embarrassment invigorated me. I rolled over and pulling my feet under me staggered fifteen yards on all-threes, my left arm dangling. Two women then hurried down the path in search of Vicki. "You husband is at the fort," they said on finding her. "He is bleeding, but he is probably all right. You better go get him." Vicki ran up and urged me to go down the hill and rest. "At times," she said, "life turns us into jackasses, but why do you persist in braying so repeatedly?" "Reading is responsible," I said. Then against common sense and Vicki's wishes I forced myself to climb to the top of Signal Hill—alas, bowed, and so bloody that each of the six people I met coming down asked if I was "okay."

That night blood and serum trickled down my arms and legs, spotting my clothes and gluing the fabrics to me. However, a change purse of scabs formed, some penny-sized but three or so dollars-worth of dandy fifty-cent pieces. I had not wandered "Russia's Elsewhere" or experienced "an indelible fear" as had Thubron. My climb had been foolish, the stuff of head-shaking reproof not admiration. But I felt euphoric. Time had not completely obliterated the old me, Charles Kingsley's green lad who once cried "hey for boot and horse" and set off "round the world away." For years in Storrs I invariably returned home from hiking bruised and bone-cracked, so frequently that instead of saying hello Vicki greeted me asking, "what have you done now, lummox?" Of course, as one ages the walls of gated communities become thicker. Moreover, people become simpler. They swallow the pap spooned out by gerontologists and think that they ought to change or "progress." On television, physicians urge older people to forgo meat. During my life I have eaten abattoirs of animals including coral reefs of crustaceans. Last year, though, aside from joining Vicki when I treated her to McDoubles, I heeded dietary suggestions and ate little meat. In St. Kitts I applauded myself after noticing slogans painted on the side of a Rasta food van, among them: "Where You Never Taste Death," "Your Health Is Your Wealth," and "Let Thy Food Be Thy Medicine And Thy Medicine Be Thy Food."

Often, I think words more interesting than what they say. Actually, I may have eaten less meat because I liked using Rasta expressions. "No more lotal (unclean food) for me," I told Vicki, "no buried food (canned goods), and don't open the door to the morgue (refrigerator)." I only used Rasta words that referred to food. When I went to the barber shop, I did not instruct Holly to hide the "Three Unclean Spirits" (combs, scissors, and razors) out of sight. Neither did I refer to Christian revivalists as racketeers although collection-plate filchings are as common in tent meetings as bank robberies in small towns. Despite dietary cheerleaders chanting, "you can do it," habits endure. Recently I've fallen off the vegetable cart. In Martinique I ate a blood pudding as long as a Billy club, and on Curacao a bowl of iguana soup.

The iguana was bony but went well with Polar beer. I slid so far off the vegetable counter that in Fort-de-France, I chopped a claw off a dead iguana. Once it stops fermenting, I'll display it on the windowsill of my study amid the miscellany of feathers, tails, snake skins, and small skulls I've collected during the past four decades.

I have written hundreds of pages describing trees and flowers. I bought shelves of guides and for half a century labored to get things right, that is, portray plants where I saw them, and as I saw, touched, tasted, or smelled them. Now I think the compulsion to be accurate a species of mental illness. People are most susceptible during their middle years. The illness dries the creative juices and shrivels the imagination. According to *The Forceps*, it clips the mind's primary feathers and keeps the soul earthbound. Mark Twain wrote that he "would move a state if the exigencies of literature required it." For my part I now move trees and alter their blooming seasons not because book-ishness requires it but simply, and sensibly, if whim suggests it. Because of my age I plant trees and flowers in a Mount Auburn Cemetery of the mind, the tomb-stones and graves providing grounding enough.

As climbing the bluff below Fort Rodney il-lustrated, I have lost the strength of youth and am incapable of devoting more than an hour a day to gardening despite my hoeing being on the page and not in the yard. In a bare spot from which I recently cleared tangles of poison ivy, I planted trumpet trees. They are good colonizers and restore topsoil. Age erodes trust and naïve optimism, and so surrounding my Mount Auburn are two protective palisades, the first composed of candelabra spurge or euphorbia lactea, the second of sweet acacia or needle bush. In an old pasture in the middle of the cemetery stand two massive trees, a great raintree, bromeliads flaring from its branches in cowlicks and then a baobab. The baobab once grew in Independence Park in Basseterre. It was the only baobab in St. Kitts, but I stole it and replanted it. The cemetery is lush with oleander and yellow bells, orange manjack, and noni, all attracting bouquets of butterflies. Umbrella trees are punk with spikes, and the paddle-shaped leaves of Indian almonds canoe the air. Only imagination limits the variety of plants. Here stands a foxtail palm, there, a dragon's blood tree with curtain walls oozing from the trunk and snaking viscous across the ground. Just beyond the entrance of the cemetery is a grove of woman's tongues. The broad bean pods are dry and gold, and in a breeze, visitors can hear them whispering. Unlike its namesake in Cambridge, which is confined to 175 acres, my Mount Auburn enjoys unlimited land. Throughout the year meadows are dazzling plats of wildflowers, the colors more various than those found in a box of crayons. "Only the blessed live scenic deaths," an acquaintance stated urging me to expand the cemetery. Last week I planted small crown flower, a milkweed common in the Caribbean. Although its flowers blossom in clusters of broad purple stars, I hadn't noticed the plant until this year.

Ponds turn through the cemetery in a string of blue pearls. The ponds are alive with fish, all the varieties saltwater. In an imaginary cemetery, the density and mineral content of water don't matter. The alert mourner can easily spot blue tangs, sergeant majors, and four-eyed butterfly fish. If he dangles his legs in the water, blue-headed wrasses will glean dead skin from his feet. While black durgeons waver by shyly, a school of bar jacks rumpuses along, their dorsal fins slicing out of the water into the air. A purple and yellow fairy basslet hovers under a ledge. A needle-fish hangs beside a sea fan, and a juvenile spotted trunkfish presses itself into the sand looking like a change purse.

Unlike Cambridge's Mount Auburn, no famous people are buried in my cemetery: no Longfellow, no Julia Ward Howe, none of the Lowells, Holmes's, or Lodges, no Winslow Homer or Thomas Bailey Aldrich. Despite my admiration for successful magazine writers, Fanny Fern and Nathaniel Parker Willis are in Cambridge. I practically worship naturalists, but sadly Louis Agassiz and William Hamilton Gibson are already taken. In comparison to those of the most recognized writers, the afterlife of a popular essayist is short. No one would notice the removal of Robert Lynd, my favorite essayist, from Belfast City Cemetery. However, accomplishing the transfer would necessitate disinterring Burke and Hare the famous Edinburgh body-snatchers. If all Rhadamanthus' horses and men couldn't piece the two back together, I'd have to draft another member of the resurrectionist lodge, preferably one buried recently and in better physical shape. Alas, such thoughts are fantasies. Unlike purloining trees, moving corpses requires reams of paperwork and numberless assuaging visits to senile ghostly relatives.

The headstones in my cemetery are upright gray granite stones with rounded tops. No names or carvings appear on the stones. Instead chaplets of lichens adorn them, firedot and rock shield among others. The stones are 24 inches tall and 18 broad and stand on small stabilizing pedestals buried in the ground. In the graveyard there are no statues, obelisks, mausoleums, pyramids, or Greek or Mayan temples. I chose not to bury university friends in my cemetery despite the importuning of several who believe the interments would save their families a great deal of money, enough, Tim said, for Audrey to buy a second-hand Honda. However. a graveyard without bodies is dead, so I've decided to raid the Pillow of Heaven cemetery in Carthage, Tennessee, and exhume hearses of characters whom I created decades ago.

They had almost turned to dust along with the books in which they appeared. But I suspect that ungodly nature of present-day Southern politics so horrified them that they hadn't quite sailed up Salt River, and they will settle happily in their new surroundings and feel reborn. How grand it will be to shovel old corpses into new graves: Hoben Donkin, Loppie Groat, Dr. Sollows, Googoo Hooberry and his cousin Cerumen, Big Mealy Timmons, the Pankeys, Turlow Gutheridge, Hink Ruunt, Proverbs Goforth, Mathuzulum Guppy, LaBelle Watrous, Vester McBee, Bevie Povey, and Clevanna Farquarhson, amid a charnel house more. The Revered Slubey Garts will preside at the reburials. Obed Eells will want to preach, but the ponds on the grounds aren't deep enough for him to sail in on The Old Ship of Zion blowing a trumpet and announcing Judgment Day. Let me assure queasy day trippers that although the corpses moving into my Mount Auburn have long been entombed in moribund books, they haven't moldered. Although they are no longer fresh, livor mortis has not turned them purple. I suspect that when I was absent writing about Scotland or Australia, they distilled several barrels of Live Forever Water

So that their new home won't be dislocating, I have already brought Barrow's Grocery, Ankerrow's Café, and Battery Hill up from Carthage. I put the grocery and café across the street opposite the entrance to the cemetery. Because the cemetery is measureless to man, I placed Battery Hill inside the grounds and sowed it with daffodils. Difference invigorates. So that my old companions won't sink into inactive ways, I fetched a Rasta lunch wagon, the Exodus Juice Bar from Marigot in St. Maarten. I placed the bar just inside the cemetery so it will be the first commercial establishment my friends see when they go for stroll on a hot day. The bar is yellow, and painted on one side is a portrait of Hailee Selassie in full dress, a raised bed of medals flowering across his chest. In Marigot the bar specialized in smoothies and made the best mango smoothie I ever drank. The bar brewed and will continue to brew twenty different smoothies, among them, carrot, soursop, guava, pineapple, kale, spinach, celery, prune, papaya, and beet. Most of my characters are conservative, and none has ever guzzled a smoothie, but I hope they'll be adventuresome. Perhaps the duppies (ghosts) manning the bar will become creative and expand their menu, adding quinoa, parsnip, turnip, arugula, and tofu smoothies among others.

Well, that's enough writing. I am tired. A drizzle is falling, and the day is cold. Branches are pasted against the sky and look like cracks scoring the bottom of a dishwater-worn bowl. Occasionally a crow flies overhead wings blinking like eyelashes. Once I drop my pencil, I'm leaving the house and neighborhood and going to Mount Auburn. There the day is warm and sunny, and the breeze is a zephyr. A year ago, I planted an alley of scrambled egg trees. They're blooming, the bunches of flowers so yellow they look like hope. I'll nap in the alley, and when I wake, I'll stroll over to a nearby walk and bath in the purple fragrance of the bauhinias or orchid trees a wealthy reader of my books gave me at Christmas. Incidentally, my readers are wildly various and live everywhere in the world: in a lamasery in Shangri-La, on one of Nova Zembla's ice floes, and in a mud hut in wind-blown Timbuktu. While a woman on the shores of Lake Titicaca raises giant frogs for the Bastille Market in Paris, a man lives in a house pasted like a limpet to a volcano on Kamchatka and heats his rooms with steam billowing from a thermal spring.

Over time readers have grown fond of me. When I was young, my thoughts were plain, and I analyzed them in a simple honest style. People bought my volumes, but nobody mailed me a gift. Now my style is often cosmetological. In one paragraph appears a beauty spot; in the next a false adjective, high on the cheekbones of a page an all-day blush. Rather than appreciative notes, readers now send plants. "Your writing," Josh explained "is a suggestive mulch." "For the literary orangery," a man wrote then quoted John Leonard Knapp who said, "The love of flowers seems a naturally implanted passion...We scatter them over the shell, the bier, and the earth, when we consign our mortal blossoms to the dust, as emblems of transient joy, fading pleasures, withered hopes; yet rest in sure and certain trust that each in due season will be renewed again." Knapp was a memorable naturalist. Would that a kindly grave robber with agrostological inclinations would ship me Knapp's bones and his knowledge of grasses.

During the month following the publication of *The World Was My Garden, Too*, hardly a day passed without a DHL truck driving to Mount Auburn carrying a flat of plants. To accommodate the plants,

I built a potting shed. I erected it out of sight behind the Rasta wagon. To prevent the duppies from
raiding it in hopes of fashioning an exotic list of floral
smoothies I hung an iron portcullis before the shed's
doors. I'm an experienced looter, and I stole the portcullis from a crumbling barbican in Wales. Although
season doesn't affect the plants, it influences me. I have
transplanted some of the plants, but I won't replant
the rest until spring settles and the temperature rises.
In most shadowy spots in the cemetery, however, I've
hung Philippine orchids or rose grapes. The blossoms
dangle in eighteen-inch bundles. Their yellow centers
flicker and backlight the flowers' petals, making them
glow like pink Depression glass, turning them into
botanic lanterns. Throughout the cemetery I intend to
plant jasmine and Indian hawthorn. Their fragrances
evoke doxologies.

No matter having been hearty eaters when alive,
the dead have small appetites. To satisfy the ghostly
need for an occasional snack, I planted dwarf Cav-
endish bananas. Because they are little and can be
eaten on the run, the bananas serve as the graveyard
equivalent of fast food. Moreover, the potassium in
bananas has beneficial postmortem effects. It slows
the production of hydrogen sulfide and methane
thereby reducing the bloat associated with decompo-
sition and mitigating what to overly sensitive nares
is a noxious aroma. No Mortuary Science university
has definitively ascertained the volume of liquid a
ghost should consume each day in order to remain
healthy. The smoothies at the Rasta bar ought to ensure that my characters stay marinated. However, hot
summer can cause fatal dehydration. To supplement
the smoothies, by July I hope to have planted pitcher
plants throughout the graveyard. I intend to plant

nepenthes truncate which has extraordinarily large pitchers resembling bedroom slippers. The pitchers collect water and will serve as water fountains. If a ghost fears becoming dehydrated, all he need do to replenish the liquids in what was his body is drink the contents of a pitcher. While on the subject of dryness, let me add that I've planted only one cactus in the cemetery, the woody torch (Cleistocactus strauseii). Its round, slender columns can grow ten feet tall. A fur of gray spines covers them, and in the moonlight, the columns look like silver fingers pointing skyward, guiding lost wanderers toward the celestial.

Religious metaphors make me uncomfortable, as they do my characters, none of whom including the preachers, will ever leave this world. Here, on the earth, they believe is where and what people should worship. So that visitors will not be led astray by rarefied metaphysics, I have strewn rooted treasure chests of flowers across the cemetery, among others, pink ball or tropical hydrangea, its flowers hanging downward in red clusters, from a distance looking like powder puffs, and blue ginger, blooming in steeples, its petals indigo, mustaches of white streaking them, their centers hunks of melted butter. Winding through trees are golden trumpet vines, the inside of the flowers' bells white, thin lines wavering down them in blushes, making them look like peppermint candy.

Beauty is ethereal and sometimes is dangerous. Too much beauty can compromise character. It may so divert a person that his roots break from the soil causing his thoughts, and emotions, to be wafted about like cirrus clouds, hazy and thin, unanchored by any grainy reality actual or imagined. As a panacea throughout Mount Auburn appears a pharmacy of plants. These focus vision on the palpable. They tether perception to the immediate and make observers marvel at the diversity of the here-and-now earth. The plant kingdom is carnivalesque. Although its shows are countless, let me give two examples of the eye and foot stoppers now growing in the cemetery. Clinging to limbs is the epiphyte anthurium Wendlingeri, sometimes called strap leaf anthurium. The plant's green leaves hang off branches in rubbery clumps. They can be five feet long and half a foot wide and look like razor strops force-fed somatotropin or human growth hormone, a "bug juice" far more powerful than the old standby three-in-one fertilizers loaded with phosphorus, nitrogen, and potassium. Also thriving is alocasia cuprea, one of the jewel alocasias. The leaves of my plants are a foot long and half a foot wide and look like waffle irons. Their upper surfaces are coppery green. They appear plasticized, and from their mid-ribs dark veins split off in pairs, on most of my plants ten pairs.

"Of making many books there is no end," *Ecclesiastes* warned. Traditionally *Ecclesiastes* was attributed to Solomon. Modern scholarship generally rejects the attribution. Would that the word *books* were an erroneous translation and that the word had vanished from the text, leaving readers to supply what they will. While one reader might fill the blank with *tales,* another might detect ghostly vestiges of *lies* on the original manuscript. For my part I am indecisive. Life is repetitive. I suspect that tomorrow Claire will come to mind. She won't write me, but she may inscribe another of my books—if she can find one. Last month flood waters in southern Illinois swept away a storage container packed with remaindered copies of my writings. The high water washed the container down the Mississippi River. For a time, the container vanished and was thought lost, but then passengers holidaying on American Cruise Lines' ship *Queen of the Mississippi* spotted it lodged on a sandbar near Natchez. However, before a river scavenger could wrap a chain around it and pull it from the bar, a current lifted it off the sand and it was last seen bobbing around an eroded wing dam. Ten days later a Vietnamese shrimper netted a copy of *May Days* in the Gulf of Mexico, but all the other volumes sank without leaving an inky trace behind. Of course, if Claire does appear, I'll probably miss her as I intend to revisit Tennessee and resuscitate more of my old characters. I will welcome them on Rogation Sunday and set out Adirondack chairs and a table silver and pink with the chalice-like blossoms of King Protea. Cups of the flowers are eight inches deep and at the lip five and a half inches wide. When overflowing with Tennessee milk and honey, that is, bourbon, a chalice could be wantonly inspiriting, dangerous to any tippler, even to skeletons that have lost their lower jaws and are only calvariums.

Maybe I can reduce alcohol's injurious effects by serving hornbill ginger blossoms. They are the size of cupcakes and look appetizing. Flowers tangle over them resembling shreds of cherry and orange icing. From the flowers long white stamens swing out loosely like strips of coconut. Beside the cakes I'll set out a platter heaped with blossoms of Napoleonaea beninensis, a shrub native to West Africa. Not only is the fragrance of the flowers buttery, but the flowers are the size of pats of butter. When my characters were alive, their appetites were conventional. Although I don't know how death has affected their palates, I hope that cupcakes and butter will still appeal

131

to them and that they'll eat or imagine eating enough to ameliorate the consequences of swilling. But on the other hand, my ornate dietary preparations might be for naught. Perhaps I won't go to Tennessee. Instead I may harrow a distant plot of Mount Auburn. In case some of my corpses are overweight, I will plant chalta or elephant apple. The fruits look like grapefruit, but the rind is thick and almost impenetrable. To extract the meat, obese corpses will have to put their scapulas to the wheel. In the process they'll grind away kilograms of unhealthy flesh. Moreover, buds on my snowflake aralias are swelling, and I should stay home and get the plants into the ground before they burst into clusters of coronets.

Roadway

While travel formed "part of the education" of the young, Bacon wrote, for the "elder" it was "part of experience." If by experience, Bacon implied that travel changed the old, rounding or deepening character and enriching sensibility, he was wrong. Vicki and I travel in search of nothing. Our formative nomadic days are over. For a month every winter we tent alongside tourist docks in the Caribbean. In summer we are dutiful residents of the nineteenth-century sea captain's house in Nova Scotia that Vicki's parents bought seventy-three years ago. We clean and trim. We paste and hammer. We scrub mildew. We struggle to keep collapse a nail's length away. The work exhausts us, and we are losing, really have lost, the fight. Trees fall, and the unruly scrub creeps closer. The roof leaks, and molding falls and shatters. Our strength has ebbed with the years, and worry smothers our spirits. We know that during the summer the water pump will fail, the telephone will die, doors will break from their hinges, and window frames will bow and splinter. The roof of the barn will begin to sag again, and the concrete floor of the backhouse will crack and furrow. All that will happen has happened before. All that we will say has been said, and thought, before.

Decades ago, I traveled and was adventuresome. Now when walking itself can be dangerous, I avoid risk. In June I fell off my bicycle. I landed on my left hip and arm. Bruises bloomed along my side, but I bounced up, bent and embarrassed but unbroken. I don't need to take chances in order to prove myself to myself. If success exists, I have succeeded beyond what others may have imagined my dreams. For my part, though, I've never been a dreamer. When I was young, I was too untalented to entertain fanciful expectations. Because my expectations were modest and sensible, if indeed I had expectations, I avoided failure's disappointments and frustrations. Long have I enjoyed the quiet of abstinence and avoidance. I studiously know less now than I once did. However, ignorance is the yoga of thought and keeps a person intellectually limber.

Ignorance's relative Curiosity is the second greatest of the eight Cardinal Attributes, only a photo finish nose behind Decency. In any case, the days of curious people are sweet with small delights. Like soft ice cream, the delights aren't the frozen stuff of opinion. They appeal to the mental palate and are evanescent and forgettable. The London plane tree, Josh told me this spring, is a cross between a sycamore and an oriental plane tree. The hybrid is more vigorous than either parent and is "a gift to city landscapers." The tree develops rapidly and thrives amid pollution. The plane tree's bark is brittle and grows slower than its trunk. Consequently, unlike other trees the plane tree isn't poisoned by grime. Before dirt blocks the tiny pores through which gases move back and forth, the trunk grows and shatters the tight-fitting bark. It drops the soiled, aging pieces in flakes and exposing fresh new bark breathes easily. As thick bark would kill the plane tree, so certainty hardens joints and hearts and causes numbing attacks of dogma.

To the wise a word is never sufficient. By the by, of the making of aphorisms there is no end. As a result, maxims intended to button subjects down behind periods trail off in a ragamuffin of colons, semicolons, dashes, and glottal starts. That aside, though, the conversation of most Americans is confined to sport or politics, fatuities that elicit soggy trite responses. The subjects dampen thought, turn the mind moldy, and inhibit inclinations to reverie. However, on the positive side of things, the subjects have enabled me to perfect the vacuous gaze, a contraceptive useful in all intimate social situations.

Early June in Storrs was an easel displaying a canvas white as fresh bark on a London plane tree. Mountain laurel bloomed in great soft mounds along the Fenton River transforming banks into Artic landscapes. The white was so pure that it swept other colors out of sight. As water broke through rapids in the river, spray shined white rather than silver. Bushes of multiflora roses bloomed in shaggy old fields. The clean fragrance of the flowers swept notions of invasive plants from the mind. Amid low grassy weeds, chickweed, yarrow, and fuzzy white clover blossomed. Tree swallows swirled and dived through the air above a beaver pond. When the swallows rose, their undersides shook in choppy white splashes only to break and tumble from sight as the birds curled away. Whitetails and spangled skimmers pulsed across the tussock sedges and muddy overflow pools at the edge of the pond, the white stigmas on the forewings of the skimmers bobbing like flags waved by railway linemen.

The world is colorful and staining. Smoothness is pot-holed, and whiteness does not last. Other colors soon animate days. They come bringing beauty and are responsible for shaded livability vital with diversity—tears, laughter, happiness, horror, absurdity, all the long and short moments with their limitless possibilities. Beyond the beaver pond goldfinches scrambled through alders. "Fussy enchanting sparklers spangled with song," Vicki said. From a ditch the stems of hemlock thrust up smooth-shaven but ridged and mottled with purple. In dry sand pinks blushed with merriment, and vetch climbed across bedstraw, its flowers stacked above each other looking like the roofs of blue pagodas clustered on a steep hillside. On many walks I started home when gnats swarmed my eyes turning my cheeks into shoals. Even though the gnats swam across my sight in waves of floaters, I saw many things. A wood turtle basked on a bicycle path. I carried the turtle four yards from the trail and put her down in an equally sunny, sleep-inducing, but safer, spot. Outside the university library, I rescued a small kit that three crows had herded into the right angle of a cement wall. I freed the rabbit in a thick patch of blue flag surrounding a sunken drain.

Alas, in my front yard, I found the body of a young opossum. A hawk or an owl had probably killed the opossum because the body was limber and fresh. I sheared off the tail, and placing it in a jar, submerged it in a blend of water and Clorox. I don't know why I removed the tail. But, of course, I cannot explain many things I do. Explaining the actions of others is easier. I think I know why a son ended the obituary of his mother, writing, "Bingo goes on as before." Bingo appeared this spring in several obituaries, the references at first startling but then spare and poignant, an observation revealing much about the pastimes and loneliness of old age. "Uncle Harold" never married, and his favorite activity, his nephew wrote, was "calling the numbers in Bingo at the Knights of Columbus Hall on Monday nights." Still, I cannot imagine what motivated a daughter to say of her mother, "She finally has the smoking hot body she always wanted." But then why did I dream last night that I was sleeping beside a wizened old tailor? His skin was brown and sagged against the bones atop his hands like tent awnings. His fingers had dried and crinkling inward turned his hands into claws. To assure him, not me, that he was alive, I patted one of his hands every hour or so. What I am sure of, though, is that after putting the jar containing the opossum's tail on a shelf in the garage, I walked behind the house and studied the nest I'd watched a robin build in a rhododendron. The bird was off the nest, but in it lay four azure eggs—finer than porcelain laid out for a stately celebration.

Curiosities abound although items people today think odd were humdrum in the nineteenth century. Hanging on the wall in the back parlor of our house in Nova Scotia is an oval gold frame. Behind the glass blooms a memorial garden composed of flowers woven from the hair of dead family members. Because many people died before growing old, the flowers are red, brown, and black as well as gray and white. In a frame upstairs is a large windowpane flounder. The flounder is more colorful than the usual bottom-dweller because its scales are the elytra of beetles common in the Maritimes. Most of the scales came from ground and tiger beetles: the bright green fiery searcher, the dark Lacustrine gazelle, and the hairy-necked tiger with inlets of cream pooling up from the margins into the brownish main of the elytra. Time and its legions of devouring mites have made many scales difficult to identify. Moreover, half a beetle is not a whole beetle. Still, some elytra are easily recognizable: the broad and robust elytra of the tunneling large pedunculate beetle and that of the orange and black nicrophorus carrion beetles. While deep groves run streaked down the back of the antelope stag beetle, the European chafer is a familiar early summer nighttime visitor to screen doors. The flounder's eyes are lady beetles. I think they're seven-spotted, but I am not positive as time and sunlight have cataracted me and them.

In the long nights of Canadian winters when chores enough had been done, people, often but not always women, amused themselves by creating curiosities. A neighbor's great grandmother cultivated a patch of wildflowers: dandelions, buttercups, pasture roses, and sheep laurel among others, all the blossoms white and fashioned from fish bones as befitting a seaside community. I wondered what fish the bones came from, probably Atlantic salmon, haddock, Gaspereau herring, and maybe beached sea ravens. Of course, the grandmother would have known the sources of her stems and petals. I hardly know a dorsal from a tail fin and didn't recognize the origin of any anthers or sepals. I haven't boned a fish in decades, and the only fish bones I come across are culinary surprises.

At night in Connecticut when I am too tired to climb up stairs and go to bed, I turn on the television and start a movie on Netflix. The movies are unfailingly mediocre. Almost never do I watch one to the end. The single benefit is that they are so exasperating that they invigorate. I mutter a rude imprecation, switch off the television, and hike upstairs to the bedroom. A hundred and sixty years ago, the inhabitants of house like ours in Beaver River occupied their weary hours with other, and from our perspective, odder things. In a garage sale in Salmon River, I once saw, and should have bought, a wooden shield eighteen inches from top to bottom and sixteen inches wide at its broadest. Extending from the shield's center was a carved right forearm and hand. The wrist was rotated slightly, and except for the index finger the fingers turned inward and bunched together in the palm. The shield was a homemade religious icon as the index finger pointed skyward. Wrapping the arm was the sleeve of a presentable coat woven from wood. The sleeve was well-tailored and stopped an inch and a half below the base of the thumb allowing room for a shirt cuff to obtrude. The coat had been painted black and the cuff white. Both were worn, and the paints were chipped although the naked wood underneath was unscratched.

Like many people I keep a Christmas or Valentine's Day list of curiosities. On the latter is "My Mistress's Hair," a poem written in the late sixteenth century by a man, whose surname may have been Whattley or Waitley. I haven't found a printed copy. Despite being composed in a sturdy, sinewy age, the poem was probably too prurient for the page. Years ago, in London while reading through cartons of deservedly neglected letters, I discovered two references to the poem. Both included descriptions of the poem and "a gentleman's sampler" of fetid lines, unquotable in the present uterine moment. Some of the sacred poems in George Herbert's *The Temple* (1633) resemble the shapes of their subjects, an Altar and Easter Wings, for example. Similarly, lines of Whattley's poem resembled hair. A trimmed ornate stanza looked like a lock tied in a ribbon while in a couplet strands dangled from a pillow like Alexandrines. Near the end of the poem appeared a quatrain composed of trochees. In a trochaic foot an unstressed syllable follows a stressed syllable. When sketched, a short straight line represents the initial stressed syllable and a curved or frizzled line the unstressed. If consecutive feet were drawn, the writers noted, the illustration would be pudendal.

As Valentine's Day now has little to do with affection but is a commercial card day, so the items on my Valentine's list don't really intrigue me. They are simply curiosities left over from bookish months I spent in British libraries in the 1970s. If I discovered a copy of Whattley's poem, I'd likely treat it as I do movies on Netflix, start but not finish it. The single literary curiosity I remain eager to see no longer exists. When Puritans plundered the monasteries in the 1530s, they destroyed the only copy of a medieval mummers play in which Satan was self-sacrificing and heroic and God fallible and viciously human. In the play God falls in love with his creation Eve. To prevent God from committing incest and being damned for eternity, Satan transforms himself into the Serpent and seduces Eve himself. He does so despite finding Eve's appearance repulsive. Moreover, he realizes that his action will arouse God's jealousy and kindle an enduring anger that will fuel the flames of Hell and condemn him to eternal misery. In sacrificing himself for Man, Satan becomes a holy Christ figure, particularly if the play is read through the iconographic filter of the *Patrialogia Latina*.

Vicki and I did not drive to Canada during the smooth white week of early June. We set off in July. By then metaphoric cockleburs clung to the hours, and days were dappled at best and pocked at worst. I can't manage an automatic teller machine and have never used a debit card. "Convenient" modern parking meters mystify me, and as a result after Vicki visits the eye doctor I refuse to stop in West Hartford for lunch. Not once have I held a cell phone. I don't have a web page, and I haven't signed on to Facebook. I am not a know-nothing recluse or a philosophic leveler. I don't smash looms. I just don't use them. For me anonymity, negligence, and the incompetence that distances me from freneticism are agreeable. Pasted on the wall of the branch of Bank of America in Storrs are two posters. On them appear employees of the bank smiling and welcoming customers. The figures are larger than life, as are, the posters imply, the employees' decency and competence. Printed on the first poster is, "Talk to us. We can help." On the second is the question, "What would you like the power to do?" If I'd had the power to do a smidgen of the things I imagined, I would never have had a bank account. More than likely, I would have spent the past sixty years of my life in solitary confinement. Instead I did what other people told me and society demanded I do. I now have three bank accounts, savings in four retirement funds, and untold monetary worries. Insofar as asking for help, I avoid problem solvers. In the shadows behind every problem lurks a battalion of raw unanticipated effects. Of course, if I came down with virulent financial dysentery and my savings began to leak away, I could consult the Bank of America's "Chief Client Care Executive." Scheduling an appointment, however, might be difficult. I suspect the Executive is always busy as I have never observed anyone wearing scrubs, much less dispensing kaopectate in the lobby of the bank.

If I mastered a toolbox of fashionable skills, I'd feel obligated to use them. In the process I'd lose me and melt into the corporate throng. However, despite his best salt-estranging intentions, no person can exist completely apart from the main. Three years ago, I got an "EZ Pass" transponder so that Vicki and I could travel to Canada and not have to stop at toll booths in Maine and Massachusetts. We used the transponder twice that summer. Since then we have not driven on toll roads. Although people eventually become immobile, their credit cards march on. I realized that before leaving for Nova Scotia I'd have to contact the turnpike authority and update our credit information. I delayed acting until dreams about problems on the Massachusetts Pike collided with my sleep and began waking me at four-thirty in the morning. Age complicates both the simplest and the hardest things. I was savvy enough to guess that I'd need the number of the transponder when I telephoned the authority. The car was in the garage. Even after I switched on the garage lights and the lights inside the car, I couldn't read the number when I studied the windshield. I then returned to the house, fetched my keys, and backed the car into the sunlight. I was still unable to decipher the number, so I returned to the house and got my eyeglasses. I moaned, said an oath which was popular with the mummers' god, and tried to read the number. I failed again, so I mouthed another oath, returned to the house and got a magnifying glass. This time I read the number. It consisted of several digits. I copied them down five times, and when three combinations were identical, I called the turnpike administration. After I supplied my name, address, telephone and transponder number, the young man to whom I was speaking asked for my pin number. "Pin number! What pin number?" I said. "I don't have an EZ Pass pin number." "Yes, you do," the man said, "make a guess." I guessed and astonishingly got the number right. "It never fails," the man said. "Old people use the same pin number for everything, absolutely everything."

The young imagine a future grander than it will be. The old imagine a past grander than it was. In part this explains the elderly's revisiting the past. They do so by resuscitating memories and attempting to repeat old experiences. For years Vicki and I have attended the 4th of July Boom Box Parade in Willimantic. Shortly after, we leave for Nova Scotia, and the parade has evolved into a personal good-bye celebration. Willimantic is a salt and pepper town, and all sorts of people march and season the day. If they own old boom boxes, people carry them on their shoulders tuning them to the local radio station that plays stirring marching music, among others, "Stars and Stripes Forever," "Anchors Aweigh," "The Marine Hymn," and the "Radetzky March." Leading the parade this year was a troop of muscular, middle-aged women on motorcycles. "Dikes on bikes," a woman leaning against a nearby wall said, her tone aggressive, daring me to saying anything negative. People's sexual inclinations are uninteresting and certainly not worth quarrelling about. "Good for them," I said.

Many people carried signs, the contents of which I agreed with: "No More Wars for Profit," "Leave Iran Alone," and "Fix the Climate." Other people turned themselves into fleshly sandwich boards and wore shirts with personal statements stamped on the fronts. A large muffin-rumped woman wore my favorite: "My Mind Says Gym. My Body Says Pizza." Men walked by pulling grocery cars and hawking dolls, balloons, and Teddy bears. "Shoe Smith" drove an ancient sports car, painted on the side of which was the question, "Feet Hurt?" Mrs. Connecticut smiled furiously perched high behind the rear seat of a white convertible. A woman pedaled a bicycle built for two. A skeleton sat in the second seat, its head rotating and grinning, legs bound to the pedals and pumping. A town hall of state and local politicians strode past, arms waving like the wings of herring gulls. Dance schools pranced. A karate club darted then suddenly froze in unnatural postures. Fencers skipped and lunged. Daycare mothers pushed trains of baby carriages. Boys led pet dogs, and a girl pushed a perambulator overflowing with kittens. In another perambulator lay Wilbur, a teenager's new pot-bellied pig. Wilbur had dressed for the occasion and wore a pink bonnet. "Wilbur is small now, but someday he will weigh three hundred pounds," his owner said.

Church congregations paraded together. Sunday schoolers distributed Tootsie Pops. While one member of the Light on the Hill Church handed me a purple rubber bracelet on which was printed "In Everything Give Thanks," another gave me two pencils. On one pencil appeared rainbows of bright crosses, on the other a miscellany of red hearts, orange stars, white doves, and green and yellow fish. In a drawer in my desk at home lay another pair of pencils. I'd received them four years ago. "Walk With Jesus," letters scrolling down the side of one urged while a sentence on the other declared "Jesus Is The One."

Television and retirement have made me an armchair detective. I'm not the sort of sleuth who solves scientific puzzles on "Forensic Files" or probes neighborhood violence in "Nightmare Next Door." I lack the energy to forego sleep in order to close cases in "48 Hours." Joe Kenda the "Homicide Hunter" is remarkably competent, but even though I admire him we wouldn't make a copacetic team because he doesn't have a sense of humor. No, I'm at home with Inspector Tom Barnaby at Causton Town Police Station in Midsomer County. In fact, I know the countryside well having been his sidekick when he solved murders in scores of unlikely places: Badger's Drift, Little Worthy, Angel's Rise, Monks Barton, Luxton Deeping, Fletcher's Cross, and Shotover and Forest Hill, among casebooks of others. Rarely does a television gumshoe get to use his expertise. But the parade offered me an opportunity to "showcase" my investigatory talents. Printed on the bracelet and pencils in minute type were "Made in China" and RINCO 02864. I donned my deerstalker and searched the online world. I discovered that RINCO was Rhode Island Novelty Company located at 5 Industrial Road in Cumberland, Rhode Island O2864, self-acclaimed as "the nation's leading importer and wholesale distributor of novelty toys." I learned that a box of one hundred Inspirational Pencils cost $13.20. Bracelets were cheaper, one hundred going for $10.20. Rinco sold a variety of religious paraphernalia—decorated folding fans, cross necklaces, and web bracelets with W.W.J.D. (What Would Jesus Do) printed on them. The company's wares were ecumenical, consisting of 26 "Themes" and 26 "Categories." Not simply acolytes but young atheists had plenty to choose from: Aliens, Pirates, Snowflakes, Cops and Robbers, Monsters, and Dinosaurs. Team Spirit appealed to junior high cheerleaders, Race Cars to aspiring mechanics, and on Labor Day strong union men and women could hand out selections from Construction Crew.

Television mysteries rarely consist of a single part. The celluloid road from Midsomer Magna winds through Marsh Wood and into Bow Clayton. One case leads to another. A marcher handed me a packet of three crayons. The crayons were blue, red, and yellow and each was three inches long. The crayons stuck out of a piece of copy paper folded into a pocket. Sketched on the paper was a series of concentric circles. Pushing into the outer circle was a triangle, the whole illustration, Vicki said, looking like a sperm penetrating an egg. People who colored the drawing and who purchased a Crossroads Café favorite meal in Mansfield's East Brook Mall were eligible for either "a kids Mac and Cheese" or a twenty percent discount on a Family Meal.

Like the bracelet and pencils, the crayons were made in China, but their distributor CrayonKing Crayons was in Clovis, California, about as far from Rinco as a company could be and still be located in the United States. CrayonKing was socially responsible. The paper wrapping each crayon assured parents that the crayons were not toxic but warned that they were "a Choking Hazard for Children Under 3." Three boxes each containing 720 packs of three crayons cost $57 a box. Bulk purchasing was cheaper. If a person bought forty or more boxes, each box cost $46. The good detective thinks long and hard and as a result figures out what things add up to. For the buyer ordering three boxes a single crayon cost slightly more than 2.6 cents. The price of a crayon for the person who bought 40 boxes was a fraction more than 2.1 cents. Forty boxes, three crayons to a pack, would amount to 86,400 crayons. "Enough crayons for, enough for what?" I asked Vicki looking at the number. "I don't know," Vicki said. "But I just heard a recording of Box Car Willy singing 'You are my sunshine.' What do you think about that?" I did not respond, but later I recalled something Cornelius Weygandt, an English teacher at the University of Pennsylvania, wrote ninety years ago about Gilbert White's *The Natural History and Antiquities of Selborne*. White pressed "the happy moments of years" into small measure. "It is no wonder they brim over between the lines." I wasn't exactly sure what Weygandt meant. I understood enough to satisfy me, however. In any case relentless exactness smothers life and ultimately is inexact.

Five packing and quibbling days later Vicki and I left for Nova Scotia. In April we bought tickets to Yarmouth on the ferry leaving Bar Harbor. Because upgrading the dock in Bar Harbor was behind schedule, Bay Ferries cancelled our reservation, and we drove to St. John, New Brunswick, and took the *Fundy Rose*, another ferry, to Digby. From Digby we pushed down the French Coast to Beaver River and our house in southwest Nova Scotia. After excluding the three-hour ride on the ferry, the trip was a hard 550-mile drive. Soothing white June had ended. Beggar's ticks and July had arrived with their barbed awns and traffic jams. EZ Pass did not smooth the drive north. Careless motorists careened from lane to lane driving like the Walking Dead or better like people intent on increasing the number of dead. Huge trucks loomed in the rearview mirror like the cannibalistic Laestrygonians, their motors roaring deep-throated and grisly, their grills mutant jaws, their fangs slathers of chrome. Overloaded logging trucks shimmied and trembled. Apart from classrooms and the censorious eyes of teachers, school buses ignored highway rules.

Stops for the dogs punctuated the trip like ellipsis, eleven times in two days. Once or twice stops made me impatient but not usually. I used canine necessity to relieve my own. I took short walks and wandered into scrub and down dirt roads. For mosquitos I was a Whopper Jr., and they gathered around me as enthusiastic as second graders bounding into a Burger King after winning an intramural soccer game. For me the mosquitos were ignorable until the itching began, something that always comes later. In contrast the effects of sights along the walks were immediate. Medicinal and awakening, they scrubbed road fatigue from my eyes: vetch so thick it looked like yarn, buttercups, Queen Anne's lace, eyebright, a ditch buttoned over by yellow cow lilies, and along the shoulder of a road seedpods of lupin silver and bristly in the sunlight. Near St. John, viper's bugloss and night-flowering catchfly transformed an unshaven chin of shore into a garden. Swollen pink calyxes of the latter looked like small watering cans racked and hung out to dry by fairy folk.

Vicki and I broke the trip with a night across the New Brunswick border in St. Stephen. After dinner at a Pizza Delight, we strolled for an hour along the St. Croix River. Across the water the lights of Calais, Maine, fluttered like small flowers in a breeze but abruptly they broke and tumbled like they'd been mowed. In the background music racketed and banged like the Interstate. In contrast St. Stephen was dark and silent, and we grew sleepy and thoughtful. "I am too old for this trip," I said. "I don't read as much as I once did. How can someone who lacks the endurance to finish most books muster the strength to move into the house? Cleaning will be impossible. Spiders will have enjoyed countless insect banquets. Graveyards of woodlice will be under every window in every room. No appliance will work. Dreadlocks of mold will decorate every wall. If the pump turns on, the water will be filled with iron and undrinkable. If we were reasonable, we'd turn around and drive back to Connecticut tomorrow." "True," Vicki said, "but how sad if after forty years of marriage we began acting reasonably. To say good-bye to Nova Scotia would be wishing farewell to life." "Nuts," I said. "Let's go to bed. We'll sleep well, and tomorrow won't be difficult. After the ferry we'll stop in Digby and have an early dinner of scallop burgers."

Vicki and I have now been in Beaver River for two weeks. The roadway has become our driveway. Rather it would have done so if there were a driveway. Instead the car sits on a patch of grass in front of the barn. Shredded plaster causes spasms in Vicki's lungs, and my nose is a leaky faucet. No over-the counter washer can stop the dripping. The dogs don't object to the well water, but Vicki and I drink bottled water. The ceiling above the upstairs hall fell during the winter. We swept up the pieces and decided not to repair the damage. "Since we can't afford a new ceiling, let's glue our eyes to the floor," Vicki suggested. After the alarm system kept the neighborhood awake for eight months, beneficent Satan took matters into his hands. He caused a thunderstorm and fried the system. We won't have the alarum repaired because it would go off again and sow inconvenience. The telephone doesn't work. Thrice Bell Aliant scheduled visits from a "technician." We did not leave the house during the appointed days. No technician ever appeared. But, so what? If a friend died, I'd like to know. But since the friend himself probably wouldn't call to inform me, waiting for his obituary is satisfactory. Some temporary things have been accomplished. Vicki has unpacked the house, and I have chopped the knotweed that threatens to smother our rugosa roses. The wood box is filled with firewood. The hummingbird feeders are up, and I have rediscovered my rusty tools.

Continuance is the rule of work here, indeed of all living. The mosquitos along the highway must have contacted their maritime cousins, black flies, and told them we were coming. Consequently, the flies delayed their vacations. Rather than decamping by the end of the first week in July, they stayed and gave us a lumpy, corpuscular welcome. In various ways days here are always buggy. Mia has regained her summertime fondness for beetles. She doesn't eat beetles in Connecticut. Perhaps the full buck moon influenced her appetite. Twice I've watched her dine upon a woodland worm and slug hunter and once upon a tasty-looking harpalus ground beetle. For her part Vicki continues her year-round charitable activity as a spider rescuer. So far Vicki has pulled hundreds of tiny spiders and their mothers out of the path of the vacuum cleaner. From the bathtub she has rescued more, most of these slipping through cracks in the wood surrounding the faucets. She scoops the spiders into empty plastic yogurt containers. She then carries the containers into the barn where the young spiders gather near their mothers like filings around magnets.

Most of what I've seen this summer is familiar aside from a breakfast sandwich in Tim Hortons. "100% Plant-Based Sausage," an advertisement proclaimed, made with "Beyond Meat." For Canada Day, Tims, as Vicki and I call it, created a Fireworks Donut. The dough was almost invisible buried under cherry bombs of red sprinkles and mushy white candies that erupted on the tongue shooting out rockets of sugar—or so we assumed, not being stout-hearted or patriotic enough to sample one. Like Vicki's urging spiders into plastic ambulances, many familiar things have made me happy: a field rollicking in a clown's coat of yellow hawkweed, the fragrance of honeysuckle rolling like water off a dry bank, and a hermit thrush singing in the spruce growing along the lane running from our house to the drumlin overlooking the Gulf of Maine.

One morning as I jogged around Cedar Lake, I surprised a hare on the shoulder of the Beaver River Road. The hare was large and heathy and his chestnut coat glowed. His nose was buried in yellow clover, and at first, he didn't notice me. Years ago, when I ran quickly and my feet slapped the ground instead of mincing like the pointed slippers of David Suchet's Hercule Poirot, the hare would have heard me approaching and bounded into the bush. This morning his ears twitched. He turned his head slightly, studied me, then returned to the pleasure of nibbling. Over the years some familiar things have improved unexpectedly. I have run the Sheila Poole 10-kilometer road race and its predecessor twenty-five or so times. Years ago, my times mattered, and I finished among the first third of the racers. I have progressed. Slowly as I slipped into and below the middle group of runners, I lost interest in my time. This year I reached a pinnacle and finished last—something that gives me much to crow about when I chat with adolescents who mistakenly believe that dead last is dead rather than quick.

Unpleasantness often surprises. Because the mold causes fits of sneezing and keeps me awake at night, I have the freedom of unoccupied hours. Consequently, I've decided to become a good utilitarian and use the excess to write a self-help book. "Maybe I'll make a few rupees," I told Vicki. "Hopeless cases are a huge market. They'll swallow any gilded bolus and believe the most preposterous claptrap. Think about the gulls who voted for the mountebank now hanging his shingle on a golf course in Palm Beach. Even after four years the tinsel still distracts them and they neither hear nor see the bunkum." "Gulls?" Vicki said, "there are flocks of them on the beach, mostly herring and ring-billed but also a few great black-backed." "Even if the book doesn't make a ton of jack," I said, "maybe the royalties will pay for a final trip to Australia. How nice it would be to sail into the sunset and there meet four or five people who 'love' my books."

Vicki's and my conversations simultaneously go everywhere and nowhere. I'd write about them, but they are too realistic to be other than soporifics. Married couples would recognize them. People buy books for diversion. Why purchase a volume that only contains what one hears every day at breakfast, lunch, and dinner? That aside, I've made a list of possible topics and chapters for my self-help book. All are efficacious Galenicals and have been tested and certified by the American Hippocratic Society and Aesculapian Lodge. Several thoughtful and practical articles describing the Lodge's Upas Tree Forest have appeared in scholarly journals devoted to gerontology. The articles are worth reading if one is burdened with aging parents or with a dotty bachelor uncle suffering from lechery senilis and wasting your inheritance on a passing fanny, as grammarians addicted to colons and semi-colons express it. "We promise," the Lodge's forester testified, "that once the last days of your wayward family member are under our suzerainty his chippie will remain a Near Mrs."

Academic research is almost always scholarship for entertainment's sake. Few scholarly articles have practical value. An exception was a "betterment" study I read for my book: an account of "globesity" published in the *Medical Repository* a hundred years ago. Cited several times was the *Ear-to-ear Bible* published in 1810. The bible's title was taken from Matthew's sage advice, "Who hath ears to ear (hear), let him hear." In the article appeared innumerable suggestions for improving the British diet. Many were quaint rather than practical. Oddities, however, are often more efficacious in remedying "Infirmities and Imbecilities of the Body and Mind" than Materia Medica. They alleviate the smothering encumbrances of convalescence and turn off color moments into sparkling holidays. The article quoted letters initially published in *The Morning Post*. Dissatisfied with the sizes of their bodies, the correspondents expressed the hope that after the Resurrection they would have, as one person put it, "a more Grecian shape." The writers ranged from portly to thin, one man being "three stone overweight" and a five-foot, six-inch woman underweight at seven stone. What followed in the article was a page and a half of "Bible Foods" which the author assured readers would be available in heaven. A regimen of these, he believed, would remedy "gross imbalances in weight." Indeed, he suspected they might be mandatory for new arrivals whose weights were "infelicitous." Among a cafeteria of other foods, Guardian Angels would force-feed the thin "the fat of the lamb, grapes and olives, first-ripe figs, dates, and caper-berries," these last an appetite enhancer. Featured in the diets of those who abused their earthly bodies by "eating bread with no fear of scarceness" would be bitter herbs, broad beans, walnut shells, red pottage, millet loaves, and carob husks seasoned with sweet cane. Sydney Smith said that the great secret of life was good digestion. For the writer of the article, the great secret of the afterlife was a proper, sanctifying diet that promoted angelic gastrointestinal rectitude.

Among the chapters suggested by my submersion in academic journals are: "Using God's Scalpel to Get in Touch with Your Inner Adult," "Elevating Thought in order to Talk about Things Less Important than Gossip," and "Christmas Tattoos Pleasing to Herpetologists, Parasitologists, and Faith Healers." People of a certain age will surely enjoy "Maximizing the Kicks of Atrial Fibrillations" and "Re-reading Paphian Novels and Not Lusting after the You Who Panted over Them Sixty Years Ago." Who wouldn't want to know "The *Comme Il Faut* Way of Telling a Goth that You Hope His Mother Won't Bite Him When He Returns to His Kennel?" "Teaching to Avoid Becoming an Inspiration" will keep soggy academic spin doctors away from the door more effectively than a pit bull. Corpses-to-be will benefit from "How to Die and Not Be Remembered by People Who Did Not Know You But Who Persist in Telling Others How You Touched Their Lives." Of course, many chapters will smack of self-help, "Lying so Convincingly that You Believe Yourself" being particularly uplifting.

The list is a teasing sampler of bon-bon. Let me reassure people duped by authors hawking snake oil that I will not use fast-food expressions like "thoughts and prayers" and "the healing process." Like plastic garbage creating dead zones in the ocean, they wash through inspirational books in waves of poisonous paragraphs causing epidemics of cultural dementia. Moreover, I've assembled an editorial board composed of five-star advice generals. Chairing the board is the wise lady from Philadelphia. Accounts of her principled advice can be found in *The Peterkin Papers*. Her life is an open book. Nothing has been redacted, and she has promised to read my pages scrupulously subjecting them to the "highest ethical and efficacious standards."

When I was a boy, I dreamed of raiding strawberry patches. Sometimes the child is the father of the man. The questionable inclinations of the boy have ripened into the scabrous doings of the adult. Time has passed. and I have become a meticulous, trustworthy plagiarist. In writing a library of volumes I plucked the juiciest fruits sprouting from the cerebral veins of strangers. Consequently, none of the uplifting regimens advocated in my book will be worm-holed or have distasteful side effects. They have undergone decades of psychological testing. Countless inspirational texts have featured them, and they have been certified by the Mind-Body Society of North America. The packaging of the advice in nouns and verbs is my own, that is, singular, but the contents of the paragraphs are familiar, plural because the material crops up often, in, among others, sermons, commencement orations, State of the Union addresses, trumpet calls to social action, and locker-room pep talks. Close acquaintance breeds appreciation. How the chapfallen will lift their eyes to the heavens and nod warmly when they recognize the old saw "The darkness vanishes when the sun rises." If mulled and swallowed with a mouthful of pure spring water, the results of adhering to my counsel will inevitably be beneficial and in many instances as remunerative as winning the lottery.

Lastly, the book will also contain self-help pastilles the flavors of which have been influenced by the summer. Shortly after arriving in Beaver River, Vicki and I went to the Walmart in Yarmouth. The day was blustery, cold, and rainy. I didn't wear a raincoat, and when I stepped out of the car, the wind jerked my umbrella and turned it inside out snapping two struts. The parking lot outside Walmart was full, and I parked a long way from the front door. Although I ran, I was soaked by the time I entered the store. Inside the store air conditioning was running, and I immediately began shivering. Aside from leaving the store, racing back to the car, and switching on the heater, I didn't know how to warm myself. My perplexity lasted only a moment, however. At the end of an aisle stood a large warming oven. It contained "Deli Hot Dogs" and "Roasted Seasoned Chickens." Readers interested in food and mathematics will be keen to learn that the hot dogs cost fifty cents each, and that the chickens were priced at $8.47 for one or $15 for two. Also interesting was the fact that the cook only prepared 38 chickens that day. The usual number, she said, was fifty or sixty. She also thought but wasn't certain that the chickens were shipped to Yarmouth from Ontario. On noticing the oven, I rushed over. The front was open, and heat billowed out. I sidled close then turned myself around as if I were on a rotisserie. I dried my shirt and the top of my trousers. Next I backed up to the oven as if it were a fireplace and melted the chill off my bottom. The naive might think sight of a strange oldster cooking his behind would be unappetizing and frustrate sales. They would be wrong. Many customers in the store were wet and cold, and after studying me several joined me forming a line before the oven. The birds sold like hot cakes, as short order cooks put it. The aroma was enticing, and practically everyone in the line bought one or two. By the time Vicki finished shopping, I was comfortable, and the oven was empty. And that, dear hearts, is my first tip: "How to Warm Yourself in a Grocery on a Cold Day." There will certainly be more proficuous tips, but to learn about them people will have to read the book.

Always Going On

"Life doesn't have a neat beginning and a tidy end," Roger a character in V. S. Naipaul's *Half a Life* says. "Life is always going on." My dogs and I grow older, and summer no longer awakens expectations of stirring change. Opening the house in Nova Scotia doesn't make me skip, joyous to shed the drudgery of winter in Connecticut. Instead I sag. Life away from Storrs now seems harder than that at home. Simple open-armed swan days have become half-gainers and flips with corkscrew twists or other dives the names of which I've forgotten and am not inquisitive enough to care about. Exhuming the frolicking summers of years past is impossible. When the porch door in Nova Scotia swings wide, a miasma of worry sweeps over me. Suppose I fall as I do every summer, but this time shatter a hip. How will I get back to doctors in Storrs and how fast can I do so? What about the other parts of my road-weary body? What will happen if my heart goes on a tear or my prostate balloons? Will the new generator in Connecticut work if an August storm disrupts the electricity on my street, as it always does? Suppose one of my friends at home dies. All are aged and stumbling, and chances are that someone will "cross the bar." The number of old boys staggering through their last days toward the sea would be higher except that their ranks have already been thinned. Last December when Vicki and I went to the seasonal bazaar at the Storrs Congregational Church, there were 22 females and 2 males in the main hall, I, constituting half the male contingent.

The house in Beaver River is 160 years old and needs more repairs than I do. Vicki and I can afford them, but what then? To whom can we pass the house? Eliza lives in California, Edward in South Carolina, and Francis is restoring his own home in southwest Connecticut. When Vicki's parents shed the house, Vicki and I assumed responsibility for its care. Because I taught school, our summers were free. Moreover, we lived in eastern Connecticut, and Nova Scotia was an easy overnight ferry ride from Maine. When Vicki's two brothers were young, they spent summers at the house. Childhood passes, however. Because they work in New York and have never had the luxury of long vacations, during the last decades they've only visited occasionally. As a result, their associations with the house have been more sentimental than actual. Sentiment binds, however, and through the years they've paid taxes and helped with extraordinary expenses. But as it always does, time has changed their concerns. They have aged into lives in which Nova Scotia is a very small part, probably, I suspect, a nettlesome part. How much longer will they, rather can or should they, remain committed to the house? The childhood memories of even the most sentimental and responsible people eventually grow dim, and burdensome.

Nowadays my children live modestly. For them caring for the house would be financially impossible. Moreover, they do not have children of their own, and no matter how they imagine doing so, they won't be able to repeat the smiling times of forty years ago. Summers were glorious. Vicki and I were vigorous and spontaneous, and age had not turned either of us cautious or querulous. We were "The Happy Family," and thinking about those years so saddens me that I push recollection out of mind. When I fail to purge remembrance, I sit motionless and ache, and, as might be expected of someone my age, worry about dark inexplicable Fate armed with arrows poisoned with the terrible things that can and do happen to all families.

Splitting logs and chopping kindling for the iron stove no longer make me fancy myself a countryman. At night when I toss the contents of the slop bowl into the bay across the side meadow, I don't imagine frightening creatures feeding on it, and me. There are plenty of mice and voles, but no big animals. When I walk back to the house, I gaze at the stars, but I don't search for Draco and Pegasus, Cygnus and Hercules. I know where they're located. If the moon is bright, I pause near the weeping willow. In the light the stone of George our dachshund is visible. George died in 2004, but it seems to me that I dug his grave last summer. I stand silent and motionless outside the house for a moment. Time dissolves, and everything and nothing appear to have happened and to be happening simultaneously. Eventually I shrug, climb the porch steps, open the screen door, and go into the kitchen. I'm puzzled, but life always goes on—diminished and different but still capable of delighting and intriguing.

Because the telephone at the house is broken, and we are not connected to the Internet, Vicki and I check email whenever we go to the library in Yarmouth. A week ago, while as I was reading email in the biography room, a woman speaking with a deep, practically unintelligible Eastern European accent and holding the sort of reporter's pad that social scientists carry approached me and said, "Are you Christian?"

"What?" I replied tentatively not sure I heard her correctly. "Are you Christian?" she asked again. "No," I said firmly, almost stridently, "I'm an atheist." She paused and staring at me asked again, "Are you Christian?" "Well," I said, "I was raised Episcopalian, but now I am an atheist." "Are you Christian?" she asked once more. "What?" I said, my tone resentful, thinking her question intrusive. Before the interrogation continued, a man working across the room spoke, "She means, 'is your name Christian?'" "Ah, ha," I said, "no, I'm not Christian." That appeared to satisfy the woman, and she left the room. Four minutes later she returned. "What is your name?" she asked. I was tempted to say my name was Buddhist, Jew, or Moslem, but I simply said, "Sam." When she looked mystified and again asked if I were Christian, I spelled my first name for her, enunciating slowly and carefully, "S-A-M." "Yes, Siam," she said, after a pause and inserting an *I* into my name transforming it into the former name of Thailand, "Yes, Siam, but are you Christian?" She was, I learned later, looking for a library employee named Christian.

Except for a note from my friend Josh, my emails were clutter. Throughout the year casual acquaintances send me scrolls of jokes swept up from leavings on the internet. I delete them unread. However, in my anecdotage I've developed a rash susceptibility to puns. One joke appeared in Josh's note. "The following tale," Josh wrote, "is a threadbare story often told and often forgotten. It is viral, indeed Shakespearean with puns and will appeal to you." According to Josh, a mother skunk had two kits. She named one In and the other Out. Whenever In was in the den, Out was usually out. Correspondingly when In was out, Out was in. One morning Mama Skunk called Out to her and asked him to go out and fetch In. Out always obeyed his mother, and he went out and brought In in. Out did not take much time. The skunks lived a thick wood, and Mama was astonished that Out found In so quickly. "How did you do it?" she asked. "It was easy," Out answered. "In stinct."

Josh's emails are lively. Only rarely does he discuss bubonic politics or athletics. But he does suffer from seasonal hypochondria and medical matters fascinate him. Recently, he claimed he read a study describing the potential benefits of "intestinal flora." When subsoil from the interiors of people suffering from autism was infused into the recesses of mice, the behavior of the mice changed; they became less social and more retiring. "The possibilities are endless. The right bacteria could be contraceptive, protecting mice from cats by minimizing squeaking and from traps by creating cheese and peanut butter allergies." For humans the research promised a cornucopia of benefits. "College admissions would be transformed," Josh hymned. "No longer would Nabobs waste money buying their children into Harvard, Yale or some Scientologist branch of the University of California. A dollop of the right flora and say good-bye to wet blanket spawn and welcome needle-minded scholars. Moreover, student loans would disappear. Students already in prestigious institutions could finance their educations by selling their flora, sterilized, of course, and seasoned with pinches of la-ti-da experiences. How the world would change! Fast runners could live like slow runners. Instead of wasting their lives mechanically revolving around tracks and spending weekends flattening their arches on asphalt, they'd have time to devote to sensible interests: collecting china, reading a book every six months, amassing candy jars lumpy with scrumptious wives and husbands, and taking service dogs to visit laity experiencing the ills of Masonic withdrawal. Drug stores would vanish. Instead of peddling tablets and salves, pharmacists would metamorphose into short-order cooks and buy lunch wagons. They'd sell delicatessens of sandwiches. The essential ingredient of all sandwiches would be the same, but it could be served on an amalthea of breads: whole wheat, rye, All-American white, pumpernickel—in bagels and pita pockets—gluten and yeast free, on and on into an endless lunch."

After leaving the library Vicki and I dropped our dirty clothes at the laundromat and went to Tim Hortons. People hanker for anonymity, but they rarely achieve it. Because we are summer residents, Vicki and I imagine we are invisible. We are not. "Been to the laundromat and getting coffee while your clothes wash, aren't you?" a stranger said when we sat in a booth. On Vicki's looking startled, the man said, "You do laundry ever week at this time." The man was friendly and good-natured. "When he speaks to you next week," Vicki said. "Tell him you are amazed he recognized because you are wearing clean underpants." I won't follow Vicki's instructions because again I have stopped wearing underpants. I say *again* because I stopped in summers past. I don't remember when I first resisted the grope of foundation garments. All I know is that I avoided wearing them when I was a child. Even worse now when I succumb to sartorial convention and don boxer shorts, I often put them on backwards, for me a small or smalls inconvenience, but for Vicki another indication that I am fast becoming "oldtarded." Alas, Vicki has a gift for the telling remark. In the Quick n' Tasty last week, she told a waitress that the ideal end would be to explode like a cherry bomb at 75. "How old are you?" the waitress asked me. "78," I answered.

Habit creates identity. In our first thirty days in Nova Scotia, we've had coffee at Tim Hortons fourteen times. Nine times we have driven to D. J.'s store in Salmon River. There we eat breakfast, share a club sandwich, or split an early-afternoon piece of pie, usually coconut cream. Eliza recently spent two weeks with us. Six times she and Vicki journeyed to D. J.'s and bought ice cream cones. On three additional occasions, they and Geoff, Vicki's brother who stayed a week, had cones. Vicki thinks such record-keeping peculiar. "Teaching was a mistake. You should have been an accountant." The remark was familiar, but I don't know how frequently she's said it. I haven't tracked the number, but I wish I had done so. In any case I was a duffer compared to Geoff. He was studying four languages online and had not missed a lesson in 489 days.

After fetching our clothes from the laundromat, we went to the Bank of Montreal, and the Jack-Pudding day continued. Members of my family give each other books. Not all are belle lettres. A goodly number have been penny dreadfuls. Stacked atop a table in the lobby of the bank and selling for twenty-five cents apiece, the proceeds going to local charities, was a stack of fly-specked volumes. To welcome Eliza to Nova Scotia I purchased *The CEO Takes A Wife*. I was so pleased I increased the sale price by forty percent and paid thirty-five cents. Silhouette Books published the book in 2008 in its Silhouette Desire line, a series celebrated for being "Always Powerful, Passionate and Provocative." Maxine Sullivan an Australian blue stocking wrote the novel. Sullivan's other novels similarly focused on the intimate doings of monied "Down Under-ers." Among her titles were *The Millionaire's Seductive Revenge*, *The Executive's Vengeful Seduction*, and *The Tycoon's Blackmailed Mistress*. I'll only sketch the plot of *The CEO* as I don't want to spoil the book for future readers. Cesare the founder of the House of Valente, a perfume dynasty, ordered his thirty-five-year-old son Alex to marry and produce an heir. He warned that disobedience would draw dire financial consequences down upon Alex and his siblings. The threat worked, and Alex proposed to Olivia Cunningham, the owner of three foundering fashion boutiques and the daughter of a bankrupt aging film star. Where love fails, money succeeds, and the novel described Alex's courtship of Olivia. Style does not do much for men and women, but it makes books. On one occasion Alex startled Oliva by giving her a Gallic or, better perhaps, an orthodontic molar-tickling Novocain-free kiss. His mouth closed over hers "taking without asking, as if it was his right. And then his tongue dipped inside her mouth and did a sweep, exploring her, getting to know her, until she shuddered from a flood of sensation that shook her world."

Eliza appreciated the gift. She is warm-hearted and generous and shortly after arriving in Beaver River purchased a present for me from Rick in the yellow barn in Port Maitland. She paid a dollar for *Chalk Talks*, two and a half times the amount I forked out for her book. Published in 1928 *Chalk Talks* consisted of 50 "illustrated talks along spiritual lines." "Our Master," L. O. Brown, the author explained, "never preached a sermon when He did not liken His truth to some everyday ordinary object so that even the children in His company could take in the power and sweetness of the truth He taught." In an encomium, St. John Halstead stated that his friend Mr. Brown "put his very self" into the book so that "all ministers, teachers, and church workers everywhere" might profit from its pages. "It is destined to have a wide circulation. To use it will be to appreciate its untold value." The talks were between 175 and 250 words long. Above each appeared an epigraph from the bible. Introducing Unseen Influence, for example, was an excerpt from "Ecclesiastes," "Cast thy bread upon the waters: for thou shalt find it after many days."

The talks were sermonettes. Their subjects were broadly charitable—Protestant but non-denominational, among others, Giving, Little Things, The Clock, Kindness, and Deeds of Life. Messages were clear. In The Lessons of the Tree, Brown urged readers to "prune away from your life the sin that will make it crooked and full of knots and gnarls." In The Lighthouse, he explained that "the business of the lighthouse is to give out the warning light which tells the mariner which way to go. For the ocean is not always smooth; great storms arise, and then it is the lighthouse that protects the ship from the rockbound coast. The light of the world is Jesus. We keep the lighthouses which send forth His light to those tossed on the billows of sin. We must keep our lamps trimmed and burning clearly."

On the pages opposite each talk appeared visual suggestions for chalk drawings. Brown said that he kept amateurs in mind when he fashioned the illustrations. A person "did not have to be an artist," Brown assured readers, "to use this material effectually." Each page represented a blackboard and was often halved or quartered. In the sections the drawings progressed from crude sketches to finished illustrations. Thus, only the rough top of a ridge ran across the first illustration for The Tunnel. The second added a curved line that looked like a small horseshoe. In the third the shattered trunks of four trees appeared on the ridge, and a faint railway track trailed into what was now two horseshoes, a large one curving over and around the initial, smaller shoe. In the last frame, grass covered the side of the ridge, bushes grew under the trees, and the jagged tops of the trees themselves spread and softened into crowns. The space between the horseshoes was darkened creating a tunnel, and the rails and sleepers became thicker, more substantial, and trustworthy. Lastly two telephone poles stood beside the track supporting four cables that disappeared into the tunnel running along its roof.

The talks were erasable, but they appealed to me. They were simple and sweet like the bread pudding that Vicki and I sometimes ate at D.J.'s. A person could not make a whole meal out of the pudding or the talks, but they both enlivened random moments. Also, little stories appeared in the talks. The tales were alluringly naïve. In one story a young woman opened her bible and calling her little sister said, "Come now, and I will help you with your Sunday-school lesson." The little girl walked over and seeing the bible said, "Let us use grandpa's Bible, sister, grandpa won't care." "Why?" the young woman asked holding her bible. "This is just the same as grandpa's; there is no difference." "Oh, yes, there is," the girl responded. "Grandpa's Bible must be more interesting than yours, for he reads it so much more than you read yours."

After leaving the bank, Vicki and I walked across Main Street to Old World Bakery to buy olive bread. On the counter lay squares of carrot cake. In part people return repeatedly to summer homes in hopes of invigorating themselves. Distant armchair sentiment softens the past and shapes happy fictions. Once people settle into their houses, however, actual recollections are difficult to recover. Cleaning and repairing dominate days and a person usually becomes too tired to enjoy indulgent leisure. "For forty years," I complained shortly after we arrived, "I have chopped Japanese knotweed. I've wrenched my back into a permanent hitch digging and chopping, and still the stuff thrives and multiples. Each year its offspring colonizes a new spot. If the devil wants to make my death a living Hell, tell him to plant knotweed on my grave. No matter the venomous bile my corpse generates, the knotweed will flourish."

During summer I recall the distant past only fleetingly. Almost always the memories are triggered spontaneously by association. Time, though, has rusted the triggers and frozen them in place so that memories misfire. However, the icing on the carrot cake was lubricating and thick, and suddenly I heard a voice speaking from the deep past urging me to examine the icing carefully to make sure it wasn't a map of fly tracks. Next I remembered country stores, black floorboards, cat hairs on barrels and shelves, and hanging over meat counters strips of flypaper. "Always wave your hand over raisin bread before buying it," a voice advised, "the raisins may have wings." "Should we buy a couple squares of the cake?" I heard Vicki say. "Oh, yeah, they look scrumptious," I said muttering "shoo fly" to myself and smiling. "What's so funny?" Vicki asked. "Life," I said, "just life going on."

The next morning, we went to Meteghan. We had coffee at the local Tim Hortons then drove to the wharf. Boats were docked throughout the harbor: scallop draggers, lobster boats, and ground fishing trawlers.

Masts and aerials jutted up sharply like dead saplings. I started reading the names of the boats: *Lindy Dawn, Wendy Gail, Lady Melansen, Captain Chef,* and *Shayleigh & Boys,* but then the boats sank from sight and I was in the switching yards in Nashville. Vicki was gone, and Daddy and I were looking at steam engines. The air was smoky and metallic with clatter. Daddy let me put three or four pennies on the tracks, and we collected them after an engine ran over them. For years a flattened nickel and quarter have sat on my desk in Beaver River. The nickel fits atop and into the quarter. I can't recall the origin of the coins. I like imaging that Daddy and I put them on the tracks. But we didn't. We saved nickels and dimes, and certainly quarters.

Life always goes on, but it generally runs on the same sleepers. Only rarely can routine be disrupted. This is especially true for people who migrate each summer and settle in the same house in same place during the same month. Because of necessity, convenience, and the influence of surroundings, my interests remain constant. In Meteghan the sound of the tide's banging and dragging below the great breakwater and the racks of boats silent and practically thoughtful in the sun did not hold my interest long. What attracted me more was a ribbon of land separating a parking lot from walkways leading to the docks. The ribbon was a low hedge of wild radish. The four petals on each of the new yellow blossoms seemed to spin like propellers while the white petals on the old barely moved apparently caught in dragnets of air.

Flowers once seemed embroidery on the tablecloth of summer. Now their blossoms frame days and support my attachment to Nova Scotia. Beside the barn late flowering white rhododendron is blooming.

Nearby blossoms trickle from the golden elder, and fall webworms are wrapping nests around leaves. Ranks of red-capped pitcher plants stand straight and helmeted above bogs. Along sandy roads collars of Queen Anne's lace have replaced July's cat's ears. Fireweed has dimmed to embers, but purple loose-strife flares from drainage ditches over the shoulders of Seaward Road. While wild mint blooms along pools at the end of ditches, nets of forget-me-nots hold the damp sides together. Amid the rocks behind the beach, the horns of bindweed are pink and white, and the stems of seaside goldenrod have stretched and broadened into thin lumpy spatulas. Reeds have swallowed rough comfrey, but tansy ragwort is un-tarnished and is a luminous gold unmatchable by the artifice of jewelry.

Through the grasses around the house creeping Jenny scatters yellow pennies, and the small lanterns of self-heal throw slivers of purple light. Along the bluff overlooking the Gulf of Maine, the seed heads of goat's beard have fluffed into airy nimbuses. In dry gravel along our neighbor Tom's drive pearly everlasting and dazzlingly pink steeplebush have appeared. Knapweed spreads in a slow sluice down the hay fields, and in the fallow field behind the barn, Vicki kneels on the ground picking low bush blue-berries. Her straw hat is ragged. The brim sags like grass, and from a distance the hat looks like a sun-flower that having outlasted its color has been tossed on to a compost pile—an unconscionably beautiful pile, nonetheless, waxy with bay and shining with flat-topped and low blue New England asters, star chickweed, and an eye's length away meadow sweet. The flowers are endlessly alluring, but to notice all of them a person would need to drench his retinas every night with eyebright. They are balms and cordials ameliorating the soul-anesthetizing sense that every day is everyday. They are febrifuges cleansing hot impatience from the mind, not philosopher's stones but naturalist's stones.

Once I wove mushrooms, sedges, reeds, and grasses into words. But as my running has deteriorating into limping, so I have lost dexterity, and they dangle like loose threads from a bed spread, noticed but not compelling me to open a sewing box and seize needle and pen. Diminution inevitably accompanies Time's passing. People become accustomed to and comfortable with getting less or nothing from something. Friends vanish faster than the blossoms of gerardia. "Losing a loved one is never easy," began an advertisement for a funeral home that appeared in the Halifax newspaper the day after Eliza arrived. "Direct Cremation" cost "$1560 + tax." "What do you think the death tax would be?" Eliza asked. "Not much," I said. "I wouldn't be useful for anything other than fertilizer. Forget burial. The stove would save you and Mom a bundle. The only hitch is that you'd have to borrow a pickup truck and haul me closer than forty kilometers to Dartmouth." "Easily done," Eliza said, "and I'd drive slowly making sure you had a smooth ride. I hate for you to drop an arm on the way to Glory." Later I learned that I was wrong about the plus tax. In Tim Horton's last week, a fellow coffee-drinker, a tall giraffe-faced cook who supplemented his earnings by moonlighting as a pallbearer, informed me that the amount of plus tax was calculated on a scale similar to the graduated levy that determined inheritance taxes. The liability of corpses who consumed extravagantly during their eating hours and on their persons stored excessive avoirdupois was "considerably higher than that assessed on the remains of the malnourished."

Our three dogs sleep most of the day. Rather than cavorting on the beach, they now trail behind Vicki and me until their muscles stretch and arthritis loosens its grip. At times I think we are running a canine hospice. Instead of nursing-home patients around a terrace humped in wheelchairs, the dogs lie on the porch steps. They are inert, and no longer must I rope them to buoys to prevent them from wandering. The decline of the dogs was expected. What is worse and unforeseen is the diminution of our microcosmic Nova Scotia natural world. Some life doesn't always go on. No longer do brocades of moths cover the front door in the evening. No more do the orbs of gray cross spiders drape like doilies over windowpanes. Showers of sparrows don't sweep across the kitchen meadow. Warblers don't rain pattering through the scrub. Frogs, toads, snakes, butterflies, and hornets have almost disappeared. Only glimpses remain: at Cape Forchu a deer from a Landseer canvas, still and golden in the setting sun, a two-lined grasshopper depositing eggs in a dirt road, and in sphagnum woods a hermit thrush low on a lichened branch, her tail bright red and in her beak a small lacewing.

Death is more visible than life: an immature jumping mouse beheaded by a cat, a seal shredded by the propeller of a fishing boat, and at low tide lion's mane jellyfish pancaked in the sand and gleaming like hubcaps. Along the shoreline of the Gulf of Maine death is not so apparent as it was when the water teemed with fish, but nevertheless sundried and preserved in salt, it is more discernible than that on land creating the false impression of seas teeming with life. From the beach I collected the heads of two cormorants cured and odorless. I'll bury them in a suitcase, take them to Connecticut, and place them on a window ledge in my study. I am not sure why I collect bones. Perhaps I do so because I avoid harming living creatures and the remnants evoke images of live animals, in this case cormorants hammering low over the water, their wings moving so fast they ripple the air. Perhaps I've succumbed to momentomania, or maybe I simply keep bones to mark my own passing. Like artifacts purchased by tourists, they remind me that I didn't always inhabit the present and lived other moments elsewhere. Lying on a shelf in the back house is a barndoor skate curled around itself into an ampersand. Its skin is brown, and spines run ridged down its back and sides. The spines are sharp, and several cut my fingers drawing blood. On the wall hang the heads of monk or goose fish. Tides have sandpapered their skin, and they look like Halloween masks. Their eye sockets droop and are large and mournful. Their mouths are saws of teeth while the mouths themselves look like slices of cantaloupe, quartered and viewed from the side. The mouth of the largest fish has sunk into a rictus six inches across and from top to bottom at its broadest one-and-three-quarter inches.

The decrease of animals is cumulative numerically and psychologically. Years ago, before leaving Connecticut Vicki and I always wondered what unfamiliar creatures we'd see. Now we wonder what we have seen and will no longer see. The causes are various and obvious: climate change, the growth of Canada's and the world's devouring, wrecking population, and, more immediately, pesticides and herbicides. Decades ago, corporations killed deciduous trees by spraying woodlots with a herbicide one of the ingredients of which was dioxin. The spray was celebrated as effective, efficient, and harmless. That assertion having been disproved, woodlots are now sprayed with herbicides laced with glyphosate, an ingredient of Roundup. Of course, apologists echo the past and say it is safe and efficient. What will come next are more echoes—new herbicides accompanied by old claims and slow prurient catastrophe. To expect Canadians not to be as venal as the rest of the world is wishful naivete. But summer people leave elsewheres to escape choking home fires, those places, as Goldsmith described them, where wealth accumulates and men decay. For a while people are successful and breathe deeply. Ignorance filters out grit and insulates from realities. The world seems kinder when time clicks past on a mantle clock and apart from the clack of radio and newspaper. Neighbors forget distant summer people, and friends creep off to the crematorium without telephoning. Alas, visiting the same place for many years eventually educates even though a person studiously attempts to remain blinkered. After decades and maybe only after decades, a person cannot avoid noticing the soiled and lamenting the diminished. In coming to an unfamiliar place people initially experience euphoria. Not cognizant of past richness, they see only newness bountiful with difference. Will Vicki and I return to Nova Scotia for more lesser-summers? I don't know. Knowledge ages a person quicker than high blood pressure.

Last Saturday Vicki and I went to the Cold Shed Music Festival on the Yarmouth wharf. As I listened to a country singer singing "Lovesick Blues," I glanced across the wharf. The yearly Shark Scramble was ending, and boats were docking. To boost tourism the town sponsored a shark fishing competition each year, the winners determined by the poundage of shark caught. The prodigal waste of the contest and its meretricious sensationalism revolt me, and Vicki and I've never attended. As I stood on the wharf, I noticed a blue shark lying on the deck of a boat. The shark was elegant, slim and smooth, long and blacker than blue. It was more attractive than any of the spectators herded on the pier. "And," I thought, "probably more cultivated and intelligent." While adults gorged on ice cream and feigned fear, their children waved balloons shaped like sharks and squealed with glee whenever an animal was hauled aloft and displayed.

I muzzled my growls. Often the better part of words is silence. Choosing not to speak may lessen self-respect. But self-respect doesn't matter to people who have lived long, wept and laughed, people whom life has taught to love and appreciate. Moreover, self-respect is a progenitor of pestilential Pride, the most virulent of the Seven Deadly Sins. In contrast to self-respect, peace and quiet matter inordinately to me. I think them more important than any bastardizing species of respect. "Vicki," I said, "it's time to go; we need to walk the dogs." In Silence, one of the essays in *Chalk Talks*, a young man lashed by "the sharp tongues" of critics consulted St. Macarius of Egypt, "Go to a cemetery," the saint advised, "and upbraid the dead. Reprimand them for their mistakes and for the sins which they committed during their sojourn on earth. Tell them that the world is far better off since they are out of it. When you have done this, listen closely to the reply which they give to you." After the young man learned the effects of his criticism upon the dead, the saint instructed him "to praise them for the noble works in which they were engaged while on earth. Tell them that they can never be forgotten." Assure them that the memory of their noble lives "will live forever and that generation after generation will praise them." "Listen to the answer," Macarius concluded, "then come to me." The young man followed the instructions. On man's return Macarius asked, "How did the dead receive your abuse of them?" "They answered not a word," the young man replied. "And how did they behave when you flattered them?" Macarius asked next. "They took no notice of that either," the man reported. "Go," Macarius then said, "and do likewise."

"The best way to take abuse is to remain silent," Brown summed up. "There can be no quarrel where only one takes part. And when someone is praising you, it is always best to keep still and let such good things that as are said be said without your comment." The easiest way to live placidly is to be silent. There is more method to inaction than to action or to put advice aphoristically: people allergic to pills should not wake sleeping doctors. In any case walking the dogs was purgative. Not once did I mention the Shark Scramble to them or say anything about man's inhumanity. But then, and there is always a "but then." As soon as prudence begins to grow like a dismal fungus in a man's brain, Robert Louis Stevenson wrote, "it finds its first expression in a paralysis of generous acts. The victim begins to shrink spiritually; he develops a fancy for parlors with a regulated temperature." Eventually concern for the self "becomes so engrossing, that the noises of the outer world begin to come thin and faint into the parlor with the regulated temperature."

After the walk, Vicki switched on the lights in front parlor. I did not regulate the temperature because the house isn't heated. The only warmth comes from the wood stove in the kitchen. Then we returned to the Festival. Before listening to the music, we ate dinner at the Red Shed, eating, shame, oh, shame, fish sandwiches. After dinner when I entered the tent, a singer was urging his sweetheart to put her head "a little closer to the phone." The song brought to mind memories of loves lost to distant area codes, and the sharks sank below thought into oxygen-less concern. Yes, life and all aspects of it, beginnings, middles, and ends, are untidy. But even diminished days are caravanserais. Spikes of cattails in the wet along the Beaver River road have turned richly cordovan, and in meadows wood nymphs are popping from the grass, the black and white eyes in their forewings blinking. Generous bouquets of pink blossoms have bent the canes of rambling roses, causing them, as Eliza put it thirty years ago, to curtsey. Last week a twelve-spotted skimmer lit on a twig near me as I walked down the lane to the drumlin overlooking the Gulf. The dragonfly is common, but on the wings of this particular insect the white patches sandwiched between the black ones were blue and phosphorescent. Our fields have been mowed and the hay rolled into huge rounded bales. I've split more wood, and bumblebees have discovered the hummingbird feeders on the kitchen porch. I flick the bees off with my index finger. They buzz around but don't sting, and eventually they fly away.

In a week, goldenrod will bloom, turning the shoulders of fields and roads into fountains of yellow. And today Vicki made brown-bread peanut butter sandwiches. She packed them in an insulated bag along with potato chips, radishes, carrots, and two Pepsi colas, and we went to the stockcar races at the

Lake Doucette Speedway. A woman sitting in front of us in the bleachers wore a shirt on the front of which was printed "God Only Answers Knee Mail." "Three years ago," another woman said talking about her husband, "They chopped Dave's foot off. When the prosthesis finally arrived, we had a party. All the family came to the house. I cooked hamburgers and for dessert bought a chocolate cream pie at Red & White. After dinner we gathered around Dave and autographed the new foot."

This was Fan Appreciation Day, and two-thirds through the program the races paused. Girls served squares of vanilla cake. Drivers parked their cars along the safety fence, and spectators strolled onto the track, studied the cars, and talked to drivers and their crews. Drivers distributed colorful posters bigger than and almost as thick as tablemats depicting themselves and their cars. They also signed the posters, and Vicki and I collected four. Mike Banks's number 95 was butterfly red, and Doug Townsend's 42 was dragonfly green and purple. MDM Boatbuilders and Pubnico Plastics were among the sponsors of Carroll Comeau's 19 while NGK Sparkplugs and Aero helped sponsor Paul Morris's hornet yellow 56. Next week our son Francis arrives at Four Winds. When Francis was small, he could identify every car on the road. Now he is thirty-eight, and his interests have changed. Nevertheless, for old time's sake, I put the posters in his room.

Neither Vicki nor I had ever touched a stock car much less looked inside. Never had we been invited to autograph the hood of a car. We didn't know a good neck brace cost $700 or that to keep a car running at a small track was between five and eight thousand dollars a year, At a large track an owner would likely spend ten thousand dollars but could be "on the hook" for as much as fifteen thousand. On the way home from the track we stopped at D.J.'s store in Salmon River and bought ice cream cones, Vicki, rum raisin, and I, death by chocolate. "What a good day—what an astonishing afternoon," I said as we stood outside D. J.'s eating ice cream. "The happiest life," I continued quoting a line from Norman Douglas's *Fountains in the Sand*, "can hardly be better than a stringing together of such odd little moments." "Yes," Vicki said, "occasionally life stalls and pitches a tire. Sometimes the muffler falls off, and the sound is deafening, but the days go on, around and around and around."

It's Thundering in New Brunswick

Whenever Jack hears thunder or glimpses lightening, he crawls under my bed and flattens himself on the floor against the wall behind the headboard. He pushes my slippers, notebooks, pencils, and any novels I've stacked next to the bed ahead of him. Often the cords for the clock and bedside lamp snag him, and freeing him is difficult. Sometimes I seize his collar and jerk him out; other times I grab his tail and nudge him along. Three years ago, Vicki rescued Mia from a kill shelter. Initially storms didn't bother her, but Jack is a strong canine personality, and now she joins him under the bed creating a snarl of dogs and wires, writing materials and literature.

I suspect that Jack cannot hear thunder in New Brunswick. It is a goodly distance away from Beaver River across the Gulf of Maine and the Bay of Fundy. I don't notice it because age has muffled my hearing. But then not hearing a sound does not mean a person doesn't hear it. An eyedropper of imagination clears ears, eyes, nose, and occasionally throat. Days are a swirl of the actual and the imagined. "To enjoy keenly the mixed texture of human experience, rather leads a man to disregard precautions," Robert Louis Stevenson wrote. To capture heard and unheard melodies, I disregard genre and rule. I scramble through paragraphs and life hunting dogs under the bed one moment, the next marveling at a feral poem printed in a community monthly, the most recent being: "The dog barks. / The hare screams. / The loon cackles. / The old man coughs and farts. / The woman hawks and pours tea. / And the moth? / The moth beats it wings / Against the pane, the pane, against the pane."

Years ago, when I taught, I rarely strayed from congruity and definition. Things are different now. I write nothing about thunder in this essay, and the first paragraph ought to be an end, not a beginning, note. In fact, I almost entitled the essay "All My Stops Are Briefly." Washington Irving introduced *The Sketch Book* by describing his, and my method, writing, "I have wandered through different countries, and witnessed many of the shifting scenes of life. I cannot say that I have studied them with the eye of a philosopher; but rather with the sauntering gaze with which humble lovers of the picturesque stroll from the window of one print-shop to another; caught sometimes by the delineations of beauty, sometimes by the distortions of caricature, and sometimes by the loveliness of landscape."

I don't fret about significance. "Everything," Marcus Aurelius wrote, "is only for a day, both that which remembers and that which is remembered." As my age and blood pressure have risen, so my earnestness has fallen. I am not a scruple-monger, and nowadays Jack's doings occupy more of my hours than conscientious prattle. During the summer Jack got an abscess in his mouth, and Vicki and I took him to the veterinarian at the Parade Street Animal Hospital in Yarmouth. Pasted on a wall was a poster equating human and dog lives. At 78 I was 14 in "little dog years." The poster seemed accurate. No longer do I scamper about and yap like a young dog. I sleep more and have given up my currish ways. I haven't

nosed around trashy places in seven little dog years. I
don't chase rabbits, but under the influence of pills, I
still wag my tail, and on the page, I hound two-legged
skunks. I'm too restrained to howl, but to be honest
I am often melancholy. Some days I feel, as Hank
Williams put it, "so lonesome I could cry." Time has
culled my pack of friends. Last week Randy cancelled
both a colonoscopy and his Wellness Exam. Earlier
in the summer the transmission dropped out of his
car, and for the first time in his life Randy bought a
secondhand rather than a new car.

Well, the remark about howling isn't quite accurate. I howled once this summer. Early in July I slipped
on the stairs racing from the second floor to pick up
Mia and carry her outside before she had an accident.
Halfway down the stairs something popped in my
leg. Almost immediately my knee started swelling.
For eight weeks it was mushy and lumpy, the size of
an Osage orange. Injuring the knee reduced my jogging to limping. In years past I washed every day after
jogging. I dislike baths, however, especially during
country summers. Frequent bathing seems a depart-
ment-store Chanel activity that fosters an urban sep-
aration of man from the natural world and, among
countless others, its perfumes of skunk and deer, bay,
witherod, and wild mint, rotting mushrooms, and
the waterlogged aroma of a toppled spruce, its bark
shells of lichens, its heart wood shredded. Whenever
the unwashed me walked the lane running beside
our house to the Gulf of Maine, I smelled Sparky, the
resident red squirrel, before he noticed me. Since boyhood I have found snakes by following my nose. Or
so I like to think, and wanting to think something
determines the tenor of life. After hurting my leg, I
began bathing every ten days, a schedule unappealing

to Vicki despite her acknowledging I wasn't redolent, smelling "green if anything." It also reduced the laundry. What person dirty as an earthworm wraps himself in clean clothes? Moreover, dress mapped my doings: blueberry and blackberry stains, twigs from the boggy woods, remnants of deerflies and mosquitos, and blood usually splattered but occasionally in small pools, their sources mysterious cuts, insignificant matters a person doesn't notice as he scrambles over collapsing stone walls and pushes through roils of brambles intent on seeing birds or hoping to break from suburban thought and maybe think something almost fresh.

Our bathtub is old and sits high on the bathroom floor. Getting in and out is difficult. There are no hand holds or railings. One side of the tub abuts the wall. The lip of the tub is two inches wide, and to get out of the tub, one lodges the palm of his left hand atop the lip and against the wall. On the other side of the tub to provide purchase he hangs a washrag over the edge. He then locks his right hand down over the fabric, and using both hands and arms pushes himself up. The process is difficult for the aged and especially for someone like me with a bum knee who must lever up slowly. Despite covering the bottom of the tub with a rubber mat and digging one's heels into it, slipping is easy. Bathing infrequently made me inattentive. Late one afternoon Vicki insisted that I wash before we drove to Yarmouth for dinner and a movie. I'd spent the day roaming wood and field looking for insects. I was tired and my leg throbbed. I put the mat down, dropped my washrag over the edge of the tub, and then turned on the hot water faucet. Unaccountably I neglected to turn on the cold. After two inches of water were in the tub, I stepped in. Impulses from my feet travel slower to my brain than they once did. Before I realized the water was scalding, and I sat down. It was then I howled. Getting out of the tub was a slow, cooking unappetizing process. "Who would have thought broiled rump would appeal to an aspiring vegetarian and unwashed naturalist?" Vicki said. "Clever, but insensitive," I said.

On a desk at Parade Street Animal Hospital stood a holder containing business cards. The only card that interested me advertised "Forget Me Not Pet Cremation" in East Kemptville. "I will stay with you for all time," the card read. During my puppy years, nice people petted me, all of whom have forgotten me. "I haven't forgotten you," Vicki said, "how could I? You are always around fuddle-lating in the middle of things." I dream a great deal. The dreams are wondrously tedious, and at breakfast against Vicki's wishes and consequently for my pleasure, I insist on describing the previous night's dream. Two nights ago, I dreamed I was boiling beet greens. Last night I ate dinner with the president of Mexico, "quite the nicest president I've ever met." Earlier in the week I founded a nursing home for dogs. Instead of human patients slumped in wheelchairs and sitting in a circle around a terrace, the dogs stretched out and dozed on porch steps. They were well-behaved, and none had to be fastened to buoys like our packlet to prevent them from wandering into the scrub and digging through the contents of yesterday's slop bowl. Vicki likes to keep me on a tight leash, but I'm a slow learner and have never mastered heeling, something that keeps Vicki thinking about me. Last month during Hurricane Dorian I went outside wearing carpet slippers, an act that provoked Vicki to exclaim "God Almighty" followed by a shrill recital of unflattering adjectives. Later that day Vicki used stronger language after wind gusted down from the roof of the barn then banged upward turning a part of my lower regions into a nozzle that washed my face as I stood on the edge of the kitchen porch relieving myself.

No matter the weather—stenciling rain or withering sunlight—every day I read. Many of my reading stops are brief. Tacked to the announcement board at Red & White grocery three weeks ago was a homemade poster announcing, "Ginny Hen Chicks for Sale." Painted on a sign outside the tourist bureau was the town's new slogan, "Yarmouth On the Edge of Everywhere." "But unfortunately, that could mean Yarmouth is nowhere," Vicki said. "What do you think?" "It's much better than that of Mansfield and Storrs, 'Your Place to Grow,'" I said. Sloganeering and branding are clichés of the "Corporate Mundane." Generally, they are committee-made and are akin to license-plate mottos, except not as memorable as "Famous Potatoes" or "Live Free or Die." When not flattering or selling, they attempt to instill municipal conformity. They flatten the terrain of place into bland acceptability—into, especially in almost affluent areas, Condo-Land. And worst of all, they inexorably reflect the wishes of salesmen and developers. "Of all the infernal uses to which a country can be put there is none like development," H.M. Tomlinson declared in *Old Junk*.

The most striking bit of reading appeared in the *Clare Shopper*. An advertisement announced an "Everything Must Go" sale at an antique shop in Bear River. Among items on the block was Charles Dickens's computer. "Obviously a Commodore," Vicki said. The cynosure of the sale was an empty three-ounce bottle of Mentholatum. Shakespeare used the ointment to prevent his lips from chapping while he was in Sicillia researching *The Winter's Tale*. Competition for the bottle was fierce. The "prize," Vicki read in a later issue of the *Shopper*, "was purchased by an associate dean of the Yale School of Medicine." Giving the lie to the widespread belief that academics are more grasping than Jonas Chuzzlewit, the dean loaned the bottle to the Beinecke Library to be exhibited beside the Bard of Avon's First Folio.

Milton recommended "books promiscuously read." Reading was the safest way people could learn about "the regions of sin and falsity." Since childhood I have read promiscuously, not to construct breastworks against the dangers of living but for entertainment and delight. Of course, reading was contraceptive. While friends were out misbehaving, I was at home reading. Pages do not lead a person astray. They simply lead to other pages. For sale in the Yarmouth Library was a collection of romance novels. What I wondered were the *Secrets of a Good Girl*. They were probably insignificant, not serious enough to make her *Hard to Tame*. No matter the temptation she would never get *In Too Deep*. More interesting was *The Billionaire in Penthouse B*. Maybe Daddy Warbucks married the Good Girl after she played a role in *Rescuing His Secret Child*. To be avoided was *The Hawk of Venice*. He was no Velveteen Rabbit and was probably the grandson of Farmer McGregor. When the Hawk was on the wing, all two-legged and four-legged Flopsy Bunnies would be well advised not to leave the domestic warren unless accompanied by the *Bodyguard to the Bride*.

A surfeit of drugstore romances can cause literary indigestion, making one wince when he sips the elixir of a good book, say, George MacDonald's magical *The*

Princess and the Goblin. One day when MacDonald's Princess Irene was eight years old, rain confined her to the nursery. She became bored and grew "so tired that even her toys could no longer amuse her." She dozed waking suddenly and tumbling off her chair when her nurse left the nursery. Impetuously, she jumped up and ran out a door, not the door the nurse left from but "one which opened at the foot of a curious old stair of worm-eaten oak, which looked as if never anyone had set foot upon it. She had once before been up six steps, and that was sufficient reason, in such a day, for trying to find out what was at the top." Irene quickly became lost and unable to return to the "safe nursery." But as MacDonald reassuringly put it, "it doesn't follow that she *was* lost, because she had lost herself." Oh, dear," I thought, "here are the ingredients of a pot-boiling romance: a Lolita in the making, an impetuous girl having suddenly grown impatient with domesticity, her childhood swept aside by an urge to explore and experience. No wonder that a worm-eaten and dangerous staircase would be more alluring than the narrow gate and straight way." As readers of romances could expect, Irene was beset by goblins. Thankfully, though, at the conclusion of the novel her life came smilingly right, and like the heroines of romances Irene proved herself still and always a Princess.

Age changes a person's perception of time. As one grows older, childhood seems simultaneously immediate and distant. Not only do oldsters scroll through memory and revisit the past but they also reread. Years will have changed their speech. They will have put away some childish things, and tempered by experience, they realize that they see through glasses darkly. But they will reread, especially the books they read as children. In Nova Scotia I reread Thomas

Bailey Aldrich's autobiographical *The Story of A Bad Boy.* The volume was given to Vicki's father "Edward Dudley Johnson" at Christmas 1920 by his "mother and daddy." First published in 1869, the book described the childhood of Tom Bailey. After the failure of his father's business in New Orleans, Tom moved to Rivermouth, "a pretty New England town," and lived with his grandfather Captain Nutter and his Aunt Abigail, the Captain's maiden sister who treated all ailments, real or imaginary, with "hot drops." Tom was "an amiable, impulsive lad, blessed with fine digestive powers, and no hypocrite." At the end of book, he confessed that he was "not such a very bad boy."

Tom was given to "high jinks," the phrase old-fashioned and applied to boisterous activities once thought engagingly innocent. Tom and his friends exploded firecrackers, belonged a secret club the Rivermouth Centipedes, and built snow forts atop Slatter's Hill over which they fought battles with boys from the South End of town. The book's appeal to me was sentimental. As men age, they grow harder and softer. "Everything," Josh once declared, "is paradoxical. Answers are beginnings as well as ends. They always provoke questions. The paradoxical nature of everything may be the only truth, and also the only falsehood." With loving appreciation, Bailey described the occupations of the Centipedes after they molted into adults. Phil Adams became American consul in Shanghai; Pepper Whitcomb a judge, and Fred Langdon who made the best licorice water in Rivermouth moved to California and started a vineyard. Jack Harris who commanded Bailey and his friends in the "famous snow-ball battles of Slatter's Hill" joined the Army of the Potomac at the outbreak of the Civil War and was killed at Seven Pines.

In the sequel to *The Princess and the Goblin*, *The Princess and Curdie*, the Princess's great chum Curdie matured with, MacDonald wrote, "the usual consequence, that he was getting rather stupid—one of the chief signs of which was that he believed less and less in things he had never seen." Curdie became a miner, and the occupation shaped him. "He took less and less notice of the bees and butterflies, moths and dragonflies, the flowers and the brooks and the clouds," MacDonald wrote. "He was gradually changing into a commonplace man." The heroes of romance rarely resemble the novels' purchasers. Almost inevitably and imperceptibly, people become their occupations. To the great satisfaction of the reader, Curdie escaped becoming ordinary. He and Irene eventually married, and on the death of her father the king, they ruled the kingdom together. They didn't have children, but that was all right because the young readers of the *Goblin* and *Curdie* were, and are, their offspring.

"Happy, magical Past," Tom Bailey exclaimed in describing his childhood. How "pleasantly" his old schoolmates lived in memory. They endured because for a time they were bad boys and had not become forgettable. So long as people did not obstinately oppose Providence's "benevolent intentions" nor "persist in a wrong course of life," Richard Graves concluded in *The Spiritual Quixote*, it "frequently makes use of our passions, our errors, and even our youthful follies, to promote our welfare, and conduct us to happiness." A little misbehavior seasons and love humanizes. In "Farewell to Nancy," Robert Burns wrote, "Had we never loved sae kindly, / Had we never loved sae blindly, / Never met, or never parted, / We had ne'er been broken-hearted." Not long ago, Hugh the son of a college friend wrote me. In his letter, Hugh recounted that "a few years back" he attended the wedding of a classmate in Portland, Maine. The morning after the wedding he bought a bagel at Scratch Bakery in South Portland. The day was "brilliantly sunny," but as Hugh sat on a bench outside the bakery, he was too melancholy to eat because, he explained, someone dear to him had died recently. Then a woman walked out of the bakery and sitting next to him began knitting a scarf. Hugh introduced himself, and they chatted. They discovered that they had both been to small colleges, in Hugh's case Sewanee, in hers a school in Minnesota. She lived in South Carolina and was in Portland to teach at a music camp. She loved music and said that years ago she attended the Sewanee Summer Music Festival. Hugh said that his "angel" had also been musical, and the conversation became personal and reminiscent.

The woman said that she had "once spent time with a wonderful man who attended Sewanee." They'd met when he was a graduate student at Princeton. She'd visited his family in Virginia and Tennessee, and they'd planned to marry, but life, "oh, life," intervened, among other things her having a year of college remaining. Hugh asked the name of the man, and on her saying the first name, he blurted out the last. I startled her, Hugh said, and she put down her knitting and we really talked about living. Hugh wrote that their conversation "was one of those unexpected soul-quenching morsels at a time I was sad and needed it. We discussed love and loss, and she assured me that no matter how dark the present seemed that in the future I would love again." "She then paused and said, 'Sam and I were once very fond of each other and probably still are in some small way. You give him my best if you talk to him again.'

With that her husband walked out of the bakery, and she said, 'You will never believe who this young man knows!' Afterward she hugged me, wished me well, and off we went in different directions."

"Tears, idle tears," Tennyson wrote, "I know not what they mean." Burns knew. "Deep as first love, and wild with all regret," I murmured as I lay Hugh's letter down. Happily, or maybe sadly, common-sensical life prevented my feelings from fermenting. Vicki ambled into the study shortly after I finished reading. Forty years have enabled Vicki to parse me like a primer. On seeing me sitting silent and pensive, she exclaimed, "Steady on, old sport. Whatever is making you look sad isn't healthy. Come help me make a pie." "What kind of pie?" I asked. "Chocolate, what else?" she said. "Hot diggity," I said and trailed after her into the kitchen.

I suspect that today bad boys like Bailey's gamesome schoolmates are comparatively rare. Telephone ID long ago freed Prince Albert from the can and the giggling inquiries of children. Nowadays does anyone ever accidently cut himself and joyously smear the red warpaint over his arms and face and play Cowboys and "Indigenous People"? "Indoctrinated virtue" has unhorsed the cowgirl, and I doubt she will ever find herself back in the saddle and in that place where a friend is a boy. Josh told me that in gated affluent communities suburban idealists encourage their offspring to play victims and oppressors. Josh said that he read an account describing the plight of one little girl who refused to be a victim. She said that she wanted to be a "Mommy like Grandma," have a pet cat, play with dolls, and someday marry "a pale male like Daddy." She is now attending a re-education academy and being treated by a child psychologist.

Do twelve-year-old's today don bandanas and imagine holding up stagecoaches? Do they rifle through the passengers' wallets and vests removing money and watches, stealing from everyone except from a little sloe-eyed girl shy and pigeon-toed and wearing a blue dress and a sun bonnet? No, they imagine wearing white buttoned-down collars. They don't wave cap pistols; they wield pens. They don't flee to bolt holds in the badlands, but instead hide in plain view in monstrous houses where undocumented workers mow the grass every day and the stable is a garage filled with cars with strange-sounding names. Intent on fleecing the incompetent and the feeble-minded, the old, the gullible, and the stupidly greedy, they ignore little girls. "Did I ever tell you," I asked Josh, "about the hut my friends and I built when I was ten? We dug holes around it to trap the wild women Mother said lived in the woods. Over the door we hung an amulet to protect us from the evil eye and a string of chicken feet to keep the boogeyman out. What we really wanted was a corpse. We talked about burying it beside the path leading to the hut and putting a rock in its mouth to prevent it from biting us if it rose from the grave. We asked our parents to give us a body for Christmas, but they only shook their heads and told us that baseball gloves and bats would have to satisfy us." "Yes, you told me." Josh said, "in another essay." "What magical days they were," I said, not listening to Josh, "days of firecrackers and snakes, jars of June bugs, and boxes of lizards. Back then I never imagined becoming a commonplace man—a university teacher for heaven's sake!" "The differences between children raised on pavement and those raised on grass are great," Josh said. "The appointments of the formers' worlds are abstract, those of the latter lyrical. The latter don't become moralists. Rarely do barefoot bad boys become men who rush to judgement. Change or the absence of change doesn't roil them, and they make good teachers."

This summer I noticed few moths and butterflies, not because my interest had failed like that of Curdie but because during the past decade the number of insects had diminished greatly. Nevertheless, I wandered field and wood as I did when I was a boy and as I have done for the past forty summers in Nova Scotia. Actually, I roamed with more urgency than I did during previous years. Most acquaintances my age were gone or going, and at my back the grinding of Time's inexorable diesel engine had grown louder. I worried that my memory would erode and recollections of the "happy, magical Past" would soften and crumble. I'd lose the capacity to imagine and appreciate. I'd become splenetic and resentful, and the life left to me would stretch into a distance as barren and desolate as the Plain of Dura.

Because insects no longer swarmed across my sight coloring hours, I turned them into jewelry. I wanted them to glitter and so distract me that I ignored loss. Initially I planned illusory charm bracelets. I associated charm with bewitch, and I pictured insects circling my wrist and glowing like the rosy berries of mountain ash. If they were not God's plenty, they could be fancy's plenty. I imagined hearing the bracelets jangle and hoped the sound would be as musical as pastures in the fall when field crickets began singing. However, although I could wield a pencil, I lacked jeweler's skills as well as files and burs. Moreover, most of the insects that appealed to me were too big to attach to bracelets. As a result, I fashioned chimeric enameled necklaces. On one the major pendant was a laurel sphinx. The moth hung head down, its wings folded together over its abdomen. Across the forewings color ran in brown and tan lines looking like sand streaked by wind gusting low across a beach. On either side of the moth hung a black and yellow argiope (garden spider). The black was jet; the yellow looked like gold polished and rubbed thin, both colors melded in a mosaic. Behind, above, and below each spider stretched its stabilimentum—silk woven into a sterling silver zigzag.

The laurel was the only sphinx moth I saw, and I didn't find any other possible pendants. Toward summer's end a few small meadow hawks patrolled the bay beside the lane, but no big cruisers or darners prowled the damp near the cow pond. Fiery searchers did not scuttle through the grass around the house, and I saw almost no click beetles. I collected a few smaller ornaments fit more for rings than necklaces: a black bee fly with a white belt cinched around its abdomen and from rose hips orange fruit flies with stripes drizzling across their wings like dark icicles. Carolina grasshoppers fed amid the dry grass growing on the sandy lip of the lane. Black with pale yellow bands at the tips, their wings unfolded like fans and would have made attractive accompaniments for pendants if gathered in sheaves and splayed out. Red admirals were more common than any other butterfly. Often, I saw them atop the white parasols of flat-topped asters. What a glass flower the pair would have made, the wings of the butterfly raised like evening and quivering silently, the red heel curving across them like the last rays of sunlight and the flowers themselves white and fuzzy and sunny mid-day yellow.

Despite the summer's seeming barren in comparison to the past, it wasn't devoid of life. One afternoon as I roamed the high bluffs beyond Cape St. Mary, I walked into a floral print of flat-topped and blue asters, lance-leaved goldenrod, sow thistle, and daisies. Over them hovered a holiday of butterflies: monarchs, American ladies, fritillaries, and red admirals. Almost every day crows waddled sassily along the road beside the barn. They shook their tails, hopped, and leaned over their toes. Twice when Thumper the porcupine was crossing a narrow ditch, he saw me and buried his head in weeds on the far side. I called him Thumper because when I stood near him, he shifted his back toward me and whacked my walking stick with his tail. And then this was the summer of the masked shrew. Never had I seen as many alive and dead, these last killed by feral cats and also ferreted out of grass mounds by Mia, our ratting rescue dog. I reprimanded Mia. I urged her to leave the shrews alone and return to earthworms, her favorite wild dish in Storrs. Mia's vocabulary isn't large, and although she rotated her ears when I spoke, I don't think she understood me. In any case she didn't heed my request and throughout the summer hunted shrews.

Tom Bailey said that Rivermouth was "full of hints and flavors of the sea." Red rust covered the roofs and gables of houses that faced the east. A salty smell pervaded the air, and dense gray fogs crept through the streets. The storms, wreckage from broken boats, the wharves and shipyards fed the imagination and filled the brain of "every healthy boy with dreams of adventure." Does a person grow younger as he becomes old? When I was a boy, I sailed with Captain Cook and landed with him at Botany Bay. I was on the *Pamir* when it was torpedoed by a German submarine in 1917. I accompanied Charles Waterton as he wandered barefoot from Guiana to Brazil. I was

Mungo Park's classmate in Selkirk and the only one of his friends who suspected he'd become a celebrated adventurer. Even though the natives accused me of being one of the "devil's children," I also wanted to visit Timbuktu. I reached Bamako on the Niger River, but then a swarm of bees attacked me. Three of my pack animals died, and my face was so badly stung that I couldn't open my eyes for twelve days. I was able to sip water, but because I couldn't eat, I became "a walking skeleton" and had to return home.

After I recuperated, I trod the safer *Royal Road to Romance* and later saw all the Marvels with Richard Halliburton. I was the unnamed traveler who shared A. W. Kinglake's audience with the Pasha of Belgrade in 1835. In fact, the Pasha paid me the highest compliment I received during my centuries of travel, saying that the catalogue of my "glorious deeds" was "brighter than the firmament of heaven." Shortly thereafter, I roamed Greece with Henry Miller and George Katsimbalis, the Colossus of Maroussi, I stowed away with D. H. Lawrence and his wife when they sailed from Palermo to Cagliari and was by their side when they explored Sardinia. Like them I was disappointed when the wild boar I ate was dry and coarse. I haven't tasted wild boar since, but if I growl and start eating meat again, I'll return to Sardinia and give boar another try.

Most memorably I was a cabin boy on Cornelius Crane's brigantine yacht the *Illyria* when he explored the "Jungle Islands" of the South Seas in 1929. In New Guinea I traded a pocketknife to a Mai riverman for a preserved human head. None of my friends owned heads, and I was very proud of Lord Byron as I christened him. Although Mother didn't believe possessing a head as vulgar as bronzing baby shoes and converting them into the bases of lamps, she nevertheless did not think, as she told members of her bridge club, that a properly raised Episcopal boy should own a collection of heads. Exaggeration was part of Mother's charm, and she seasoned plodding truth with high-spirited untruth. But to keep the accounting straight and honest: although I hankered for a Keats and a Shelley, Lord Byron was the only head I owned. Preserved heads are good childhood conversation pieces. But they themselves are too silent to hold interest of a lively boy for long, and eventually I stored the head in the attic. Many years later when I was teaching in Jordan, Mother and Father moved into a condominium. Before moving Mother cleaned out the house. Among the many items she sent to the dump were the head and, alas, two cigar boxes packed with love letters.

Never did I suffer from "a fugitive and cloistered" imagination "unexercised and unbreathed." I did not dream of running away, just occasionally shedding the "curse of Tranquility" and wandering off. Bad boys who have dear parents become dutiful sons. The only times I sallied out of respectability were when I opened books. In reaction to the buttoned-down "hopelessly sane" days of office and desk, bad boys emeritus often become fond of nonsense, not the sort that provokes disrupting cacophonous guffaws but that which causes quiet, private smiles, for example, a poem like Mervyn Peake's "The sunlight lies." A hearty allergic sneeze caused by mold brought the poem to mind one rainy day. I recited it silently, chuckled, and forgot about the dismal state of the house. "The sunlight lies upon the fields / It lies upon the trees / It lies upon the hills and clouds / And on the flowers and fleas. / It lies on everything it can, /

For that is how it's made. / and it would lie on me, except / That I am in the shade." In the shade and sunlight of pages, I suddenly found myself steering a felucca on the White Nile and then afterward a stowing away on a tramp steamer entering the La Plata River. Home may not be where the imagination is, at least all the time, but it's where the heart hangs out.

Despite my meanderings, no plant or insect is named after me. On no island is there a mysterious Pickering Cave. Still, I have made discoveries, not those that cause fame to flicker but small things that entertained and suited me. In Nova Scotia I missed the boat and did not sail with Tom Bailey and three other Centipedes and become marooned on a rocky shore. Unlike Curdie, nowhere in field or wood did I stumble across a creature whose body was a "mass of incongruities": a short trunk, and long legs "made like an elephant's." Not even in dreams did I talk to an animal with dark green eyes and whose lower teeth swept up like icicles from its jaw and covered its upper lip. Sadly, no beast whose head resembled that of a polar bear one moment and that of a snake the next rode a high wave onto Bartlett's Beach and accompanied me to Black Point, tumbling and scampering, rumbling at sea crows and hissing at gulls.

Instead I accompanied Vicki on her shopping adventures, visiting Walmart, the Dollar Store, Canadian Tire, Sobeys, and Dayton Fruit and Vegetable. In a grocery cart at the entrance to Bulk Barn, overflowing with items discounted because their "Sell By" dates had almost expired, I discovered a package of sixteen vegan chocolate cookies. The price had been cut 75% to $2.26. I am an intrepid traveler. I ignored Vicki's thumbing her taste buds and bought the cookies. I carried them back to Beaver River. They were wonderful. I finished the package in three days sneaking them out of the pantry when Vicki was upstairs. As real explorers know, one discovery leads to another. The next week I again insisted on serving as Vicki's first mate when she returned to Bulk Barn. Discoveries may be original, but not all are appetizing. The vegan cookies had vanished, but in the cart, I found a Sproos Bar, a "Double Chocolate Beet" bar. Initially priced at $3.99; it, too, had been reduced 75%. The bar contained "wild-caught North Atlantic fish collagen," "plant-based fats," and was sweetened with dates. Each bar contained 240 calories but no cholesterol. The list of ingredients was long and natural although not all were familiar, inulin, for example, a starchy material found in several fruits but which is commonly obtained from chicory.

"Here I go," I said to Vicki, smacking my lips and biting into the bar as we left the store. "Don't," Vicki warned. She spoke too late. I should have kept my mouth shut. In any case one bite proved enough, and I didn't swallow. All discoveries, even the unappealing and the failed, invigorate and lead to other discoveries. At the bottom of cart lay boxes of "goodcook" Marshmallow Sticks. Each box contained eight, thirty-one-inch long bamboo skewers "Made in China." Initially a box cost $1.69, but to stimulate sales they'd been reduced 50%. "Alders grow beside all the roads surrouding Yarmouth and are the eczema of neglected fields," I said to Vicki. "Half the fun of roasting marshmallows is cutting your own stick. Who'd buy these?" "Clearly, no one hereabouts," Vicki said, "maybe people who live in cities and cook marshmallows on the porches of condominiums."

"Taste is not only a part and an index of morality; —it is the ONLY morality," John Ruskin wrote. "Tell me what you like, and I'll tell you what you are." Ruskin was intelligent, presumptuous, and often wrong. A person does many things habitually, not because he likes them but just because he does them. More palatable to me is Robert Louis Stevenson's remark, "When a man's heart warms to his viands, he forgets a great deal of sophistry, and soars into the rosy zone of contemplation." Dinners at the Wheelhouse in Digby bookended our arrival in and departure from Nova Scotia. Both times Vicki and I shared a scallop platter and ate Greek salads and baked potatoes. Each of us also drank a twenty-ounce glass of pale ale. We'd spent two days on the road when we arrived and were tired, so we split a slice of coconut cream pie. We are fur grandparents, and to monitor the dogs locked in the car we sat by the back window of the dining room overlooking both the restaurant's parking lot and the Annapolis Basin.

Such little doings shaped our days in Canada as they do in Connecticut. Ignoring high seriousness and taste—moral, cultural, or culinary—creates a sense of freedom. Moreover, it sometimes makes me think myself one-up on people who succumb to believing such matters important. Of course, Pride is a devil, its hold on people so paradoxical that escaping its clutches is impossible. "Sensible folks," Josh has long said however, "always prefer the low to the high." Be that as it may, and Josh may be wrong, I tracked the summer's gastronomical activities. Doing so occupied my pencil. Vicki called it my summer's crossroad puzzle. In any case I anticipated the delight of watching boredom settle like mist on the faces of people who later asked how we spent our weeks in Canada. We went to Tim Hortons 31 times, two of the stops actually in New Brunswick, one near St.

John on the drive up, the other at St. Stephen as we left. Twice we went to Tims in Meteghan, nineteen kilometers north from Beaver River, and twice to a franchise on Starrs Road, this after buying vegetables at Riverview Produce. The rest of the times we went to the Tims between Main and Water streets. We always sat in a booth and drank medium-sized coffees. While Vicki ate a cupcake, I was abstemious. Late in the summer when breakfast sandwiches went on sale at two for five dollars, I joined Vicki if the sandwiches were served on biscuits. The pleasures of repetition are small but real. Coffee regulars recognized and chatted with us. One man showed me pieces of kidney stones that a doctor had broken with "sound waves." They were hard and brown with a soupcon of cream, "the color of coffee," Vicki observed. The man kept them in a small coin purse which he carried in the breast pocket of his jacket. "If I pass any more pieces," he said, "I'll add them to my collection. I have a friend who keeps her gall stones in a jam jar in the kitchen. But I'm the only person I know who takes kidney stones with him when he leaves the house. I think they bring good luck."

I'm preternaturally approachable, and throughout my life strangers have told me startling things, many of which were fishy. In Tims, one dreary afternoon, a gnarled old man whom I hadn't seen before invited himself into Vicki's and my booth. He asked the usual questions: where we were from and how long we had been in Nova Scotia. The questions were prelude to the man's describing his life. He said he'd grown up in Pubnico where his father was a fisherman. When he was a boy, his family's favorite delicacy consisted of small fish his father extracted from the stomachs of larger fish. "They were partially digested and soft

and juicy. We ate them raw," he said. "Mother believed they were good for treating a medicine cabinet
of ailments." Among those he mentioned were white
mouth, convulsions, mildew, boils, rickets, and stuttering. "My four brothers, six sisters, and I never saw a
doctor," the man added. He didn't describe the symptoms of white mouth, but if pushed to a diagnosis,
I'd guess strep throat or diphtheria. The mildew, I assume, was a fungus, and as for stuttering, the man
spoke clearly and enunciated carefully. Whether he
told the truth didn't matter. He was entertaining, and
I bought him a large coffee and a bran muffin. His
mother was his favorite subject. Her kitchen "smelled
like paradise," and she was so accomplished that she
"could change a periwinkle into a strawberry." She
also managed the family's finances. "So that we children were able to wear decent clothes to school, she
cooked in the same house dress and apron for a year."
Once, he recounted, "she resuscitated a dying hen."
Neighbors misunderstood and thinking she raised
the chicken from the dead, began bringing sick animals by the house for her to cure. "She wasn't able
to help them," the man said, "but so many people
talked about Mother's medical powers that the local
veterinarian complained to the parish priest, saying
Mother was ruining his business."

  "I'm glad the man told us his stories were true,"
Vicki said later. "If he hadn't, we never would have
suspected they were. But do you think he really married a woman named Peanut Hooberry?" "Sure," I
said. "The Hooberrys are a distinguished Nova Scotia
family. Macadamia Hooberry immigrated to Halifax
from Greece late in the eighteenth century. In 1918
his great-great-great grandson Acorn was one of the
sponsors of the Women's Franchise Act. In fact, tele-

vision prognosticators routinely predict that Hazel Hooberry will be Nova Scotia's first female premier. The Hooberry doesn't fall far from the tree."

Vicki and I dined in Yarmouth 23 times. Seven times we ate on the waterfront at the bar at Rudder's. We shared a pitcher of Rudder's Red or Blonde Rock beer, a Caesar salad, and bar chips, these last potato chips soaked in oil and fried. The chips looked a little like the sort of scabs my boyhood companions delighted in showing friends. They always threatened to charge a nickel to see them or any of their other marvelous scrapes or cuts. But being bad boys, they were so proud of their wounds that resisting showing them off was irresistible and amid the admiration of friends the nickel was forgotten. Dipped in cream cheese, the chips were scrumptious, a little like memories of childhood, the edges smoothed and softened as a person's taste becomes sentimental. Perhaps the sentimental is the "rosy zone of contemplation." Maybe sentiment is also the index of the best morality, the morality that tolerates and assuages, the morality that enables dreaming, and doesn't dissect and destroy in the name of a fluorescent abstraction, say, truth. It is the morality that dethrones bloody Moloch. Christianity, G.K. Chesterton said, was the "stupendous triumph of sentiment."

I prefer coffee house to bar acquaintances. Too often the stranger sitting on the next stool announces that one is his new best friend, this after the question, "where are you from," the answer swiftly accompanied by physical camaraderie, an arm slung over one's shoulders. "At the end of the summer, I'm coming to Connecticut to see you," a man declared one night. "We'll have some good times. What's your name?" "My name is Troy," I said, sliding back off my seat and pulling Vicki behind me, "But you'll have to hurry. I'm old, and by the time you get to Connecticut, I'll be dead." "That remark certainly ended the conversation," Vicki said when we were outside. "It was meant to," I replied.

A half century ago when I started teaching, I sometimes chaffed at routine. "Freshman English today, yesterday, and all the tomorrows," I said, my hours spent with people too young to be companions, my luxuriant thoughts mental topiary tamed to suit classroom protocol. Life seemed ruled by margins and lines. I imagined absenting myself from the university, particularly when winter was white and blank as typing paper. I romanticized other lives and dreamed of plucking one of the moon's silver apples and striding "over the hills and far away." At such times in the teetotaling silence of my study, I occasionally recited Kipling's verse. Never, though, was I tempted to emulate his "Seven men from out of Hell," "Rollin' down the Ratcliffe Road drunk and raising Cain." "Besides," I said to Vicki as we abandoned my new friend and escaped into the car, "it's time to go. We've finished our chips. Let's head to Tims and swill coffee."

Keeping track of anything distorts. I spent more time in August and September picking blackberries than I did sipping coffee. I talked more to crabs than to strangers. I was, I suppose, overly familiar. I plucked crabs off the beach at low tide and slipped them beneath curtains of seaweed hanging from boulders. If I had not done so, gulls would have eaten them, but perhaps the crabs were old and longed for oblivion. Maybe they were seventy-eight in human years. Maybe open beaches were crab hospices, and the crabs were tired of tides, burrowing into sand,

and diets of worms and snails, fish parts and mussels. When asked if they wanted me to remove them from the beach, the crabs answered in sign language waving their antennae and shaking their legs and pincers. Because I could not understand them, I hid them amid the rocks and seaweed, perhaps condemning them to a few more unpleasant days but making me feel better about myself. "Saving crabs," I thought, "like Vicki's saving insects from the vacuum when she cleans house."

Ten minutes northeast from our house was D. J.'s store and diner in Salmon River. We went to the diner nineteen times. On Sundays Vicki and I ate eggs and bacon for breakfast. During the week we sometimes ate lunch sharing a club sandwich and afterward a helping of bread pudding or a sliver of chocolate cream pie. On thirteen other occasions Vicki and family members visiting us drove there for ice cream cones. Because death by chocolate was usually sold out, I abstained from the cones. The rest of the family ate every and anything, Vicki's brother Geoff's favorite being maple walnut, Vicki herself eating privateer's bounty, a blend of caramel and black liquorish, and our son Francis, moon mist, a farrago of grape, banana, and bubble gum. We often saw neighbors there whom we did not know but who knew us as summer residents of the old house across from the church in Beaver River. During and after hurricane Dorian, electricity and the telephone in our part of Clare County went out for three days. During one of the days the Salmon River firetruck pulled into our driveway. "I am driving around to check on everybody," the fireman said. "We've opened the firehall and are serving sandwiches. You can also wash." The fireman paused then said, "I know you. I've seen you at D. J.'s. I hope you are all right." "I know you, too," I answered, "We are okay, and thank you for coming by. I expect I will see you at D. J.'s sometime soon." "You will," the man answered.

Dorian stormed through Nova Scotia shortly before we left. For a day rain pounded and slapped, and wind gusted and roared. The sound was frighteningly harsh and primitive—akin in noise at least to the primitive that man labors to escape by establishing governments and passing laws so that diverse tribes can live beside each other without exploding into uprooting and felling clashes. Desire to avoid the primitive permeates life. People become vegetarians and vegans. They transform pets into humans and become angry when their dogs act like dogs. They realize that honesty disrupts and is dangerous, and they learn to lie and live quiet lies. Like Fred Rogers, they think "silence is one of the greatest gifts we have." They become reclusive and more comfortable with fictional than actual people. How easy it is to do one's duty by writing checks and never leaving home. Afterward a person can put away his pen and give "his little grey cells" a rest. He can cavort with Blotpage, Quibble, and Dash. He can wear yellow slacks, a sky-blue shirt, and brown and white sports shoes. He can eat double chocolate sodas and drink champagne until he becomes red in the face. It doesn't matter if he forgets the names of Chiasmus and Hendiadys. He can kiss Miss Spelling and not worry about Syntax. What fun it is to associate with gadflies like Sir Dilberry Dibble and Lady Jon Frisk. How greening to discuss gardening with Pottle the Mole Catcher. What a delight after two hours at church to rush to the country club and eat dumplings with Betty Careless and tell naughty stories about Zeugma.

In any case during Dorian trees in the windbreak lapped the ground. In the spruce woods they toppled over in rows. I kept farmer's hours going to bed at 8:00 and getting up at 4:00. The damp swept into the house making it cold, and we piled six blankets on the bed. Our chimneys did not topple, and for a day we thought we'd escaped damage. We did not. Dorian shook our 160-year-old post and beam barn rattling beams loose from the frame. Although the beams were bigger and heftier than a circus fat-man's thigh, the storm twisted and splintered them, causing the loft to drop to the floor of the barn, spilling a pile of mysterious trunks and a junk store of antique furniture.

In sixty-five years of driving and forty years of owning a house, I'd never filed an insurance claim. But once telephone service returned, I called our agent in Yarmouth. An adjuster came to the house and took pictures of the barn. The following day we locked the house, drove to Digby, and the next morning boarded the ferry for New Brunswick. We arrived home four days before my birthday. I stayed up late that night and read through three post office cartons of mail. Actually, I only opened eight envelopes. I threw everything else away unread. I got up early the following morning and mowed the grass. The next afternoon I walked along the Fenton River. Blackberries season was over, but berries were so thick on autumn olive that the trees sagged and their limbs brushed the ground. The berries were astringent and left a chalky aftertaste. They were also sweetly tart and beautiful with maroon skins freckled with pearl making the sweetness more visual than gustatory. I ate a handful and watched a great blue heron swallow a small trout.

I ambled home across the campus. For the first

time I noticed the cones of golden larch, green origami rosettes shaped like small artichokes. One bright sight leads to others, in my case one tree to another. Panicles of seeds on sourwood stitched up and out looking like threads torn from elfin slippers. Seven-Son Flower tree was blooming. Lacebark elm was awash with driblets of seeds tinged with pink, and the limbs of kousa dogwoods were vegetable counters sagging under baskets of raspberry fruits. Repairing the barn in Beaver River was bound to be expensive, but I forgot about the stuff of high blood pressure as I strolled home. On my birthday the children telephoned to wish me good tidings. Jet Blue, Holmgren Subaru, Retirement Security, and Holland America Cruise Line emailed me. My friend Raymond gave me a bottle of wine, and I received cards from Vicki, the dogs, an old sweetheart, three running companions, only one of whom is still able to run, and from Billy, a childhood acquaintance born in Nashville on the same day and year I was born.

Dinner that night was popcorn, a tofu hot dog, and a piece of a chocolate pie Vicki made that afternoon. I opened a bottle of Red Stripe beer. Vicki stuck a candle in the pie, and we ate in front of the television and watched "This Beautiful Fantastic," a cheerful Netflix movie. That night in a dream I dressed conservatively. I wrote a green and red plaid shirt, pressed khaki trousers, and brown tasseled loafers. Initially shaving cream covered my face, later, peanut butter, creamy, not crunchy my favorite. During the dream I walked a huge tortoise on a leash. The tortoise behaved better than Vicki's and my dogs. It did not jerk the leash. Instead it swiveled its long neck around and affectionally rubbed its head against my leg. The next morning Vicki and I drove across state to the university hospital in Farmington where a dermatologist scraped off our barnacles. When we checked in, a receptionist asked if we had been out of the country during the past three months. On my saying we'd just returned from Nova Scotia, she looked puzzled. "Nova Scotia," she said, "that's in Europe, isn't it?"

A Joke?

Toward the end of his long writing life, G. K. Chesterton worried that contemporary ethical and economic problems would change the essay, making it restrictively cogent and dogmatic. St. Thomas Aquinas, Chesterton wrote, "said that neither the active nor the contemplative life could be lived without relaxation in the form of jokes and games. The drama or the epic might be called the active life of literature, the sonnet or the ode the contemplative life. The essay is the joke."

The spirits of the age and of age shape essays. Neither wholeheartedly celebrates the joke. George Moore said that his *Confessions of a Young Man* was "merely the evanescent haze by the side of the wood, the enchantment of a May morning." "Youth goes forth singing," he explained, admitting that such songs were often crude and superficial but adding that they babbled spontaneously and truthfully. May turns to November. Asphalt smothers babbling brooks, and the haze becomes a smoky fog. The songs remain true, but they become dirges and laments for those fabled times when one's heart was young and gay. For retired oldsters even the most satisfactory life seems unsatisfactory if one has the leisure and a brain active enough to ponder. Moreover, it is impossible to relax by the side of a silent copse and ignore the blather of hyperbole and branding, propaganda, celebrity, and commerce. Not even social eremites are immune to the anxiety spread by radio and television. The narrator of "Stopping by Woods on a Snowy Evening" got things wrong. He should have ignored his promises. Instead of pushing through the snow and deep woods, he should have turned about and retraced his steps. He could have returned on a sunny morning in spring when bluebells and trillium were blooming. Then perhaps his promises would not have seemed onerous. Of course, in life off the page reversing direction isn't possible. One tolerates the miles and the weather and endures.

People my age dream of the Elysian fields of assisted living. They imagine material ease, days of no mowing or raking, no shoveling, no picking up sticks, no calls to plumbers, electricians, or roofers who never appear. They also dream about the blossoming time before the Cherry Orchard was chopped down. They romanticize the past and places they forsook for, as Washington Irving put it, "new objects of wonder." They question why they absented themselves from felicity or at least what seems felicity when glimpsed through the mazy wood of memory. Like that of Rip Van Winkle their absences seem naps, albeit the dozes often lasted longer than Rip's twenty years. They yearn to visit their former homes or at least see them again. But they know that's impossible. The streets and houses have changed. Strangers live in them. Indeed, they themselves are strangers, and the companions of boyhood are unrecognizable. Even when former friends meet, they have little to talk about. Memories of high school sports evoke a smile then a shrug as teammates recollect broken acquaintances. No matter how large the team once was, not enough benchwarmers remain to plug gaps on the field and in the mind. "How have the years treated your old roommate Jacky?" I wrote a college classmate last Christmas. "I haven't heard anything about him for decades." "He founded an advertising company and was a great success," the classmate replied. "He never married and devoted a lot of time to charity. He became an ardent environmentalist and for years worked to keep the Caney Fork River clean, especially the stretch flowing past Rock Island." "But now, alas, you wouldn't recognize Jacky, and he wouldn't recognize you. He has hogged all the illnesses. But thankfully," my correspondent concluded, "he, rather his remnants, won't suffer much longer." Are the elderly the only people who understand that while days often seem interminable, life itself is but a flicker? "Cancer, Dementia, Coronary, Parkinson's, the Four Pale Horses of the Apocalypse," Josh said. "A person grows accustomed to their names and to their ways like 'breathing out and breathing in,' as Professor Higgins put it in *My Fair Lady*."

People hanker for the bygone in order to escape the dislocating appointments of their presents. My friends in Storrs are retired academics, and changes in grammar irk them more than the meretricious doings of the political canaille in Washington. Setting their red marking pencils on edge at the rhetorical moment are the ear-grating infelicities of the Lesser Pronoun Shift. Last week I received an email announcing a lecture sponsored by the history department. The speaker was a professor from a nearby college. "They," the notice read, "will be present for a lecture" in early November. The professor, the notice continued, "will preview their forthcoming book." Recently I read an article attacking sexist language, among other things the phrase "animal husbandry."

In another but related article a "Gender Specialist" urged people to refrain from using the "carceral words" *man* and *woman*. To avoid sexist language, a right-minded person should instead call "their" friend "womanion," the first five letters drawn from *woman* and *man*, last three imported from *companion*. "The times, it are and are not changing," Josh remarked, explaining that despite being widespread and contagious, voguish grammatical fervor was a mild verbal flu quickly cured by a dose of writing job applications. Instead of celebrating humor's high rationality, its questioning and playful doubting, its capacity to kindle change, and its being a panacea for enervating anxiety, social egalitarians, he wrote the next day, "tried to browbeat the under read into believing all levity is questionable."

I don't know if Josh is right or wrong. But certainly, brave new grammar and its neologisms cling to mind longer than statements coined by philosophers. Like me, many oldsters react strongly to bruised syntax and morphology. Last week when a football pundit fumbled his language and praised a coach's "trickeration," I kicked the game out of bounds and snapped off the television. Because Vicki left the radio on in the kitchen, I overheard a woman testify on National Public Radio that she'd been "invisibilized." "'Words, words, words'—unfortunately I know what they are supposed to mean," I mumbled, went outside, and shoveled snow. In Albert Bigelow Paine's *The Hollow Tree*, Story Teller told bedtime tales to "the Little Lady." She was "four years old, going on five" and was very fond of stories. Sometimes she wanted a new story, and but more often than not she wanted an old story. These last, Story Teller said, "must always be told the same, because the Little Lady, like a good many grown up people, does not care for new and revised editions, but wants the old stories in the old words that sound real and true."

Change dislocates and disturbs, especially the elderly who long for stability, that is, for what they believe to be and to have been real and true, in stories, in words, and in daily life. Instead of "Give me that old time religion," they sing "give me the old times." Even in my own neighborhood I think myself an alien or at least a visitor from a distant era. In the Willimantic Co-op last week, I saw a card advertising "Dr. Hempdog." "Hemp Oil Tinctures," the card said, "Comfort for Our Furry Friends," "Especially Rich in CBD and Terpenes." "I don't belong in Now," I said to Vicki. "Swallow a handful of CBD gels, and you'll soon feel at home," Vicki said. "I know what CB's and CD's are, and I've known a pharmacy of SOB's, but what's a CBD?" I asked. "What a Diplodocus!" Vicki exclaimed. "I thought people like you were extinct." In the mail that afternoon an advertisement arrived asking if I was using "the catheter that is really right for you." That night I thumbed *The Harvard Magazine.* Under "Crimson Classifieds" appeared advertisements for "Massachusetts Real Estate." For sale on Planting Island at Marion an hour and twenty minutes from Cambridge was the "perfect vacation starter home." At 1306 square feet, the house had three bedrooms, two bathrooms, a dry basement, an attic, was heated, and was only steps away from the beach—all for $590,000. Initially the price provoked an exclamation featuring the name of the son of the Great First Cause. This was followed by "Holy Cow," a genuflection to the biblical Golden Calf, and lastly by "what a joke," said as I showed the advertisement to Vicki. "Not a joke," Vicki said, "but the way of the changing pecuniary world." "No," I said. "You'll see," she answered. Two days Eliza telephoned, and I saw. She and Travis, her husband, had returned to California from a week in Portland, Oregon. "Portland is a wonderful city filled with coffee shops, bookstores, and bakeries," she reported, "and, best of all, you can get a nice house for only half a million dollars."

In his history of the Dutch settlers of New York, Diedrich Knickerbocker noted that when life weighed heavy hen-pecked husbands in the Catskills wished "that they might have a quieting draught out of Rip Van Winkle's flagon." "There comes a period when one lives less in future dreamings," Norman Douglas wrote, "when one requires, in short, to be distracted." For my part, I'll pass on the high alcohol of Rip Van Winkle's flagon and confine my quaffing to a single beer, a side dish accompanying Netflix and dinner. My ordinary life is simultaneously boring and stimulating, resembling the lives of most oldsters. Accordingly. I don't dream about the future. As a result, although I sometimes suffer from bouts of scouring spleen, I don't become melancholy and long to escape the everyday. When observed carefully, the commonplace can distract, in fact almost intoxicate.

I was "gifted" with an "ineptitude for consistency" —a character trait that vaccinates writing against cogency and dogmatism, the ills Chesterton warned that would weaken the essay and elevate it into yet another literary bauble. I am my grandmothers and grandfathers—smart people, sensibly unambitious and content with "enough," people who realized that taking a thing seriously often embalmed it. The biggest difference between us is that they grew up in the country and in small towns whereas I grew up in a city. In cities community is fluid; neighbors are strangers, and people become what they do, not who their family is or was. In cities worldly or recognized achievement defines, and competition thrives—who's up and who's down, who is on the way in and on the way out. For a while I, too, wanted to be somebody, albeit the *some* remained undefined. But then shortly after I graduated from Sewanee, my DNA awakened. I ceased caring about winning or losing. What mattered was doing, and doing for enjoyment. I didn't want to squander living by struggling for position or power. I applied to graduate school, not because I wrote well. I didn't, a fact I thought that would protect me from being whirled into any competitions that existed in English studies.

Things rarely evolved the way a person thinks they did. However, teaching freed me from ambition. Occasionally, I caught a cold and coveted recognition. Happily, fevers were always short-lived, and I swiftly returned to common sense and wandering the stacks of everyday life. Last week I accompanied Vicki on a mall Odyssey. In fact, I steered the trireme—well, actually the Subaru. Our first stop was at "The Consignment Superstore." It lacked the allure of Polyphemus' cave. Instead of the aroma of meats and cheeses, it reeked of sway-backed dresses and dry cleaning, and I left quickly. While Vicki mooned through the clothes racks, I returned to the car to take a nap. A woman saw me leave the store, however, and approached me before I reached the car. She was laden with clothes that had belonged to her husband. He died recently, she explained, noting that he and I appeared to be the same size. "I've cleaned out his closet, and I'm taking his best clothes to the consignment store, but I think his shirts would look good on you," she said. "Would you like to buy a few of them?" Aside from shirts given to participants in road races, I haven't owned a new shirt in two decades. On most days I wear my son Francis's hand-me-downs. Vicki bought them for Francis when he started high school twenty-six years ago. She purchased the extra-large size so that Francis wouldn't outgrow them immediately but instead would be able to wear them for several years. "I'm practical," she said at time, "I always think ahead." The shirts looked like shower curtains, and rather than outgrowing them, Francis never grew into them. Consequently, when I inherited them, they were slightly mildewed but otherwise new.

Next Vicki and I went to Buckland Mall. While Vicki picked up eyeglasses in LensCrafters, I wandered the mall. Music in the building was loud and choppy. Unlike the songs of the Sirens, it repulsed, and to shield myself from its dislocating cacophony, I behaved like Ulysses's crew and plugged my ears. Later I beached myself in an aisle at a table beside Gloria Jean's. I sipped coffee and watched passersby, among others, mall walkers, aged men in trains of two always wearing baseball caps and blue jeans, caregivers guiding the simple-minded, old husbands and wives limping and tottering, not planning to buy anything but simply away from home, and then pairs of women, one usually pushing a baby carriage and looking unhealthy—unhinged, as if birth had ripped all the taunt ligaments in her body, stretching them into ropy lassoes. Because my ears were plugged, the mall was as quiet as the island of Djerba. No Charybdis spun dizzily; no six-headed Scylla nipped me, no mob of teenagers swirled past shouting guttersnipe words, and no femme fatale leaned backwards over my table, shook her hair, then tangoed away.

In a way the mall was a modern-day Lotus Land.

Small booths ran down the middle of its aisles in a commercial chain. Proprietors sold non-prescription eyeglasses, earrings, nail polish, purses, watches, scarves, and "Fresh Baked" pretzels. One man took photographs and preserved "Life's Moments." Another pierced ears, and several repaired and sold used cellphones. "We Fix Phone," a sign declared. Adelbrook Bark-ery specialized in "Treats for Your Best Friend." Bamboo Pillows mitigated the effects of insomnia, snoring, asthma, neck pain, migraines, and TMJ, a joint or sliding hinge that connects a person's jawbone to his skull and which, a salesman informed me, can go on the fritz and cause pain. A machine at KeyMe stamped out keys. Displayed at The Smile Exchange were fifteen gumball machines. The machines dispensed M&M's, skittles, jellybeans, and "dippin' dots," balls filled with round bits of candy that looked like buckshot. Among the chewing gums parceled out were Double Bubble, Blueberry Smoothie, Green Apple, Watermelon, and Cry Baby, a hard shelled, taste bud curdling chewie. At Passport to Adventure if a person consented to receive phone calls and text messages, he could sign up for a $55,500 Sweepstakes and the chance to win a white Nissan SUV. At Cruise Your Way, one might win a cruise if he agreed to similar conditions. The booth was a wooden replica of a white cruise ship. The ship had six levels or decks of balconies and three of portholes, these last running down to the waterline and ranging from small to smaller to smallest.

Almost as if their morning granola contained prophylactic grounds of moly, people ambling the mall resisted the Circean attraction of the booths. The single booth that had costumers sold personalized T-shirts. Purchasers could decorate shirts with statements they composed or a picture or remark selected from an array on display around the booth, such things as "Trust Me. I'm A Dentist" and "I Love You Mommy," the *love* a cartoon Valentine's Day heart, not a word. Intoxication of the literal sort was popular. A family of four—mother, father, son, and daughter—bought the same shirt, in different doses or sizes. Printed on the front in capital letters was "Enjoy Weed." Below the words appeared a jar from the top of which exploded a constellation of starry green marijuana leaves. I was no longer a Diplodocus. In the booth nearest Gloria Jean's, a woman topped by a purple headdress managed an apothecary's shop of CBD products—ointments, creams, and drops that created synergies "known as the entourage effect." Among other beneficial things the products helped manage stress, supported "healthy inflammatory functions," made skin look youthful, and relaxed a person so that he fell asleep easier and woke up refreshed.

I experienced the "proximity effect" because I fell asleep and woke up refreshed when Vicki found me at Gloria Jean's. The sights I saw in the mall were unexciting, but unlike the things Ulysses claimed to have experienced while returning from Troy, they existed. Only folks up to the "goozle pipes" in CBD oil or with their snouts submerged in the wine-dark contents of amphora could have believed such stretchers. Among other monstrous lies Ulysses told the mumping citizens of Ithaca were his meeting the ghosts of Achilles and Agamemnon, being given a bag containing unfavorable winds, seeing half his sailors turned into swine, spending seven amorous but supposedly tedious years with that popsie Calypso, and experiencing an unpleasant cannibalistic to-do with Polyphemus who because of his one eye was popularly known to folks skeptical of tall mythology as Lighthouse.

I lead a balanced CBD-free life. Perhaps to compensate for the abstemious intoxication I experience during the day, dreams often muddle my nights. After arriving home, disembarking from the Subaru, and being greeted by the dogs, all of which are old but not quite as feeble as Ulysses's Argos, I buried yesterday's compost and scattered an armful of corn shucks in the wood behind the house. For dinner I ate a mixture of yoghurt, almonds, and coconut. Afterward I watched an episode of "The Durrells in Corfu" on television then went to bed. I started rereading Somerset Maugham's *The Moon and Sixpence*, but I soon fell asleep. My sleep was exciting and troubled. In a dream I stood near a dock from which a boat loaded with malefactors and explosives was preparing to sail. The crew intended to sink an oil tanker by steering their boat into the side of the ship. However, their intention had been discovered. Attached to the hull of their boat was an explosive device set to detonate once they sailed half a mile from land. I don't know how deeply involved I was in foiling the miscreants' plan. However, I was pleased that the villains would be "Blown to Kingdom Come and their bodies shredded like confetti." But then I discovered that the only female in the crew was actually an undercover police agent. Because of an oversight, "typical of the federal government," she had not been informed about the bomb and was on the dock preparing to board the doomed boat.

Standing near me on land, though, were her parents. They were old and feeble and had come to wave a fond goodbye to their daughter. When I discovered the woman's identity, I rushed over to them and putting my arms around their shoulders pulled them close. "Go down on the dock. Kiss your girl goodbye," I whispered, "and tell her to jump overboard once the boat is offshore." "What?" they said. "Tell her to jump overboard," I repeated. Alas, they were deaf. "Tell her to jump overboard," I whispered again. "What?" they asked once more. No matter how close I pulled them, no matter how I raised my voice, they remained mystified. In fact, my urgency frightened them, and they tried to twist out of my grip. At this point I am afraid, I broke the Third Commandment. I jerked them into my chest, probably wrenching their necks, and began shouting, "Tell her to jump overboard. Tell her to jump overboard." I don't think the secret agent received the message. In any case I will never know. I woke up, covered with perspiration, saying, "Tell her to jump overboard" and simultaneously thinking "those poor parents."

Unlike the novel life lacks a plot. Waking and sleeping, the rational and irrational slide into each other. A person sips coffee at Gloria Jean's one moment and stands beside a dock the next. Chesterton recognized that cogency is imposed. Because the essay in Chesterton's terms is a joke and eschews high seriousness, it allows reader and writer to ruminate without feeling compelled to interpret. Mulling for the sake of mulling is a pleasure but one often criticized as indulgent. In a competitive society shaped and propagandized by believers and doers, it seems anti-social, too rarefied a pleasure to benefit either an individual or a community. For my part I think the best essays do not instruct, inspire, or convert. They simply awaken sensibility.

Before time put a hitch in my gait, I did not wander malls and my dreams were earthier and unprintable. As a boy I imagined roaming the badlands east of the sun and west of the moon. After leaving Tennessee, I visited many distant places, the names of which I thought poetic: Patmos, Damascus, Bucharest, Tbilisi, Samarkand. Unlike Byron, however, I never became the wandering outlaw of my own mind. I met a few banditos, but they have now aged into gray wheelchair presences. And if I recall them, I don't think of them as often and with the fondness I remember friends in Nashville. "Those who have lived all their lives in remote places do not feel the remoteness," Richard Jefferies wrote. Similarly, visiting the exotic strips away exoticism and homogenizes. Once upon a time, I thought markets in Caribbean towns romantic. In fancy I envisioned tables sagging under the color spectrum of fruits and vegetables. Choruses of market women with come-hither voices and wearing rainbow colored dresses invited me to sample and buy.

In the local Price Chopper employees wear bright red aprons. On display are the contents of a tractor trailer's load of flowers, fruits, and vegetables: among others, roses, orchids, amaryllis, carnations, daisies, purple and green grapes; and red, yellow, russet, and white potatoes. A wooden divider separates avocados from yellow and sweet onions. Stacked in a bin are quarts of strawberries, blueberries, blackberries, and raspberries. Piled on tables are starfruit, papaya, limes, lemons, oranges, clementines, pomegranates, and Anjou, bosc, Asian, and red pears. Some tomatoes are as big as softballs, others look like yellow and red gumballs. The aisles are plantations of tomatillos, bananas, plantains, kiwis, passion fruits; Chinese, baby, and graffiti eggplants; green and snap beans, corn, Brussel sprouts, turnips the color of frostbite, and green, nappa, red, and savory cabbage. The variety startles and erases the recollection of Caribbean markets. People my age patronize supermarkets. They have aged beyond youth's white-washing enthusiasm for flies and the natural. They like convenience and appreciate the artificial. The words *real* and *genuine* have lost allure, and neither the taste of germs nor the fragrance of marijuana makes them eager to bite into the unwashed, be it food or life.

If an Eve who has a crush on Adam hankers for zesty serpentine doings and shops at Price Chopper, she can tempt him with an orchard of apples, Even if he is a picky eater, one of the several varieties should appeal to him, if not honey crisp or gala then Granny Smith, Cortland, empire, Fiji, Paula red, ambrosia, jazz, or smitten. If an apple doesn't inflame Adam's hormones, then Eve should try hotter items, say, a candy jar of peppers, green, red, yellow, serrano, hung wax, finger hot, cherry, or poblano. The appetites of young men today are more sophisticated or at least different from the appetites of the companions of my youth. If Adam still refuses "to get up to something," then Eve should threaten him with a week of squash for breakfast, lunch, and dinner: buttercup, butternut, dark green and white acorn, carnival, yellow, and spaghetti. Such a diet would have forced my friends, even those with saints' palates, to misbehave. After one meal, I'd have waved the white napkin and acceded to Eve's desires. In the unlikely event, however, that Adam continues to be unwilling, Eve ought to pretend to lose enthusiasm and make him a salad. Toss in radishes, cilantro; green leaf, red, and hydroponic lettuce; endive especially Belgian endive, watercress, frisee, chopped leeks, escarole, radicchio, and sprigs of ornamental parsley. Throughout the salad sprinkle nuts—almonds, hazelnuts, walnuts, and roasted peanuts. Nuts are invigorators although in my salad days I thought them greatly overrated. In any case if the nuts don't do the trick, Eve should escort Adam to the door and welcome good old Enos. If dealing with Adam has exasperated her beyond caution into recklessness, she could invite Pan to dinner. As a last resort if Enos turns out to be a vegan and the sound of the flute hurts her ears, perhaps she could corral one of the Erotes so tired of flying around that he's not adverse to a respite of messing about.

In speaking about Joshua Reynolds, William Blake said, "the man, either painter or philosopher, who learns or acquires all he knows from others, must be full of contradictions." People see and learn from their surroundings, be these composed of books and a reading family, an outback and a rain forest, or a grocery store and aisles in a mall. The essay's strength lies in mirroring surroundings, reflecting contradictions, and awakening the imagination, that is, in capturing life's inconsistent meanderings, the relaxing purposeless saunters during which a person notices troves of objects and ideas. No man lives without embracing contradictions, and those that struggle to do so fence themselves in and miss the grand variety of living. Although essays represent life as it is more accurately than other types of writing, their dependence upon words runs through them in a grand fault. Like pyrrhotite in concrete, the inadequacies of words cause the essay and, indeed, all genres to crack and crumble.

Schools purport to teach things that can't be taught, decency, affection, indeed, how to teach and then the importance of telling lies which seem truer than life itself. Schools do better with facts, truths, and regimented thinking. However, facts change rapidly, while truths deteriorate, sometimes into falsehoods, other times into sluggardly truisms. As for regimens—they look good on lined fields and pages, but don't fare well when days rumple out of regularity and rise into hills and slide into valleys. But "then, then, then," the wells of inconsistencies and contradictions never dry. Unregulated days may lead to unregulated thinking and sometimes to creativity. Never does the creativity last long. Responsibility, disease, and leaden duty eventually regiment behavior. The imagined becomes conventional. Days become gelatinous, and the mind loses the ability to fabricate appealing extravagancies.

As a result, oldsters revisit the past in hopes that memories will cause days to bud. "Our parents," a childhood friend wrote me recently, shared a special bond "as we do or 'as do we?'" Old people wander malls and groceries wishing that something would awaken fancy. They read hoping that pages will prove hallucinatory. Above all they regret losing the capacity to populate their daily lives with astonishing characters. Once upon a time, Josh told me, he might have been able to create "the land of the Crotalophoboi." "They were cannibals and necromancers," Norman Douglas wrote, "who dwelt in a region so hot, and with light so dazzling, that their eyes grew on the soles of their feet." Then there were the M'tezo and the Bulanga. The former ambled about naked, swopped wives every new moon, and "ate their superfluous female relations." A week after three hundred of the latter were baptized, they "ate up old Mrs. Richardson, our best lady preacher," a divine testified, "the poor dear! We buried her riding boots. I remember there was nothing else to bury." "I have neither the time nor the energy for such high junketing nowadays," Josh said, "I must call Tim to clean the gutters, Bruce to wash moss off the roof, and Tom to service the generator. And, alas, the house needs a new furnace. I want to buy one before winter sets in, but I know I'm already too late." For my part, my hankering in boys' books ran to sunny climes populated by anthropophagi. As a footnote, let me gratify Hebraic antediluvians by acknowledging that the literary sins of the child will out. My daughter Eliza has renounced my Hellenistic taste and is a vegetarian.

I understood Josh's incapacity to set out for distant fanciful places. The local world is also too much with me. I spent yesterday afternoon in Willimantic at the Department of Motor Vehicles. Two years ago, when I bought the Subaru, I neglected to include Vicki on the title. "I'll never get out of probate court with the car if you die. I'll be housebound and not able to drive where the action is," she said as she bustled me off to the DMV. Employees at the DMV were gracious and patient and even called me "dear." But I got so flustered that I almost cried. Four times I filled out the forms incorrectly, once because I didn't write my last name then my first name. Instead I wrote my first name first and my last name last. The other times I wrote on the wrong lines. On three occasions I returned to the car to fetch my insurance card. Because I did nor wear my reading glasses, I returned with the wrong cards, initially the card that expired in 2018 and later the new card that did not take effect for two weeks. Finally, I dug the current card out of the glove compartment though it took me a long time to find it. Eventually Trudi took the forms away from me and filled them herself. She said the rest of my day would be easier and assured me that many people got confused in the DMV.

Trudi was a kindly liar. Once I could have filled

the forms out swiftly. I could easily have imagined cannibal islands and, indeed, cannibal queens, and of course stomach-devouring cannibal coconuts, guava, and breadfruit. Seventy years ago, I was Sammy, Robinson Crusoe's more adventuresome and capable Man Friday. Despite stumbling through adding Vicki to the title, there were red letter aspects to the day. After dinner, I went to the library. Exactly thirty years ago, Stephen a librarian told me, he bought Stella his box turtle at a pet store in Massachusetts. "Stella was old then," Stephen said, "but she is in grand health and has outlived the pet store by twenty years. Yesterday I bought some of her favorite worms at Walmart, and when the library closes, I'll go home, and we'll have a feast and celebrate."

The inability of words to capture man's doings accurately does not bother me. The failure enables me to relax and not take days or thought so seriously that I miss living. What I regret more is the incapacity to paint the transcendence of Nature, auratic moments, glowing experiences, the mysterious essences which are encapsulated by the trite phrase "words fail me." For me such things are ostensibly simple, in autumn, the fan dance of gingko leaves falling to the ground, the leaves of red oaks chewed into scarlet facets by gypsy moths, breezes rinsing the fronds of hay-scented ferns, and then sunlight shining high through hemlocks, their needles glistening like slivers of ice, above and behind them bare white oaks, the trees worn brushes, their upper branches bristles stretched and loosened from ferules, lints of mushrooms soiling them, turkey tail and milk white toothed polypore rough and curdled. At the edge of a field stands a solitary beech, a robe of lemony leaves silky over its blue limbs. "The joyous sister of Leuce,

New England's counterpart of the Greeks' white popular," an unidentified transcendentalist said in the nineteenth century. How can I describe the demure appearance of a small meadow katydid without sounding silly? I lack the words to make readers appreciate the moth-eaten twill of toothed hedgehog mushrooms or November's oak leaves, shot-holed like discarded clothes distributed by the Salvation Army.

I don't probe deep into my actual everyday thoughts. If I did, no one would be scandalized, but a few would certainly reckon my ponderings inconsequential. People realize, for example, that insects communicate. They mate and give birth. They feel pain, and die from disease and exposure. But like people, do they suffer from dementia? "I believe they do," I told Vicki last night. "In late October and early November, and only then, do I find female praying mantises on the running track behind the gymnasium. I know they're dying, but they also seem confused. I pick them up, hold them against my chest, and warm them. Once they stir and bite, I free them into the deep scrub beyond the track. But they never fly." "No," Vicki said. "They age and die, but nothing is the same." "Not the same perhaps but similar. Aren't we all crawlers of one family or another, most of us beetles, some Passalidae, others Curculiondae, but nonetheless beetles?" I said, influenced by a letter I received on Monday in which a friend described the gradual abrading death of Frank an almost forgotten, library companion, a man whose books once brightened early summer nights like a swarm of fireflies. "Frank," my correspondent wrote, "cannot get off his back. He can't talk and just lies in bed and wiggles his arms and legs." Oh, well, as the evening passed, remembrance dimmed. Vicki and I watched an episode of "The French Village" on television, and later in bed I read Eric Ambler's *Epitaph for a Spy*. Today, early morning is bright and almost warm. A titmouse is perched on a branch outside my study window, and the low scrub along the property line is damp with color, the orange leaves of Japanese barberry and the pink leaves of winged euonymus shaking slightly like droplets before breaking into quiet, soothing drizzles.

Chesterton was right. The essay is a joke. In the gaming world of prose, it relaxes by distorting or, if one must tell what appears to be the truth, by lying. Three times in the past month I've come downstairs in the morning to a kitchen seasoned with the aroma of skunk. I associate skunks with barefoot boyhood, and the fragrance makes me smile. The aroma also permeated the garage. There it was more highly seasoned than a vindaloo. People who are urban and not at ease with the stercoraceous don't appreciate skunks. "You have to find that animal. Chase it away and make sure it doesn't return," Vicki instructed me on the third morning. "Finding it won't be easy," I said, "but I'll do my best. If I succeed, I'll make sure it hibernates away from the house." The truth was I knew the whereabouts of the skunk. Winter was coming, and I didn't intend to bother it. Mr. Polecat is "quite a nice gentleman" except when he gets excited, Story Teller said in *The Hollow Tree*. "But when he does, he loses friends."

Moreover, I liked sharing the yard with animals and was lonely. I had not seen my fox in two years. The rabbits of early summer had disappeared, and in late September, a careless driver hit my favorite doe. When I buried compost, I imagined racoons and opossums moving into apartments in the woodpile or in the yawning trees behind the house. I studied the ground looking for the trails of small animals and walked around the woodpile in hopes of discovering burrows. If I were fortunate enough to see darkly, maybe I'd discover traces of one of the ancient human gods, a god with animal friends and familiars, a god of grove or stream, of the near and the immediate. How wonderful it would be to meet a god who misbehaved and laughed, who damned asceticism and theology, a god who encouraged people to treasure this bruised earth, man's only home and the only earth he'll ever have.

For its part the skunk's burrow was off a drainage pipe that ran from the front of the garage down into a patch of pachysandra. At ground level the pipe had cracked open creating an entrance for the skunk. I stuck my arm into the pipe and rotated my forearm. When I removed my arm, it was redolent with skunk. "The skunk has decamped," I assured Vicki before dinner. "Are you positive?" she asked. "Absolutely," I said. "Boy, the kitchen smells good! I am really looking forward to your nut loaf and curried butternut squash soup, and by the by did you know that Vachel Lindsay called the grasshopper the Brownies' racehorse and the fairies' kangaroo? Do you think I can call katydids grassland fiddles?" "No, too precious," Vicki said. "Call a grasshopper a grasshopper, a katydid a katydid, and a chamber pot a chamber pot, not a cookie jar."

Mockingbird on the Wreath

Early in December my son Edward and his wife Erica put up and decorated their Christmas tree. "From the farm where we cut the tree Erica bought pine boughs to make a wreath as she does every year," Edward wrote. "After making the wreath she adds sprigs of holly from one of our holly bushes, and this year as in all the previous Christmases a mockingbird raided the wreath for berries." Christmas is the season of continuance. In his letter Edward asked me for my eggnog recipe, a request he makes every December. The recipe is a version of one that appears in *The Joy of Cooking*. To save the hearts of Christmas toppers I cut back on the cream and beef up the booze, blending a fifth of cheap bourbon, say, Kentucky Gentleman, with a pint of rum, a pint of brandy, and two quarts of half and half. I also toss in a pound of confectioner's sugar and a dozen eggs, white and yokes not separated. Sitting and fermenting for a day or two not only helps the eggnog but also whets the livers of canonical celebrants.

As I do every year, I warned Edward that although the eggnog slipped down the gullet smoothly, it packed a punch. "Hide the car keys of people who have more than two cups and don't allow them to drive. If they become obstreperous and demand their keys, agree but, "for friendship and Good King Wenceslas's sake," pour two cups "for the road down their throats. There is no better immobilizer." Additionally, I warned Edward against short cuts, that is, for the half and half substituting store-bought eggnog. "Commercial ipecac—a fundus stripper and pyloric canal dynamiter, gourmands call it," I wrote.

I also related a family anecdote, one Edward must had heard several times. When I was a boy, Grandma Pickering drove down from Carthage and spent Christmas with Mommy, Daddy, and me in Nashville. On all other occasions Grandma was a fervent teetotaler. At Christmas, however, Mother always assured Grandma that her eggnog was non-alcoholic. "It's a tonic," she said, "rich with natural, herbal invigorators." Mother was a splendid fabricator, but I don't think Grandma swallowed her description of the eggnog's provenance. What she did swallow, and swallow with gusto, was the eggnog, cup after vivifying cup, an elixir that made Christmas magical, effervescent with stars and shepherds, camels, mangers, and around them all the Herald Angels singing "peace on earth, and mercy mild." What I didn't tell Edward was that I no longer made eggnog. Age has sobered and sombered me. Instead of bringing joy to the day, eggnog now saddens evoking memories of lost bygones, Christmases in the company of those three wondrously nice people, Mommy and Daddy and Grandma.

Early in December I read Arthur Conan Doyle's *The White Company,* an historical romance set in the fourteenth century. Illuminating the pages were cudgels and long bows, chain mail, broad swords, and low, smoke-blackened forest inns hot with burning faggots, collops, and pots of wine. Among the characters were mountainous, bearded fighting men, pusillanimous abbots, knaves, treacherous siblings, "brothers through blood comrades," and, oh, yes, a damsel with jet black hair, at first glance a wild woodland sprite but withal a grand lady and "the most beautiful and graceful creature that mind could conceive of." The book was narrative eggnog. It dissociated readers from the analphabetic mutterings of the worldly and momentarily silencing night and day calmed armchair hours. Unlike eggnog the story was not addictive. In winter, weather compels a person, no matter how much he reads, to close his book and abjure swords and bucklers and to strap on work boots and woolly gauntlets and seizing a shovel venture outside to joust with snow and ice.

In the book Doyle described a princely feast in Bordeaux. Among the dishes displayed were "roasted peacocks, with the feathers all carefully replaced, so that the bird lay upon the dish even as it had strutted in life, boars' heads with the tusks gilded and the mouth lined with silver foil, jellies in the shape of the Twelve Apostles, and a great pastry which formed an exact model of the king's new castle at Windsor." As I now eschew strong waters, so I have aged into vegetarian days. Sampling Doyle's groaning board would have caused an attack of gout. The only dish that wouldn't have made my toes swell were the jellies. On my mentioning the jellies in a letter and comparing them to the Holy Families who once populated automobile dashboards in papist New England, a friend who in frolicking boyish days was a fixture on the Southern Debutante Circuit, described a formal dinner he attended decades ago.

The banquet table centerpiece was a nativity scene consisting of figures covered with royal icing, not only Jesus, Mary, and Joseph, but also a manger bulging with a cow, an ox, a ewe, and two lambs. Perched on the manger's roof was a dovecote of "bible birds," several with springs of olive in their beaks. From atop a bale of hay a mouse stared at the holy baby. Beside the manger stood three camels. Sitting astride them looking like Arab cowboys were angels. Instead of a pistol and lasso each angel held a shepherd's crook in one hand and a lantern in the other. "At such dinners," my friend wrote, "liquid spirits flowed and human spirits rose ebullient and at times memorably." By the end of the meal, Mary had lost her head; the Chief Marshal polished off Jesus, the crib, and Joseph's toolbox in single bite, and someone "fed the mouse to Abraham Lincoln the household cat."

Brides and grooms no longer dance atop wedding cakes, and I haven't seen an ornate pastry decoration in fifty years. My friend Josh informed me, however, that molds for garish jellies are popular among people who follow athletic teams at football universities, among others, Georgia, Clemson, LSU, and out of the region Ohio State. The molds depict almost an entire offensive squad, among them a massive lineman down on all fours, a quarterback raising his arm to pass, and a halfback in the classic galloping pose, football under left arm, right arm extended to fend off defensive players, left leg planted, and right leg raised high and crossing in front of the left. Josh said the jellies formed by the molds served as dessert at pulled-pork barbeques usually as accompaniments to chants of "Go Tigers," "Roll Tide," or a verse of the "Buckeye Battle Cry."

The Bells of Christmas Day may sing "peace on earth, good will to men," but Americans rarely hear them. Unlike war, peace does not sell. At the beginning of December seventeen books lay on the display table inside the front door of the local Barnes

& Noble. Two of the books analyzed the terrorist attacks that occurred on September 11, 2001. Eleven of the remaining books discussed war and war's alarms. Among them were descriptions of battles like the Alamo and Vicksburg, memoirs of an army life and of years as a Seal, and a how-to book examining military leadership. "The world would be better off if every man were brave enough to be a coward," Josh said on reading the title "Every Man a Hero." On the other side of the table facing the inside of the store rather than the entrance were eighteen books, all by or about women and appealing to women. "I suppose men only enjoy books about war, and women books about themselves. The stars are not brightly shining," Josh said.

Occasionally, however, starlight penetrates the corporate miasma. Late in November I ordered a pair of running shoes from Amazon. The shoes were supposed to arrive in five days. After they did not appear for eighteen days, I assumed the shoes were lost. I telephoned Amazon, and that night my money was refunded. Two days later the shoes appeared. On three occasions a delivery man had dropped them at the wrong address. On receiving the shoes, I called Amazon and told Surabhi to reinstate the charge. "I don't want something for nothing," I said. "No," she answered, "you can keep the product as well as the refund. There is no need to pay us again as it has already been refunded back to you. For the inconvenience you have experienced I request you to accept this as a token of apology from Amazon." "Did that really happen?" Josh asked me. "Yes," I said. "What a surprise!" he exclaimed then emended the old hymn, saying, "You should go tell that on the mountain."

After people stop observing, they often slide into

indifference or certainty. Life is easier both when one doesn't care or cares so much that he becomes inflexible. However, certainty is more anti-social than indifference because it often turns a person into an idealist or its dangerous facsimile a zealot. Along with arteries, age hardens opinions. I have approached distastefully close to the full-stopped stage of opinion. I have almost become house and hide bound, a mental state exacerbated by winter. In hopes of keeping ourselves and our thoughts limber—of seeing mockingbirds and blue birds, maybe even a glorious purple backed jay on an imaginary wreath—every winter Vicki and I leave Storrs for three or four weeks and cruise the Caribbean. We are not adventuresome, and the places we visit are familiar. Yet, they are different enough, and warm enough, to please and intrigue. They don't startle, but they awaken and thrust us into an appreciating Christmas mood. Throughout Haiti, legendary miracle trees thrive on barren hillsides. The trees' leaves are green and dazzling, and veins melt through them bright as butter. The branches of each tree are a tangle of spirals and limbs bending under baskets of Caribbean fruits: guava, mango, green soursop, violet plums, red cashew apples, carambola, sweet oranges, and scarlet pear-shaped ackees.

Our cruise was pedestrian. The intrepid and the young would think it arid. But when grafted together like fruits on the miracle tree, our doings transformed meanderings into the memorable—at least for us. Nothing we did or that happened was legendary or momentous. But as the cruise loosened the crystalline grasp of winter, we become more malleable and receptive to the small nothings that compose every person's days. How startling it was to be waited on in a small restaurant in Nassau by Lancelot. The restaurant was a round table family affair. Lancelot's brother Galahad was the main cook, and his sister Guinevere the hostess. How pleasant to sit on a terrace in the shadow of a palm and eat two of Kermit's chocolate dipped key lime pies on sticks in Key West or drink Montana beer and spoon through stew bony with iguana in Bon Smak Bistro, a dark out of the way restaurant in Willemstad. The only other customer was an electrician who taught courses in electricity in the Pennsylvania prison system. Squirrel was his favorite meat, and in the past year, he shot 56 near the bird feeders in his yard.

The next day I banged my head against the roof of a cave in Curacao. Inside the cave small honey or nectar feeding bats roosted. The bats pollinated the columnar cacti on the island and were endangered. Vicki and I shouldn't have entered the cave, and the bloody whack I received was deserved. But the "country" bats that swarmed my childhood had vanished, and I longed to see bats. I wanted to imagine that the natural world was not so diminished as I knew it to be. Indeed, seeing the honey bats made time scroll backwards. It evoked sweet memories of evening games of No Bears and Steal the Pig and walks through woods during which I frightened myself into pleasure by imagining copperheads lurking under the trunk of every fallen tree.

Many people we saw during the month away from Connecticut had turned themselves into fleshy manuscripts, usually primers. Tattoos wrapped arms like papyrus scrolls. Generally, the scrolls were not written on rot resistant cellulose but on cellulite. Inevitably the ink leaked and spread forming what looked like pools of blue algae. Even when tattoos remained clear, they were unpunctuated. Like run-on sentences they flowed into each other and conveyed the impression that the people they adorned were illiterate, both visually and verbally. Other people wore clothes decorated with drab slogans or startling pictures. Printed in capital letters across the chest of a T-shirt worn by a woman was, "Run Away With Me." The woman was elephantine and couldn't lift her heels off the ground no matter the incentives proffered by a potential playmate. "Reflecting an unfulfilled wish," Vicki said glancing at the shirt, "the wistfulness of incapable age." Oblique references to incapacity marked several shirts. "Growing Old Disgracefully" appeared on the shirt of a man too feeble to do anything gracefully or disgracefully. A big man whose muscles had gone to fat wore the colors of a fictional motorcycle gang on the back of a black vest. Printed across the shoulders in the top rocker was "Sons of Ibuprofen." Below appeared the club logo, a winged skull clutching a thermometer between its teeth. On the bottom rocker was "Arthritic Chapter."

Vicki's and my experiences smacked more of miracle weeds than trees. "Are you over eighty-five," a group of high schoolers asked me in Fort Lauderdale. "We are on a scavenger hunt, and we have to take a picture of somebody over eighty-five, and you look really old." "Are you Indiana Jones?" a woman asked me on St. Maarten. She was trying to lure customers into a branch of Diamonds International. I was wearing a floppy hat to protect my face and neck from the sun. I didn't resemble a swashbuckler, but being addressed as Indiana Jones was better than being confused with Methuselah. Christmas was in the air, and during the trip several people offered me presents. In Dre's bar on Barbados a mixologist blended rum, Coca Cola, and Banks beer. He called the drink a bicycle and after sampling the mix offered me a ride. I thanked him but demurred. On previous rides the man had lost his teeth, and his gums were seasonably white as snow. Inside the Cathedral Basilica of Saint John the Baptist in San Juan the air was thick with the fragrance of incense, outside with marijuana. "I've never smelled such strong marijuana," I said to Vicki. "Would you like a hit?" a devotee of aromatherapy sitting on the steps asked. Medicinal religion had put the man in a happy smiling mood. "Enjoy San Juan," he said. "Are you sure you don't want a hit?"

Not all the people who offered me presents were appealing or good-natured. In Jamaica, Vicki and I always eat a lunch in the Jerk Center in Ocho Rios, usually a quarter of a chicken apiece, sweet potato fries, two Red Stripe beers, and a mystery dish, on this trip a gizzada, a diabetic bomb, a patty or tart in a pastry shell filled with sweetened coconut and seasoned with nutmeg and ginger. After the meal while Vicki swirled a last sip of beer around in her mouth to wash away candied shreds caught between her teeth, I walked outside and stood on the sidewalk bordering DaCosta Drive. In the past when I appeared on DaCosta, hawkers gathered around me selling bootlegged tapes of Caribbean music. The disks were terrible, but the sellers were poor, and I bought a couple. I like Bob Marley's music, not quite so much as the man I met on St. John who wore a rectangular gold earring on which "Marley" was spelled in small diamonds. "I also named my son Marley," the man told me. "but instead of B. Marley, he is D. Marley." "What does the D stand for?" I asked. "D," the man replied, "it stands for D."

On this occasion, the music vendors stayed away. Instead a big man leading a small pubescent girl by the hand approached me. The girl wore a pink blouse and tight shorts and smiled tentatively. In contrast the man seemed a threatening presence. He pushed the girl at me and asked, "Do you like her?" Not simply have eaten lunch but being out to lunch, I said, "Like her? I don't know her." The man then put his hand in the small of the girl's back, rammed her forward against me, and said, "She's my sister. Do you want her?" I suddenly realized the man was a pimp and was setting the little girl as bait in a honeytrap. If I had my druthers, I'd confiscate every gun in America. But I was raised Christian. As a result, beliefs in justice and just desserts linger in my character. At that moment if I'd been "weaponized" and certain that I wouldn't be left behind when the cruise ship sailed from Ocho Rios, I would have subjected the bastard to a high caliber course of ballistic therapy. Instead I behaved mildly and shouted, "Get the Hell away from me."

"What was that about?" Vicki asked leaving the restaurant and hearing my voice. "Heartburn," I said. "The chicken was too highly seasoned." In truth I felt soiled. To cleanse myself when Vicki and I roamed the town later, I gave money to every beggar I saw, purging myself of a clogging wad of bills. What I couldn't expunge was the realization that the manacles wrapping Jacob Marley's ghost in *A Christmas Carol* were small links in the ancient iron chain fettering poverty to crime and degradation. No Scrooge would send the family of the girl outside the Jerk Centre a prize turkey for Christmas. No one would become a kindly second father to her as Scrooge became to Tiny Tim.

When he was five years old, John Masefield discovered that he "could imagine imaginary beings complete in every detail, with every faculty and possession." These beings, he explained, "did what I wished for my delight, with an incredible perfection, in a brightness not of this world." Imaginary beings are easier to write about and live with than actual people. On cruises Vicki and I are each other's single acquaintance. We never dine with strangers, and once off the ship, we wander on our own. Of course, on a ship with 2600 passengers, no couple can be an island alone. They are always part of the Main Deck. In a sauna, after hearing me answer a question about university teaching, a man sitting nearby said, "I don't believe in tenure." The man was truculent and assuming me to be a card-carrying Democrat was spoiling for a political argument. In part I go on cruises to escape politics and the shuttlecock jabber of newspapers, radio, and television. "That's too bad," I said to the man, "because I have just awarded you tenure. To criticize tenure now that you've got it would be incredibly stupid." Invertebrates don't have backbones, and because my reply startled the man, not being the apologetic academic response he anticipated, the man did not answer. Shortly afterward he left the sauna.

Because I am old, some leaves on the weeds near the trunk of my miracle tree are brittle. Others have dried into being sharp-edged. In "On Some Verses of Virgil," Montaigne advised that "a young man who spent his time discriminating between the taste of wine and sauces" should be whipped. "There is nothing I ever knew less or valued less than this [judging wine]. At present I am learning it. I am much ashamed of it," he testified, "but what should I do? I am still more ashamed and vexed at the circumstances that drive me to it. It for us [the elderly] to trifle and play the fool, and for the young to stand on their reputation and in the best place. They are going toward the world, toward reputation; we are coming from it." In past years I've attended a score of cruise-ship wine tastings. I always thought them precious. Attending embarrassed me, but I participated because like Montaigne I didn't know what else to do. I wasn't so much coming from the world as having left it. Now, however, my rehoboam has overflowed. At an age when people suffer from a plethora of palsies holding a glass by the stem, not the bowl, is initially messy then impossible. Checking the color of the wine, sniffing its "perfume," and swishing it around to study its "legs" seem trifling. What does it matter that Champagne is a fine accompaniment for caviar? I haven't tasted caviar in half a century. At my dinner table being aware that white Burgundy goes well with escargot, duck, and goose while red Burgundy or a Zinfandel is dandy with camembert is not essential knowledge. I want to know what goes with Netflix. What wine goes best with unbuttered popcorn? What's a good accompaniment for a midday excursion and Happy Meal at McDonald's? I'll never bastardize strawberry shortcake with a sweet Vouvray or dose myself with a Riesling while eating a hot dog. On cruises sommeliers have foreign accents, these generally adopted after they move away from Queens or Staten Island. Unlike Beaujolais which ostensibly goes well with the contents of a butcher's display case—liver, pork chops, ham, sweetbreads—the sommelier on the cruise could not answer the meaty questions that I pondered. No longer was I interested in the pairings of wine and food. Instead I was curious about pairings of wine and behavior. "Madeira with fruitcake is a ho-hum subject," I said, "but is Madeira the right accompaniment for lively, fruity, jocular behavior?" What wines, I asked, stimulated curiosity, prevented people from filing fraudulent income tax statements, tempered amorousity, and made people intelligent companions for their pets. What wine, I wondered, should I serve in order to provoke or quash quarrels. "I don't give a rat's ass that stuffed artichokes and Sauvignon Blanc are a good pairing," I said. I wanted to know what wine "loosened the buttons of a stuff shirt." I thought my tone both sparkling and velvety, but it was too robust for the sommelier and he absented himself from my company before I could really breach my cellar of questions. Was Pinot Noir a good choice when dinner guests were game old birds? How about people of my kidney—perhaps a California Cabernet? In oenophile terms the man made a quick finish, that is, watery and tailing off weakly, saying he was late for a meeting.

On exhibit in the Art Museum in Fort Lauderdale was Mimmo Rotella's "White Blank," a five by ten-foot canvas consisting of layers or thin white paper pasted atop a sign board. On the canvas were four small prominent splotches. Two appeared in the upper right of the canvas, one resembling a band-aid, the other a mermaid mangled into a hook. On the lower left side of the canvas the splotch looked like an itch scratched into a scab. To the right the fourth prominent marking was a smear, say, dried blood left after a boy fell off a bicycle and whacked his elbow. Displayed nearby was Jules Olitski's "Main Squeeze," another large canvas. The painting was a caramel rectangle, its color that of crème brulee, the surface smooth and custardy, unbroken by hardened sugar. I asked the gallery guard what she thought about the paintings after having stood near them for six hours. "Oh, my god!" she exclaimed. "Oh, my god!"

The guard said nothing more. Vicki and I cruise to break routine and to embellish the canvases of our days. In *Macbeth*, the first murderer addresses Banquo, saying, "it will be rain tonight." "Let it come down," Banquo replies. Away from Connecticut, we become more receptive and hope variety will rain down and color our days with things we haven't seen or heard before. Most are natural. "In the presence of nature, a wild delight runs through the man," Emerson wrote, adding, that "in the woods, we return to reason and faith." Emerson overstated. In a brutal world, it is difficult for people to have faith. When man purged gods from the earth and banished them to Never Lands, the sacral no longer shielded the natural world and nature became vulnerable to utilitarian exploitation.

Aside from protesting which more often than not saps hope and seems bootless, the best a person, rather I, can do is observe and delight: the blood orange red of Julia butterflies in Jamaica, red-tailed squirrels in Tobago, and in Curacao whiptail lizards scurrying across the sand beneath limestone ridges, the blue dots along their sides shimmering, breaking the definition of the animals' bodies and confusing predators. Sharing the escarpment was a multitude of tudora rupis land snails. They fed on cacti and manchineel trees, and their shells resembled braided miniature turbans. I took a handful of shells back to Connecticut. I put them in small souvenir dish I bought in San Juan. The dish is green and yellow and shaped like a lily pad. Perched on the lip of the pad is a coqui frog, this despite the frog's being a tree not a pond frog. Life is unlivable without imaginary license, and at night if I listen intently, I can hear the frog's two note call "co-qui," the second note higher than the first. I set the dish on the windowsill of my study next to the shell of a wood turtle who clears her throat and grumbles occasionally but never speaks.

On my canvas I loosed an aviary of birds most of which were unfamiliar. I do not understand bird language. As a result, unlike the illiteracies of human speech, bird song doesn't irritate me although the cries of trumpeter hornbills batter the eardrum and the honk and grind of flamingoes reminds me to take my car for its yearly "wellness" service. Recently after hearing a "branding officer" discuss "optionality" with a panelist who began a presentation saying, "Her and me believe," I left the house and went on a purging jog. On the canvas I painted a background for the birds, cluttered and colorfully chaotic like Henri Rousseau's dreamy art. I did not include many animals, only a small jumping guabine fish pulling itself out of a trickle of water to reach a small pool and then two rats, one alive, the other on its back, dead and festering, the way tourists generally see rats in the Caribbean. A branch from a cocoa tree hung above the dead rat. Extending the memento mori theme, seed pods on the tree had been infected by a fungus and were black not green.

Like the birds, I hadn't written about most of the trees. I transplanted a few familiar trees on the page to fill the canvas and provide roosts for birds and plants. Snaking its way through a massive kapok was a monkey ladder vine. On the kapok I also hung Swiss Cheese vine, an epiphyte, the leaves of which looked like those of a philodendron and were two and a half feet in length and pocked by oval holes, creating spectacular spooky green masks. I included a tall tyre palm because from a distance its accordion-shaped fronds looked deceptively unkempt like truths, indeed like memorable essays. For aesthetic reasons a geiger tree grew in the foreground heavy with clusters of nuts and orange and red flowers. The flowers resembled those of the African tulip tree, a favorite of Caribbean guides but one over which I exhausted my capacity to swoon several books ago. Behind the geiger loomed a motillo. It served as a roost, and I liked watching its gray buttressed roots serpentine across the rain forest floor.

Once I was a two-legged tamandua adept at spotting termite nests high in the rain forest. Now because I have begun to slump, I notice more things closer to my feet than my head. Leaf cutter and army ants trailed across the floor of the canvas. Outside their paths I scattered a sampler of seeds: from tan-tan a cluster of long thin corrugated pods, split pods of yellow trumpetbush releasing seeds with pale wings, knobby fruits of the casuarina looking like conifer cones, and a chain of cloaked seeds from fish poison tree. I scattered the seeds of this last far from the pool to which the guabine was creeping. On the ground I also spread a coverlet of leaves, most immediately recognizable, the splayed broad multi-lobed leaves of the trumpet-tree, the ones I scattered crumpled and black because they'd lain on the ground for a longish time, the broad green paddles of almond, and the big glistening sliced leaves of breadfruit. My favorite leaves were those of miconia or camasey. The leaves looked oiled, and three big veins ran their length giving them a rumpled mattress appearance. I planted so many trees I stapled an addition on the canvas to accommodate them, for example, a blue mahoe with its rigorously straight light blue trunk, and a genip heavy with fruit, the rinds green, the pulp orange and a mild laxative, not a medicinal necessity if one dines on Caribbean street food.

Along a dirt road ran a line of glory cedar or quick stick. Cuttings from the tree regenerate swiftly and throughout the Caribbean form living fences. The tree's flowers dangle in purple clusters and from a distance look like wisteria. Immediately behind my fence sunshine bathed a pillow of grass. In the grass grew constellations of white star sedges turning the small plot into an earthy firmament not a blue yonder that evoked dreams but a green place one could touch. Although I sowed wild morning glories along a river bank, I didn't plant many flowers. In the past my pages bloomed like gardens. But this year, winter's remnants lingered in my mind, not the ice I shoveled before leaving Connecticut but thoughts about friends whose lives had blown. In a sense the morning glories were therapeutic. They evoked memories of simple days when I explored abandoned cabins and climbed over collapsing fences, almost always finding, and sometimes entangling my feet in, strings of morning glories. The flowers were also mildly depressing as they humped over the river bank looking like a pall.

The variety of Caribbean plants startles and shatters moods. It also teaches that consistency is imposed. As man poisons by spraying pesticides and chemical fertilizer in hopes of managing nature and limiting surprise, so he attempts to impose consistency on his life, or when that fails as it always does, upon the lives of others. Consistency is a socially utilitarian fiction. My canvas was nonfiction. Habitats disappeared, and plants migrated whimsically delighting me and, if one has been influenced by television programs investigating the paranormal and accepts their absurd findings, then also delighting the shade of Emerson. Along the edges of my rain forest, for example, cacti thrived: sky scraping columns of kadushi pressed together making a sandy plain appear urban, pipe organ rising in tall scouring brushes, and Spanish Lady, bearded with long black-tipped spines, an autocratic marquesa with whom familiarity should be avoided.

Josh believes that collecting birds, that is, keeping a list obliquely reflects an attenuated version of the capitalist imperative to aggrandize. It especially appeals to people who have money enough to live comfortably and who don't desire anything material, people repulsed by the oily sheen of celebrity and the meretricious display of excess. They are people who no longer think their secular achievements triumphs, about which any celebratory thoughts they might have once had are now soiled by guilt and an eroding sense of life misused. "It is a quieter, subtler, more civilized form of hoarding, one in which older people can participate without undermining their self-esteem," Josh once said. "Baseball cards when they attended elementary school, birds after retirement." Two years ago, he quipped, "Know birds. Know thyself." Does an interest in birds increase as one deserts people and as solitary observation seems truer, saner, than explanation? For my part glimpses of birds make me less forlorn. Eventually, of course, cognizance of the destruction of the green world saddens me. But for a moment as I scanned bush and shrub, I wasn't a trifler sitting at the bar in the Barrachina restaurant in San Juan thinking "there's too much pineapple in this pina colada."

Like the trees I sketched, some of the birds on the canvas were familiar: a troupial in formal dress, orange and black with white epaulettes, a red legged thrush, the primaries on its wings layers of geologic gray and black, and a caracara atop a limestone outcrop, despite his beak being closed his voice clear, clicking like small metal balls swinging into one another. From Grand Turk I lifted Red Salina with a tricolored heron fishing its shallows and a score of black-necked stilts standing along a rock wall that once surrounded a salt pan. I appropriated them because their legs attracted me more than the legs of any wine, those of the heron bright, almost shellacked orange, and those of the stilts long and delicate, raising the birds' bodies so high they looked like patches of cloudlets.

Most of the birds I put on the canvas were rain forest natives of Trinidad and Tobago. To inhabitants of the islands they were pedestrian, that is, if a creature that flies, serenades, and whose dress is often more colorful than that of Harlequin can be thought ordinary. Rarely had I seen most of the birds before the cruise and seeing them exhilarated, actually and metaphorically elevating my attention above the ground. There were exceptions; not all birds were above the forest floor: the rufous-vented chachalaca Tobago's turkey and national bird scratching through leaves searching for seeds and the West Indian whistling duck silently paddling through mangroves his black and white underparts camouflaging his movement. A blue-crowned motmot perched on a limb, the middle feathers of his long tail hanging down and ending in blue pendulums looking like weights removed from a small grandfather clock. While a blue-backed manakin donned an azure cloak and a scarlet cap, a barred antshrike wore the black and white uniform of a chain gang. A colony of crested oropendolas built bola nests in immortelle trees, and bearded bellbirds bounded joyous through the crowns, their calls hammers banging anvils into raucous sound.

To attract my favorite hummingbird the white-necked Jacobin, I sketched a bouquet of heliconia—parrot's beak, hirsute, Easter, and lobster claw. With an iridescent indigo head, a starched white breast, a back that shimmied between green and blue, and a white line cutting across its neck, the Jacobin looked less like a suspiring animal than a porcelain figurine painted and displayed on a mantlepiece. On the right side of the canvas I hung a Christmas wreath. Adorning it were berries from miconia and Jamaican nettletree. I wanted to attract small purple and green honeycreepers not the larger and colorless tropical mockingbird. The honeycreepers looked like ornaments and were brighter than handblown glass bulbs, the head and chest of the purple, smoky violet, its wings black, and legs daffodil yellow. While the head of the green resembled a black cap with ear flats, the rest of its body was a mutable turquoise, green in one light, blue in another.

In filling blank days, I didn't escape invasive humans. In the Ardastra Gardens in Nassau I watched a turtle pull itself onto a mud bank. Unable to tell whether it was a Jamaican or red-eared slider, I muttered, "I wonder what that is." My male friends in Storrs are partially deaf, and to talk to them I raise my voice. As a consequence, my mutter was better suited to Connecticut than the Bahamas. A man standing fifteen feet away overheard me and addressing me said, "That's a turtle." The remark took me aback. I couldn't right myself swiftly enough for a memorable rejoinder, so I nodded slightly, and said, "That's nice to know. Thank you." "Good golly," I said to Vicki later. "The man must have thought me a nincompoop." Josh believes that wives are apostates. Certainly, Vicki is not an ardent defender of the faith, that is, of me. "Well," she said, "you were wearing white socks, muddy running shoes with broken laces, cargo shorts shredding into scraggily beards, a hiking vest stained with tea, blood, and chocolate ice cream, not to mention that your haircut was five months old." "And," she continued before I could defend sartorial inelegance, "you have a Southern accent, the sure indicator of a person's being a dope." "Yes, I have an accent," I said, "but I don't vote Republican." "Nowadays that accent identifies you as a dope, and much worse," she said. "At least," she added, "you are to be commended for not telling the man to have a nice day."

Both being and being thought a dimwit are good for a person. They diminish ambition and restore balance to the mind. They lower blood pressure and are prophylactics shielding a person from the importuning of others. Moreover, being a dope frees a person to behave in ways that dullards think dunderheaded. For most of the cruise I had a sinus infection and a rib-loosening cough. In Ocho Rios I went to a drug store and told the pharmacist that I wanted a week's supply of antibiotics. "I cannot sell those without a prescription," he said. "Are you sure?" I responded adding that I'd purchased pills illegally in many countries. On the man's repeating his refusal, I said, "too bad" and turned to leave the building. "But wait," the pharmacist said rushing from behind the counter. "If I don't record the sale," he said, "I might be able to sell you some." We agreed on a price, and the man handed me what he identified as a week's supply of amoxicillin. "How do you know he gave you amoxicillin?" Vicki asked. For all I know the man gave me birth control pills. But I took them because that was an essential part of the holiday experience. In any case the pills did not cure the sinus infection, but then neither did I become pregnant.

Vicki and I are home now. For the first time in five years at the end a holiday trip, the car battery wasn't dead, and the engine started at the airport. Early the next morning Vicki removed the Christmas wreath from front door. She stored the red bow in the downstairs closet, and I threw the wreath on the woodpile in the back yard, sailing it like a Frisby. Next, we fetched the dogs from the kennel. When they saw us, they bounded about shrieking. By the following afternoon they'd settled into their usual pattern of sleeping in the kitchen and for variety napping in my study. I, too, quickly slipped into the habitual. When we arrived, there was little snow on the ground, but I haven't put the shovel in mothballs. Twice a day I scan the yard hunting dog droppings. I scoop them up and toss them into the forsythia hedge that runs along my yard hiding my house from the gaze of people who rent the home next door. Every other day I dump vegetable compost in the woods behind our house for the deer. They eat everything except onions and banana peels. Before lunch I go to the university gym and jog four miles with David. Afterward I eat yogurt, pepping it up with almonds, wheat germ, and either blueberries or raspberries. Four days after Vicki and I came home, Raymond and Michael, former teaching buddies, and I had our monthly dinner meeting at Dimitri's in Coventry. We studiously arrive at six and leave by seven-thirty. Each time we sit in the same booth and share a large pizza. It must have a thin crust and can only be a pepperoni pizza because Raymond won't eat another kind. Michael and I also split a Greek salad. For his part Raymond eats lettuce with a few croutons tossed on top, nothing more, no tomatoes, broccoli, or celery. If the cook mistakenly adds anything else to his salad, Raymond sends it back to the kitchen. The same waitress helps us. She is very nice and knows our names. Her daughter is on the high school soccer team, and her husband is in the National Guard.

At night Vicki and I eat in the television room and watch something on Netflix or Prime, the lighter the program the better for digestion, preferably an English show, "Blandings" being a particular favorite. Usually we eat salads or veggie burgers. Sometimes I get Indian take-out, the seasoning always between mild and medium. My shipboard education has become corked, and I have not sipped wine since returning to Storrs. With every dinner, I have a single beer never in a can but always in a bottle. The beers don't have legs, but they have good knees. Vicki selects them. Now cooling on the lower shelf of the refrigerator door are Modelo, Bass, Red Stripe, and Beck's. In bed at night I read for half an hour, at the moment S. R. Crockett's *The Surprising Adventures of Sir Toady Lion with Those of General Napoleon Smith, An Improving History for Old Boys, Young Boys, Good Boys, Bad Boys, Big Boys, Little Boys, Cow Boys, and Tom-Boys*. "Aunt Minnie" presented the book to "Charlie E. Busby" at Christmas 1897. The book is a children's novel and the going is slow and saccharine. But that's all right; no longer can I stomach the blood and body parts that gush through contemporary crime novels. Books enjoy mysterious lives, and I don't know how or when the *Adventures* got into the house. I had an Aunt Allie, an Aunt Betty, an Aunt Lucille, and an Aunt Amanda but not an Aunt Minnie. Furthermore, none of my acquaintances were or are named Busby. I simply stumbled across the book while rummaging through my library searching for soporific under-the-blankets reading.

Soon after we settled in, Josh dropped by to welcome us home. He introduced us to his new puppy Mr. Happy Pants and reported that no controversy roiled the university during our absence and that campus life was placid. "Things were different elsewhere," he then said, punctuating the sentence by rolling his eyes and shaking his head disapprovingly. To assure us that the academic globe had remained stable in its off the wall orbit, he told us a whooper Because of the popularity of the television programs "The Bachelor" and "The Bachelorette," student groups on many campuses had staged collegiate equivalents. Such programs differed slightly from those on television. Instead of supplying twenty or more contestants from which the bachelor or bachelorette could select a true love, campus shows rarely provided more than a dozen. Additionally, because of the morphing sexual climate, possible selection was not restricted to a single gender. Thus, the dozen candidates usually included six males and six females. As could be predicted reaction to the college shows was mixed. "While inclusionists lauded the intersectionality, the cisgendered remained silent, the non-binary uncommitted, and football fans oblivious."

Although retired, Josh still tracks educational doings. Shortly after visiting us, he'd audited a lecture on human rights. The address was informative, but he said he'd rather be knocked off the perch by the coronavirus than attend another such meeting. "When chatted with individually, people in the audience were interesting," he reported, "but as a group they gave me narcolepsy. My jaw sagged; my eyelids drooped, and I didn't know whether to laugh or cry." In the question and answer period following the lecture, one man began, "I don't have a question, but I'm sure that if I talk long enough, I will think of one." "With the crowd, the remark passed for high academic wit, and they chortled appreciatively," For his part Josh remained silent. He then stood and grimacing apologetically left the room pretending to suffer from old man's incontinence. Once in the hall outside, he chatted with passersby. A supply-side economist told him that mortuary experts thought all the effects of coronavirus weren't terrible. So many old people would buy the farm that Social Security would suddenly become solvent. The economist also noted that savvy real estate dealers were advising customers to sell nursing home stock and invest in bone orchards. While emptying wards of beds in the former, the virus would cause a shortage of dirt beds in the latter. Days later, after the coronavirus transformed gallows humor into reprehensible left-handedness, I recalled the effects polio virus had on my childhood. To protect me every summer my parents sent me from our apartment in Nashville to my grandfather's farm in Virginia. I was quarantined in dirt-road country— not an isolation that limited but one that expanded my life immersing me in a world resplendent in Aphrodite's love-awakening green Girdle.

Josh said that the economist would have said more about the equity market futures of Silent Cities had he not been interrupted by a lady agronomist. An aficionado of both pigs and pig tales, she entertained Josh with an account of "Pork-Eaters' Paradise." According to the story, pigs in this culinary fairyland were born roasted with knives and forks protruding from their hams. Until they became dinner table centerpieces, they scampered about squealing "Eat Me" and gorging on corn and soybeans seasoned with potato chips and fat-producing estrogen. Just as the woman began to suggest which pigs were best suited for pulled pork, Josh decided his absence from the human rights discussion had lasted long enough for him to visit "lavatories on three separate floors of the building." Accordingly, he excused himself from the porcine canticle and returned to the lecture room. The interval was too short. The man was still expounding his way to a question. "I couldn't stand it," Josh said. "I winced and left again, this time limping, leading people to assume my prostate was as big as an avocado. The speech fiend who overdoses on words does not harm himself, but he renders those who cannot avoid listening to him catatonic." "Josh shouldn't be too harsh on the guy," Vicki said later. "Everybody has an inner twit, and as could be expected, gabblers have twins."

While I was cruising, Bob who worked in the ticket office in the university athletic department died. For years I spoke to Bob every weekday, except Wednesdays when he played golf. His death was unexpected and erased part of the ritual of my daily life. A childhood friend in Tennessee also died. He had been sick for four years. When he first became ill, he wrote me a taking-stock goodbye letter. "Because you taught English," he stated, "you will understand my saying that I enjoyed playing with words more than with tits." Reputations are created quicker by words and last longer than those raised on deeds. Because the man's language was often colorful and rough, people who knew him slightly thought him a rakehell. In truth, in comparison to silent hypocritical acquaintances who kept their tongues gated behind electric fences, he was saintly: devoted to family and a charitable member of the community albeit a poor choice for after-dinner speaker.

Because so many friends have died since I retired, my mind seems a catacomb. The deaths have drained my tear ducts. No longer can I grieve on demand, and in the presence of morose widows all I'm able to do is mutter embalmed consolations. The pharmacy in Ocho Rios sold packs of "Funeral Drops." They'd come in handy in Connecticut, and I regret not buying a supply. Each pack contained three amber glass bottles and three droppers. Put a drop in each eye before entering a funeral home instructions on the bottles advised. "Never more than two," the label counseled, "and DO NOT," it warned in capital letters, "INSERT DROPS INTO THE EYES OF THE CADAVERIC." "Who would do that and what would happen?" Vicki asked after I read her the label. "Well, the eyelids of the corpse," I started to say but then stopped. Non sequiturs are generally the most sensible elements of conversations.

I know nothing about the anatomy of the eye. But I suspect the surprising doings of cornea and macula would induce mourners to fling their prayer books into the air and skedaddle. Conclamatio mortis would shake the rafters of the church. Pablo R Corpse would tumble out of his Montezuma serape, and the bereaved would rise from their knees and head for the door vaulting over pews and trampling the sick and the aged, all the while moaning and wailing, imploring "the Lamb" to help them. I wondered if the crowd who witnessed Jesus's raising the son of the Widow of Naim from the dead reacted similarly. Did the lame drop their crutches and run? Did the most athletic of the halt gallop with inspired abandon into the wilderness hurdling camel's thorn and Apples of Sodom until they reached the summit of Mount Tabor?

Did Blind Bartimaeus pocket the spoils of his begging and high tailing it into the nearest vineyard, imbibe a water pot of calming demons? Who knows? Anyway, I wasn't able to answer Vicki's questions, so, I quoted four lines from the Jamaican poet Evan Jones's "The Song of the Banana Man." "Up in de hills, where de streams are cool, / an' mullet an' janga swim in de pool, / I have ten acres of mountain side, / an' a dainty-foot donkey dat I ride." "A Caribbean Road to Mandalay," Vicki said. "I suppose you'll quote Kipling next." "Yes, but instead of the Moulmein Pagoda and the Burma girl, I'll see you and 'four Gros Michel, an' four Lacatan, / some coconut trees, an' some hills of yam.'"

Friends die; people are misjudged; hurricanes sweep bananas from hillsides, but robocalls continue. Four times one afternoon last week a solicitous woman warned me that because of illegal doings my Social Security was going to be docked. If I'd provide her with requisite information, she said she would insure that I wouldn't lose any money. "This is a hidden camera world," I told Vicki, "the authorities must have been watching when I bought the amoxicillin." Insofar as financial matters are concerned, two days after coming home, I paid our charge cards. For the record I pay on time and have never been charged interest. I also gathered all 1099-R forms and calculated the year's income tax. Because I am "admirably" responsible, Lisa has telephoned twice urging me to sign up for a Chase Bank card. I haven't heard from the IRS office in Lagos, but Michael and Raymond have, and I don't expect to be forgotten.

Since returning to Storrs, I have received only one personal letter. Archie sent me a picture of a bobcat perched on a window ledge outside her husband Paul's bedroom. Paul has dementia and is bedridden. "I know sight of the cat shouldn't thrill me, but it did," Archie wrote. "Was it a spirit animal making sure Paul was all right? Of course, it wasn't. I don't believe in the numinous but entertaining such thoughts occasionally is very heady." Yesterday I looked out the kitchen window and watched a Carolina wren gleaning the gray branches of the lilac at the corner of the garage. Barren winter is flowering. Across nearby hills the green mosses that lurk unnoticed in spring and summer are suddenly visible making granite boulders blossom green and yellow and turning rocky slopes into gardens. Almost every day when I push away from my desk, lean back in my chair, and gaze lazily through the window at the web of bare limbs outside, I notice crows beating across the sky. "Harbingers." I told Vicki, "but I'm not sure of what, and I am too tired to think about the matter." "Maybe," I said the next afternoon, "harbingers of a cruise to the Land of Everlasting Evening." This morning I got confused and called Groundhog Day Porcupine Day. "Oh, Sam," Vicki said.

About the Author

Sam Pickering was born and raised in Nashville, but he has spent the past fifty years of his life living and teaching in New England, most of these last years at the University of Connecticut. He resembles an old tree knobby with burls of books and worm holed by hundreds of articles and reviews but thriving, host to greening mosses, startling polypore funguses, and to paragraphs rich with observations and thoughts. "Writing," he once wrote, "has enriched, if not made my life—not quite as enriching as dressing a field with manure, but nevertheless enabling me to harvest almost endless nourishing days. I hope my pages will similarly perk up readers' curiosities if not their digestions. If they don't fancy corn or cornpone, maybe apples will do. 'Of all the delicacies which Britons try / To please the palate or delight the eye,' William King wrote at the end of the seventeenth century. 'Of all the sev'ral kinds of sumptuous fare, / There is none that can with Apple pie compare.'"